35.00
17.88

D0554143

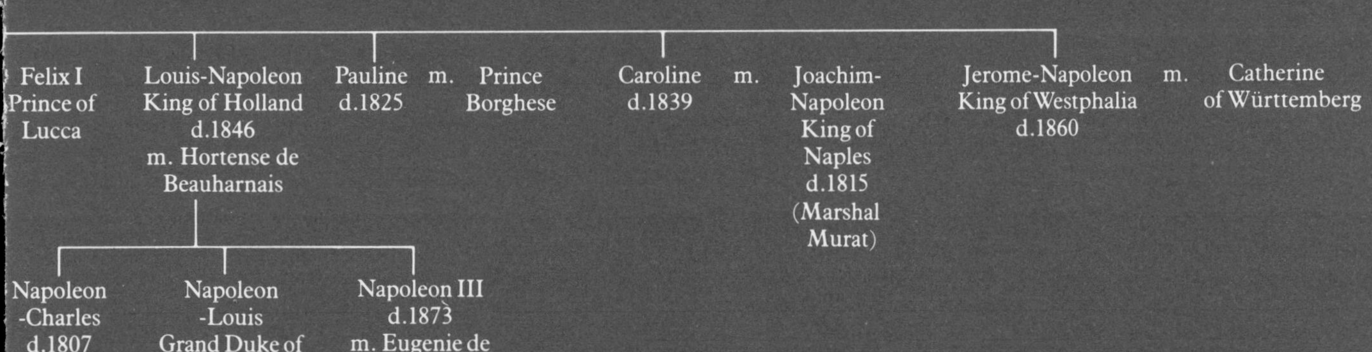

Felix I Prince of Lucca
Louis-Napoleon King of Holland d.1846 m. Hortense de Beauharnais
Pauline d.1825 m. Prince Borghese
Caroline d.1839 m. Joachim-Napoleon King of Naples d.1815 (Marshal Murat)
Jerome-Napoleon King of Westphalia d.1860 m. Catherine of Württemberg
Napoleon-Charles d.1807
Napoleon-Louis Grand Duke of Berg d.1831
Napoleon III d.1873 m. Eugenie de Montijo
Prince Imperial d.1879

THE Eagle in Splendour

NAPOLEON I AND HIS COURT

Philip Mansel

George Philip

British Library Cataloguing in Publication Data

Mansel, Philip
The eagle in splendour: Napoleon I and his court.
1. Napoléon I, *Emperor of the French*
2. France — Kings and rulers — Biography
I. Title
944.05′092′4 DC203
ISBN 0-540-01121-5

First published by George Philip,
27A Floral Street, London WC2E 9DP

Printed in Hong Kong

Contents

Acknowledgements

The author wishes to thank all those who have helped with information or illustrations. In particular he would like to thank Princesse Minnie de Beauvau, G. Burlamacchi, Rupert Cavendish, Dr O. Clottu, Jacques Descheemacher, René and Béatrice de Gaillande, Georges de Grandmaison, Nicola Howard, Gérard Hubert, Comte F. de La Bouillerie, the Marquess of Lansdowne, Ulla Lind, Nicholas McClintock, Major and Mrs J.C. Mansel, Comte Louis-Amédée de Moustier, Comte G. de Montesquiou, Jacques Perot, Jean-Michel Pianelli, the Countess of Roseberry, Adam Zamoyski and Charles-Otto Zieseniss. He is especially grateful to David Higgs and Katherine McDonogh for reading the manuscript, and to Michael Weinstein for his help with the maps.

Illustration Acknowledgements

Colour

Civica Galleria d'Arte Moderna, Milan p. 115 (above); Levens Hall (photo Jeremy Whitaker) p. 113 (above); Musée Marmottan p. 119 (above); all other colour photographs are from Réunion des Musées Nationaux, Paris.

Black and White

Ader, Picard et Tajan pp. 42–3; Archives Nationales, Paris p. 36, p. 76; Bayerischen Staatsgemäldesammlungen, Munich p. 211; Bayerisches Armeemuseum, Ingolstadt p. 179; BBC Hulton Picture Library pp. 194–5; Bibliothèque Marmottan, Boulogne-sur-Seine pp. 138–9, pp. 150–1, p. 199; Bibliothèque Nationale, Paris pp. 24–5, pp. 28–9, p. 33, p. 37, p. 47, p. 80, p. 155, pp. 170–1, pp. 192–3, pp. 200–1, pp. 206–7; British Library p. 69, p. 105; British Museum p. 54, p. 75; Ann S.K. Brown Military Collection, Brown University Library, Rhode Island pp. 144–5; Christies, London pp. 100–1, pp. 186–7, pp. 190–1; Civica Raccolta Stampe 'A. Bertarelli', Castello Sforzesco, Milan p. 32 (above and below); Hermitage Museum, Leningrad pp. 44–5; Hotel Richemond, Geneva p. 154 (left and right); Kunsthistorisches Museum, Vienna p. 55; Mansell Collection pp. 110–11; Musée Bertrand, Châteauroux p. 108; Musée Carnavalet p. 13, p. 39, pp. 62–3, pp. 176–7; Bibliothèque de Grenoble p. 97; Musée d'Unterlinden-Colmar (photo O. Zimmerman) p. 90; Musée Marmottan p. 65; Museo Correr, Venice p. 68 (below); Museo del Risorgimento, Milan p. 31; Museo di Milano pp. 66–7; Museo Glauco-Lombardi, Parma p. 122, p. 213; Museo Napoleonico, Rome p. 78, p. 125, p. 128, pp. 160–1; National Museum, Warsaw p. 88; Ny Carlsberg Glyptotek, Copenhagen p. 92; Photographie Bulloz p. 52, p. 83, p. 147; Private collections p. 40, p. 41, p. 82, p. 84, p. 85, p. 91, p. 133, p. 143; Réunion des Musées Nationaux, Paris p. 16, pp. 18–19, p. 20, p. 26, p. 38, p. 46, p. 48 (below), p. 49, pp. 50–1, pp. 56–7, p. 58, pp. 72–3, p. 74, p. 81, p. 86, pp. 94–5, pp. 102–3, p. 123, p. 136, p. 152, pp. 164–5, pp. 174–5, p. 180, p. 198, pp. 208–9; Rijksmuseum, Amsterdam p. 149; Royal Collection, Stockholm p. 30, p. 68 (above); Rupert Cavendish Antiques p. 48 (above); Soprintendenza delle Belle Arti, Naples p. 2, p. 22, p. 71, p. 157, pp. 158–9; Soprintendenza delle Belle Arti, Pisa p. 135.

1 Steps to the Throne

'Every one complains of Bonaparte; every one talks of the Court.'

Diary of Bertie Greathead, Paris, 1 January 1803.

ON 19 FEBRUARY 1800 a procession of carriages drove through the streets of Paris to the Tuileries palace. The carriages contained councillors of state, ministers and, in the grandest carriage of all, drawn by six white horses presented by the Holy Roman Emperor, the three Consuls of the French Republic. The procession drove past a barrier surmounted by an inscription saying 'Royalty has been abolished in France, it will never return' and into the courtyard of the Tuileries. The First Consul, General Bonaparte, then held a review of the Guard of the Consuls. That night he slept in the Tuileries. It was to be his official residence, and the seat of his court, for the next fourteen years.[1]

The Tuileries, begun in the sixteenth century, and enlarged and redecorated under Louis XIV, was a long grey building, which stretched between what are now the two westward-protruding wings of the Louvre. Louis XVI had lived there, half king, half prisoner, at the beginning of the French Revolution, from 1789 to 1792. Its walls were still scarred with bullet and cannon marks from the uprising on 10 August 1792 which had resulted in his overthrow and the establishment of the first French Republic. Siéyès, an ex-priest turned revolutionary politician, reminded Bonaparte of the Tuileries' unhappy memories of the fall of Louis XVI a few days after his move to the palace. The First Consul's fierce reply revealed his determination to stay in power: 'If I had been Louis XVI, I would still be Louis XVI, and if I had been a priest, I would still be one.' As Siéyès realized, sooner than most people, France now had a master; and in the next four years its master acquired a court.

It was Siéyès who had helped Bonaparte to become First Consul. Bonaparte, although only thirty-one, was the most celebrated general in the French army. Born in 1769, the son of a Corsican noble, he had been educated at military schools in France under Louis XVI — where he was disgusted by the disdain that pupils from older and grander noble families showed for those less well-born than themselves. After he left school he was bored by the prospect of service in a peacetime army: he became so discontented that by 1789 he felt republican as well as anti-French.

Although Napoleon had benefited from the old regime which had existed before 1789, like many nobles he found new opportunities under the Revolution. He supported every stage, including the overthrow of the monarchy and the Reign of Terror. Robespierre's brother Augustin called him 'an artillery officer of transcendent merit'. Bonaparte helped suppress revolts by royalist enemies of the Republic at Toulon in 1793 and Paris in 1795 (when they tried to storm the Tuileries).

After 1795 France was ruled by a new, less blood-thirsty government called the Directory, headed by five Directors. They sent General Bonaparte to command the French armies fighting Austria in Italy. He rapidly showed himself to be a brilliant, self-confident, ambitious and above all consistently victorious general. His sense of publicity was almost as extraordinary as his military genius. He subsidized newspapers in France, with titles like *Journal de Bonaparte et des Hommes Vertueux*, which helped publicize his victories.[2]

By 1798 he was so popular that he was an embarrassment. The Directory, which was temporarily at peace in Europe, sent its most successful general to invade Egypt. It was hoped to threaten England's trade with India; and Bonaparte was happy to remove himself from contact with an increasingly corrupt and unpopular regime. After a dazzling year of conquests in Egypt, his army was checked by British and Ottoman forces at the siege of Acre in Syria. He returned to France in October 1799, a sun-tanned young conqueror. He did not have any orders: but the government of the Republic had by then lost the respect of the majority of the French nation.

The Republic was at war again, with Britain, Russia and Austria. The economy and much of the countryside were in chaos: some of Bonaparte's own servants were robbed by bandits on the way back to Paris. Royalists and left-wing politicians were working for the overthrow of the corrupt ex-revolutionary politicians, headed by the five Directors, who had ruled France since 1795. The government had no committed supporters. Everyone was discontented, even the Directors themselves, of whom Siéyès was one.

Nevertheless, there was a constitution with two parliamentary chambers, the Councils of Ancients and of the Five Hundred, which still inspired a certain respect. So the coup which Siéyès prepared with Bonaparte and Talleyrand (the brilliant, corrupt politician who was already a legend for spotting the winning side) needed to preserve a facade of legality. At first everything went as planned. On 9 November a member of the Council of Ancients declared the country in danger: the chambers should move from Paris to Saint-Cloud, six miles outside. The leading Director, Barras, resigned on the advice of Talleyrand. The next day, in Saint-Cloud, which was packed with troops, the Council of Ancients began to turn against Bonaparte after he had made a disastrous speech denouncing the government: his strong Italian accent did not help. The Ancients, who were wearing their uniforms of red togas, began to shout 'Outlaw him! Outlaw him!' But General Murat entered at the head of the Guard of the Legislative Body crying: 'Grenadiers, forward! Expel them all!'[3] The deputies fled through the park of Saint-Cloud, shedding their togas as they went.

The chambers were dissolved. Bonaparte became First Consul under a new constitution, which he drew up with the help of Siéyès: two able and obedient politicians, Cambacérès and Lebrun, became Second and Third Consuls respectively. Siéyès, a weak and expendable personality, was paid off with part of the money left behind in the Directors' account. The legislature under the Consuls was composed of a nominated Senate, an elected Tribunate and a Legislative Body, sitting in Paris in three former royal palaces. Parisians paid little attention to the new constitution, the fourth in ten years. A Prussian diplomat reported that the population was blasé about everything except peace.

Indeed, by 1800, despite the confident inscription above the entrance to the Tuileries, France was ready for a return to monarchy. The Revolution had killed thousands of people, caused many more to emigrate, and precipitated catastrophic wars and inflation. For most Frenchmen by 1800, the events of the Revolution were a powerful argument against a republican form of government. Bonaparte and his ministers were careful, at first, to maintain an appearance of commitment to the republic. Nevertheless, they told foreign ambassadors that they were convinced that 'monarchical government is the only one suitable to large associations of men'. If it had been overthrown in France, the fault was 'the weakness of the ruling family'.

The real strength of the republic lay in the fact that the abolition of feudal dues and the sale of the property of the Church and émigrés had resulted in a massive redistribution of wealth which had benefited many Frenchmen, particularly the richest peasants and bourgeois. After ten years of continuous upheaval, France wanted a rest from revolution, at the same time as confirmation of its material gains. For most Frenchmen after 1800 Bonaparte seemed the best guarantee of both. An official proclamation had described the new Constitution as based on 'the sacred rights of property, equality and liberty'.[4] The sequence of words was both significant and reassuring.

The return of a court to France seemed almost as natural as a return to monarchy. A splendid court was as necessary to France as a well-drilled army to Prussia or a powerful navy to Britain. The Bourbon kings' glorious court at Versailles had had an immense impact on the manners and customs, the social structure and the economic and artistic development of France. Frenchmen had been proud that it was the grandest court in Europe. Many of the officials and servants of the old court were still living in and around Paris after the Revolution (which many of them had supported), as were the employees of the luxury trades — making china, silver, embroidery, tapestry and furniture — which the court had encouraged.

A former First Woman of the Bedchamber of Queen Marie-Antoinette was running the smartest girls' school in France, the Institution Nationale de Saint-Germain, outside Paris. Among its pupils were the First Consul's youngest sister Caroline Bonaparte and his wife's daughter by her first marriage, Hortense de Beauharnais (a particularly quick learner). The school also included members of the new rich and the old nobility, such as Agläé Auguié and Félicité de Faudoas, who were to marry two of the First Consul's most famous generals, Ney and Savary.

Through her school Madame Campan, clever, worldly and moralizing, provided one of the many links between the old and the new regimes. They were not two separate worlds: one was simply a redefinition of the other. Indeed in the future Madame Campan would help former servants of the Queen and the King's aunts to obtain jobs in the households of Madame Bonaparte and her daughter; and she would be used as a mine of information about the habits and etiquette of the court of Versailles.

Another figure from the past who frequently entertained under the Consulate was Madame de Montesson, the morganatic widow of a Bourbon prince, the Duke d'Orléans. Among her guests were members of the old nobility and the new élite, and artists and architects of the old regime in search of commissions under the new. Men first started to wear silk stockings and buckled shoes again in her house, after ten years of boots and trousers under the Revolution. She gave a splendid reception in 1802 in honour of the wedding of Hortense de Beauharnais to the younger brother of the First Consul, Louis Bonaparte. The 800 guests admired the valets wearing full livery and powdered hair, and the Duchess d'Abrantès (then Madame Junot, wife of a general of the Republic) remembered it as 'a model of what happened later'.[5]

Clearly the new world which had arisen from the Revolution, as well as the world of the old regime, was ready for a court. The masters of the Republic were proud of their newly acquired wealth, and their brilliant careers in the army or the administration, and needed somewhere to display themselves. A police report of 1802 suggests the attitude of the new élite to their revolutionary past. General Lefebvre, a republican officer who had risen through the ranks, was infuriated by a worker's complaints about the price of bread. Lefebvre said that they were no longer living in the days of Louis XVI or the Convention, and that the rabble should no longer think that they were the only people worth worrying about.[6] Like the pigs at the end of *Animal Farm*, the new rulers of France were beginning to seem no different from the old.

The government as well as the élite wanted a court. Visual splendour, one of the basic components of a court, was as necessary for a government in 1800 as a good television image is for a politician today: in 1795 even the government of the Republic had shown that it felt a need for splendour by creating garish costumes for its officials and holding regular receptions at which they could be displayed. Most members of the élite of power and wealth, whether royalist or republican, would have agreed with Bonaparte's mother when she wrote to her son: 'You know how much external splendour adds to that of rank or even of personal qualities in the eyes of public opinion.'[7]

A court is the magical result of a combination of power, visual splendour, outward deference and a personal household staffed by members of the élite. Bonaparte had power thanks to his *coup d'état*, and his power was, in appearance, legitimized by the plebiscite of January 1800, which approved the new constitution by 3 million votes. It has only recently been discovered that in fact Bonaparte's brother Lucien, the Minister of the Interior, simply added 1.5 million affirmative votes to the real, far from unanimous result of 1.5 million (out of an electorate of about 7.5 million voters).

After Bonaparte moved to the Tuileries he had the second element of a court, visual splendour. Although scarred by revolution, the Tuileries was a royal palace and, like most royal palaces, radiated an atmosphere of hierarchy and deference. As the horrified liberal writer, Madame de Staël, wrote after Bonaparte's move: 'it was enough, so to speak, to let the walls do the work.'[8]

Bonaparte was keen to help the walls. His architect Fontaine wrote in October 1801 of his interest in the decoration of the Tuileries, and of his insistence on 'the magnificence due to his rank'. Very soon his apartments were furnished with 'eastern magnificence' in yellow and lilac-blue silk, with white and gold fringes. There were old masters on the walls, Sèvres vases mounted in ormolu on the tables and his wife used Queen Marie-Antoinette's jewel-cabinet. In 1802 Mary Berry wrote: 'I have formerly seen Versailles, and I have seen the Little Trianon, and I have seen many palaces in other countries, but I never saw anything surpassing the magnificence of this.' In the next few years, as Fontaine records with delight in his diary, the Tuileries and its surrounding area were cleaned up. Unsuitable houses and inscriptions were removed; people not directly connected to the personal service of the First Consul were expelled. The whole

Swébach-Desfontaines,
Review by the First Consul at the Tuileries
Everyone wanted to watch this dazzling military ceremony: the windows of the Tuileries are packed. Bonaparte is to the left, on a white horse which had belonged to King Louis XVI.

quarter was beginning to resemble a royal palace and its precincts.

After a few months Bonaparte also began to be surrounded by the outward forms of ceremony and deference. Every ten or twenty days, after a review of his awe-inspiring guard, he held a reception for senior officers and officials which provided a startling visual display of his position at the head of the French Republic.[9]

In the state apartments on the first floor of the Tuileries, overlooking the courtyard where the guard was reviewed, access to the First Consul was determined strictly by official rank. Captains were admitted into the first antechamber preceding the First Consul's official reception room, senior officers into the second, generals into the third and councillors of state and ambassadors into the fourth. Bonaparte's receptions were a vehicle through which senior officials and officers of the Republic could satisfy their longing for recognition of their own importance. They were also a convenient meeting-place and centre of news. Above all, the hierarchy of antechambers, as well as the presence of his guard in the courtyard below, were a visible sign of the power and authority of the First Consul. Officials and officers were linked in a chain of authority which culminated in him.

The English visitors who inundated Paris after the return of peace in 1801 were delighted by such signs of a return to normality and monarchy in France. 'None of the levées of the European courts can vie in splendour with those of the Chief Consul', wrote one English visitor in 1801, and many other foreigners were equally impressed. Strict etiquette and military might, always the most remarkable features of the Napoleonic court, were there from the start.

In September 1801 the Prussian Ambassador wrote that 'the household of the First Consul is increasingly taking on the appearance of a court'.[10] The last element of a court, household officials from the élite of power and wealth, now appeared at the Tuileries: in November, two sons of pre-1789 financiers, Didelot and de Luçay, were appointed Prefects of the Palace, and Bonaparte's most intimate friend and confidant Duroc became Governor of the Tuileries.

In March 1802 ladies began to be presented formally to Madame Bonaparte. An Irish visitor noted that 'The etiquette of a Court and Court dress are strictly observed' at the First Consul's audiences. Indeed, life in the palace was now so formal and so respectable that a former actress, the wife of Bonaparte's great admirer Charles James Fox, could not dine at the Tuileries, as she had not been presented at St James's.

The First Consul was at the height of his popularity. His government had startling achievements to its credit. The institution of Prefects by a law of 17 February 1800 gave the central government a permanent executive agent in each department, for the first time since 1789. The new Prefects, recruited mainly from former members of revolutionary assemblies, could correspond directly with Paris by telegraph. They soon established themselves as the masters of their departments, and helped to provide France with the strong government for which it yearned. The budget was balanced for the first time in a decade in 1802. The government could now pay holders of government stocks in gold, instead of in discredited paper currency. A new law code was issued in 1804. In clear, concise French it ensured equality before the law, the right to civil marriage and divorce, the equal division of 75 per cent of a testator's property among his children, and the abolition of all forms of legal privilege. It was essentially the work of professional jurists, and was the culmination of years of preparation, begun under the old regime. Nevertheless Napoleon presided at thirty-six of the eighty-four sessions of the Council of State devoted to the Code, and it was renamed the Code Napoléon in 1807. It was more modern and efficient than any legal code in force at the time.[11] At the same time treaties had been signed with Austria (defeated at the great victory of Marengo) and Britain. The First Consul had restored order to France and he was at peace with the rest of Europe. After the horrors of the past it seemed like a miraculous rebirth; and Bonaparte chose to celebrate it by assuming the role of a monarch.

The moment of truth, when the First Consul and his court appeared in all their glory to the people of Paris, came on Easter Day 1802. The signature of a Concordat with the Pope and the re-establishment of Catholicism as the religion of state in France were celebrated by a Te Deum at Notre Dame. Napoleon went to Notre Dame wearing his magnificent red Consul's uniform and a ceremonial sword, in whose hilt gleamed one of the most famous French crown jewels, the Regent diamond. As in any monarchy, his family was beginning to be prominent and the appearance of his wife Josephine 'in a blaze of diamonds' created a sensation. The Te Deum was 'the grandest thing I ever heard', according to an English witness. Notre Dame was hung with Gobelins tapestries and there were 'two canopies of crimson and gold towering with plumes of white feathers' above the First Consul and the Papal Legate. The preacher at the Te Deum was the Archbishop of Aix, who had delivered the sermon at the coronation of Louis XVI.

When the First Consul and his court returned to the Tuileries after the service, the cheering crowds saw his carriages driven and escorted for the first time by footmen in his livery of green and gold: colours of youth and power which would soon be familiar throughout Europe. According to one eyewitness they exclaimed: 'Oh how beautiful it is, how we love it! It is like the old days, at last our country is itself again!' Bonaparte was giving them what they wanted.

This was indeed his calculation. According to Madame de Staël, when he returned to the Tuileries after the Te Deum, he asked a general: 'Is it not true that everything seemed back in place today?' The reply was: 'Yes, except for the two million Frenchmen who died for freedom and whom one cannot bring back to life.' But the general represented a minority of republican officers. Most Frenchmen accepted the return of a monarch and a court with relief.

Below the sumptuous surface of the Napoleonic court there was always a military reality. The Austrian Ambassador noticed that there was a much greater display of force at the Te Deum 'than under the old regime, which had more respect for the populace than they do now . . . Bonaparte was greatly cheered as he went by'.[12] The army was the real basis of Bonaparte's power. However, the cheers of the Parisians, and the result of the plebiscite of 1802 showed that he had popular support as well. About 3.2 million voters out of 7.5 million agreed he should be First Consul for life, and the result was not doctored like the plebiscite of 1800.

His move to the old royal palace of Saint-Cloud was another sign of the increasing formality of his court — and of his designs on the throne. Hitherto his main country residence had been Malmaison, Josephine's enchanting house a few miles west of Paris. It had symbolized the relatively relaxed court of the Consulate. Here the First Consul had worked and relaxed by watching his aides-de-camp act in amateur theatricals with Josephine's friends and relations in the evening.

Malmaison was not a palace. It was a house, furnished by Josephine with elegant and expensive simplicity. It was bigger than it appears today, for the gallery which housed her magnificent collection of paintings no longer exists. Many of these paintings were in the romantic neo-gothic troubadour taste which she helped to make fashionable (her collection also included pictures taken from Italy and Germany, among them three Rubens and four small Leonardos). The study of the First Consul was relatively simple, decorated with striped material which made it look like the inside of a tent.

The chief glory of Malmaison was its enormous park — hard to imagine today, since most of it has been devoured by the advancing Paris suburbs. However, when Josephine was alive, it contained lakes, fountains, a Temple of Love, the facade of a gothic chapel, a Swiss dairy staffed by milk-maids in Swiss costume, a menagerie with gazelles, tropical birds and flying squirrels, and a hot-house. Josephine had acquired a love of flowers during her childhood in the Caribbean and her hothouse, as big as that at Kew, was filled with rare plants sent to her from all over the world. It was decorated by a former protégé of Marie-Antoinette, Redouté. He is chiefly remembered for his illustrations in the magnificent botanical books which preserve the memory of the park at Malmaison.

Despite its charm and convenience, Malmaison was not grand enough for a court. Although Napoleon continued to visit it occasionally, by 1801 he had already decided to use Saint-Cloud, six miles west of Paris on a hill overlooking the Seine. It was a large and beautiful palace, where Louis XVI and Marie-Antoinette once lived. In September 1802 the First Consul moved into Saint-Cloud. As Isabey, another artist formerly employed by Marie-Antoinette who had become a friend of Josephine, wrote: 'Farewell the lively dances, the entertaining charades! . . . etiquette had arrived.'[13] On 14 November Mesdames de Luçay, de Rémusat, de Lauriston and de Talhoüet, all ladies of the lesser nobility, were appointed ladies-in-waiting of Madame Bonaparte.

Although still only First Consul of the Republic, Bonaparte now had most of the elements of a court; and his new grandeur began to affect his personal behaviour. He started to hunt in the old royal forests around Paris. At mass in Saint-Cloud, after what was now a weekly reception of senior officers and officials, it was noted that 'he gives little nods to right and left, like the Pope gives benedictions'. Like the Bourbons, he walked with a waddle, because it was the only way he could notice who was at his reception.[14] Madame Bonaparte, for the first time, took precedence of the Second and Third Consuls: a personal connection with Bonaparte was becoming more important than positions in the service of the state.

In Paris, traditionally a grumbling city, there was

criticism of the new court from both royalists and republicans: in January 1803 an English visitor noted that 'Everyone complains of Bonaparte, everyone talks of the court.' One outstanding characteristic of the Napoleonic court, which would be remembered long after it had disappeared, was the splendour of its official costumes. Even under the consulate French officers' uniforms were more lavish than those in other European armies. But this did not please everyone. The only general who approached Bonaparte in military ability and popularity, General Moreau, flaunted his distaste for the First Consul's court by wearing a plain dark coat to a reception in the Tuileries. He said: 'Moreau's uniform is not to wear one.'

In 1804 Moreau was implicated in a royalist conspiracy to seize the First Consul. Many Parisians supported him when he was put on trial, and anti-government crowds surrounded the Palais de Justice. Experienced politicians were reminded of the virulent public criticism of the government of Louis XVI in 1785, a few years before the outbreak of the Revolution. The Queen's name had been dragged through the mud over the Cardinal de Rohan's purchase of a diamond necklace, allegedly on her behalf. When Henri Beyle (better known as the great novelist Stendhal) went to the theatre, he noted that the public eagerly applauded any lines in the play which could be construed in favour of Moreau and against Bonaparte.[15]

Despite this support, however, Moreau was sent into exile. Ironically, the crisis enabled Bonaparte to seize the throne. On 18 May he was proclaimed Emperor of the French as Napoleon I, with the right to choose his successor from within his family. The proclamation of the hereditary Empire was approved by a plebiscite in 1804, which gave the result of 2.5 million in favour. With such popular support (even though this was less than in 1802) and Napoleon's own genius, who needed the legitimacy conferred by a hereditary right to the throne? Indeed, the Emperor often proclaimed his pride in the fact that he owed his authority to the people: 'Soldier, magistrate and sovereign, the Emperor owes everything to his sword and his love of the people', he said in 1805.

Isabey, *The First Consul at Malmaison* *The First Consul is wearing the uniform of the Chasseurs of the Guard. The artist Isabey was an intimate friend of Josephine Bonaparte and had arranged her purchase of Malmaison.*

This was, in theory, true. He had used plebiscites to legitimize his power in 1800, 1802 and 1804. His Empire was formally a constitutional monarchy with (until the suppression of the Tribunate in 1807) a tricameral legislature. The Senate, the most important branch of the legislature, even had two commissions whose purpose was to safeguard individual liberty and the liberty of the press.

But this was the public facade. The Senate commissions had little real power. The Senate was composed of about 100 tired old men, the immense majority of whom, despite their previous support of the Revolution, were prepared to endorse any measure proposed by the government which had nominated them. Its theoretical powers, over legislation and elections, increased during the Empire simply because the government knew it could rely on the senators' obedience. From 1802 elections to the Legislative Body and the Tribunate were closely controlled by the government and electoral colleges composed of the richest citizens.

In reality power lay with the Emperor and his ministers, and increasingly with the Emperor alone. Once he became Emperor, Napoleon I did not hold any more plebiscites. He had the right to 'interpret' laws after 1806, and assumed the right to make war and peace.

He was master of France. Under him were eleven (occasionally twelve) ministers, in charge of the ministries of war, foreign affairs, police and so on. Each ministry had between 100 and 200 employees, except for the two most important, the Ministries of War and Administration of War, which had 750 each. Most ministries were located in former aristocratic *hôtels* in the Faubourg Saint-Germain on the left bank of the Seine. The ministers chosen by Napoleon were competent politicians with experience of both the old regime and the Revolution. Gaudin, for example, Minister of Finance from 1800 until 1814, had been an important financial official before and during the Revolution.

Despite their experience, Napoleon's ministers were above all administrators, who had no desire to initiate policies independently of their master. The only ministers with minds of their own were Talleyrand, the Minister of Foreign Affairs, and Fouché, Minister of Police (except in the years 1802–04). Fouché, one of the most bloodthirsty of all revolutionaries, had calmed down, but he was nevertheless held to represent 'the men of the revolution'. Napoleon made sure that not even Fouché had his own independent power-base. He

Isabey, ***Visit of the First Consul to the factory of the Sévène brothers at Rouen in 1802*** *The First Consul, talking to a worker, is surrounded by a minister, the local Prefect and Mayor and General Bessières of the Consular Guard. The aides-de-camp and, on the right, Josephine and her lady-in-waiting, Madame de Luçay, are still kept at a distance. On the far right, with only his eyes visible, is Isabey, drawing this scene; Bonaparte was followed by artists recording his movements just as a modern leader is pursued by photographers.*

balanced Fouché's influence by creating his own private information network under Duroc, and building up the Prefecture of Police of Paris as a rival police force.

One of the Emperor's secretaries, Baron Fain, remembered that meetings of the Council of Ministers (usually held on Wednesdays) were like lessons, with the Emperor as teacher. Outside these meetings, every minister had to keep the Emperor supplied with *livrets* or handbooks, renewed every two or four weeks, which informed him of the state of their department — the numbers in each regiment, the price of wheat, the yield of taxes.[16]

Another important instrument of government, in addition to the Ministries, was the Council of State, composed of the fifty least stupid men in France according to Stendhal. They gave their opinions on government projects and policy with astonishing freedom. But they were nominated by the Emperor and the subjects under discussion were chosen by the Emperor. They were his servants, and they met in a room in the Tuileries.

Napoleon I was now a monarch with almost total power; and his true nature became increasingly apparent. The Emperor was a political and military genius, who had risen to power through the Revolution. He used to say that his nobility dated from the *coup d'état* of November 1799. But this was only a figure of speech. In reality he came from an ancient Italian noble family from Sarzana in Liguria, which had moved to Corsica in the late fifteenth century. As he recalled on Saint-Helena, the Bonapartes had been so proud of their birth and position that they felt they were the Bourbons of Corsica.[17]

As he grew older, and the temporary intoxication of the Revolution wore off, Bonaparte's fundamental aristocratic and monarchical instincts began to assert themselves. The means he had used to become Emperor — a coup, plebiscites, the support of ex-revolutionaries — were revolutionary. But the end — a hereditary throne for himself and his family — was traditional. Indeed, by becoming a monarch, Napoleon I realized the dream of many other ambitious nobles throughout European history. He belonged to (and was the last of) the long line of noble founders of royal dynasties, which included Gustavus Vasa of Sweden in the sixteenth century, and Michael Romanov of Russia in the seventeenth. Napoleon's genius was unparalleled, but not the use he made of it.

Once on the throne Napoleon I was determined to be a better defender of monarchical and aristocratic principles than his feeble Bourbon rivals. A splendid court would be a particularly effective means of strengthening monarchy and aristocracy; and the Emperor needed a splendid court more than most monarchs. Out of loyalty to their exiled sovereign, or hatred of the French Revolution, many members of the old ruling classes, both in France and in the newly conquered territories of Belgium, the Rhineland and Piedmont, did not accept Napoleon I. A splendid court might win their support. It would also demonstrate that the Emperor was quite different from his disreputable predecessors of the Directory and the Republic.

One of the main differences between the court of Napoleon I and others is that his court was a conscious creation of the monarch's will. It was not the product of centuries of traditions and accumulated 'rights'. It was formed at the beginning of the nineteenth century and all its officials were selected, often to their own surprise, by the Emperor himself. Thus the court reveals as much about the Emperor's character as it does about the society of his day. It shows how the greatest genius to sit on a throne interpreted his role as a monarch.

In July 1804 the *Maison de S.M. l'Empereur*, the Emperor's official household, was set up in six departments, known as 'services': the chapel, the palace, the chamber, the stables, the hunt and the ceremonies. Each service was directed by a Grand Officer: the Grand Almoner, Grand Marshal of the Palace, Grand Chamberlain, Grand Equerry, Grand Huntsman and Grand Master of Ceremonies respectively. The uniforms of the officials of each service were a different colour (with the exception of the priests, who wore ecclesiastical dress): red for the palace, scarlet for the chamber, blue for the stables, green for the hunt and violet for the ceremonies.

The chapel was responsible for the religious life of the court, but it was never an important department. The Emperor always kept religious ceremonies to a minimum: he attended Mass only once a week, whereas the kings of France had attended it every day. In 1813 the department contained only thirty priests and employees. They celebrated Mass in the palace chapels, and dis-

Gérard, *General Moreau* *Moreau, the ablest French general after Bonaparte, was described as 'remarkably simple in his dress and manners'. He refused to attend the growing court of the First Consul, saying that he was 'too old to stoop'.*

tributed the Emperor's contributions to charity.

Duroc, promoted from Governor of the Tuileries to be Grand Marshal of the Palace, was head of the largest service of the court, with 224 servants in the kitchens and 474 in the palaces. They were responsible for feeding the court and for the maintenance of the palaces. Since the Emperor had more palaces than any contemporary monarch (see Chapter 3), this was an immense task. The Grand Marshal was helped in supervising the kitchens — which, like many royal kitchens, were a hive of dishonesty and waste — by four Prefects of the Palace.

The service of the chamber (258 people in 1813) was in charge of the Emperor's state and private apartments on the first floor of his palaces. No other department was so closely connected with the person of the Emperor. It was responsible for his clothes and jewels and his social relations with individuals. It included valets who looked after the apartments, ushers who stood at the doors and announced visitors' names and the servants who shaved and dressed the Emperor. There were also a number of chamberlains (107 in 1814), who presented people to the Emperor. Most of them were of noble birth, and their rank and number added lustre to the household.

The transport of the court was the responsibility of the stables. Since the Emperor was the most mobile monarch of his day, this was an immense task, and this department was larger than many regiments. By 1813 it included 1113 horses, 180 carriages and 630 people: grooms, coachmen, footmen, and equerries, some of whom can always be seen in the battle pictures of the Empire, since it was they who had transported the Emperor onto the battlefield. The School of Pages also formed part of the stables, and pages accompanied the Emperor on his travels and onto the battlefield (one was captured at Waterloo). In 1813 a staff of 37 was educating 60 pages to be officers in the army.

Gérard, ***The Emperor in coronation robes***
Napoleon is depicted in the Tuileries, in front of his throne, with his crown of golden laurel leaves on his head. This majestic official portrait was painted in 1805. It appealed to him so much that he gave copies of it, in preference to any other, to relations, allies, courtiers and every French mission abroad, both diplomatic and consular.

Hunting was held to be a particularly royal form of exercise, and the Emperor, like the kings of France, often indulged in it. His hunt was much smaller than theirs had been before 1789; it contained only 93 huntsmen and servants. Napoleon I was a bad shot, frequently endangering people's lives: Marshal Masséna lost an eye owing to the unsteadiness of the imperial aim. Moreover the poaching and tree-felling which had been going on since 1789 in the old royal hunting-forests around Paris meant that the hunting available was, by royal standards, second-rate. As late as 1812 it was noted that the hunts of the King of Saxony were far better than those of the Emperor of the French.

Whereas the service of the chamber was responsible for the Emperor's receptions for individuals, the 18 people in the service of the ceremonies organized his receptions of institutions, such as the Senate and the Council of State. They also regulated the great formal ceremonies of the reign, such as the Coronation in 1804, the receptions for the feast of Saint-Napoléon (a saint the Pope had hastily rediscovered when the First Consul had become a good Catholic) every 15 August, and the Te Deums for his innumerable victories.

Apart from this civil household, the Emperor also had a military household of 13 aides-de-camp and 13 ordonnance officers. They acted as his eyes and ears in military matters. At the battle of Bautzen in 1813, for example, the Emperor sent off so many ordonnance officers bearing orders to his generals, or in search of news, that none were left around him.[18]

The Imperial Guard was also, in a sense, part of the Emperor's court, since it was devoted to the personal service of the Emperor and his family, and he kept it distinct from the army by innumerable privileges of pay, rank, splendour and imperial attention. Its connection with the court was confirmed by the fact that its four Colonels-General, Marshals Bessières, Mortier, Soult and Davout, officially formed part of the Emperor's military household, as did its eleven senior commanding officers. The Imperial Guard was an essential part of court life when the Emperor or Empress was in residence. Its splendid rigid soldiers (usually about 120 at a time) were always on duty at the entrances to the palace. Its uniforms and music added incomparable glamour to the Napoleonic court.

In addition to his civil and military households, the Emperor's court also included a number of outer departments, with 811 employees. They ran the forests, parks, museums, buildings and furniture of the Crown, and those legendary generators

Isabey, *The coronation in Notre Dame* *The Emperor is putting the crown on his head. The Pope, who came from Rome especially for the occasion, is beside him. The Empress, Napoleon's brothers Joseph and Louis and senior officials are in front of him. This is a more faithful record of this dazzling ceremony than David's celebrated picture.*

of French monarchical magnificence, the Crown factories of Sèvres, Aubusson, Savonnerie and Gobelins. Although these departments were not directly connected with the person of the monarch, and indeed had continued to exist throughout the Revolution, they were nevertheless officially regarded as part of the *Maison de S.M. l'Empereur*. So was the Emperor's private secretariat, known as the Secretariat of State.

Napoleon's desire for complete personal control meant that the household of the Empress was also part of his court. As a regulation of 1804 explained, 'His Majesty has decided to have only one household and only one administration.'[19] The chief of each department of the Empress's household was under the authority of the chief of the equivalent department in the household of the Emperor — a great difference from the almost independent households of the Queen and other members of the royal family under Louis XVI.

The Empress had a First Almoner, a lord-in-waiting who escorted her on all public occasions and a First Equerry in charge of her stables. The most important figure in her household was the Dame d'Honneur, or principal lady-in-waiting. She organized the Empress's household, supervised the servants and was responsible for her social life. Below the Dame d'Honneur were a number of Dames du Palais, or ladies-in-waiting. The Empress Josephine had 20 in 1809; the Emperor's second wife, the Empress Marie-Louise, had 36 in 1814. Marie-Antoinette had only had 16 in 1789.

Including the senior officials of the Household of the Empress Marie-Louise, there were almost 2000 people in the Emperor's Household in 1813. If the staff of the outer departments of the court are included the total rises to 2751, and it increases even further if those employed outside France are taken into account. As the French Empire expanded during the reign of Napoleon I, so did the number of his palaces and the size of his court. In 1813 775 officials and employees were working in the Emperor's palaces and museums in Piedmont, Tuscany, Rome and Holland. Thus the Household of His Majesty the Emperor and King employed an astonishing total of 3526 people throughout the French Empire.

In addition, since the Empress Marie-Louise, the Empress Josephine, the Emperor's mother Madame Mère and his sister-in-law Queen Hortense all lived in or near Paris, all the members of their households could also be considered as part of the court. Although exact figures are not available, the total number in the Emperor's court in 1813 was probably over 4000.

The cost of the court was borne by the Emperor's civil list, fixed at the start of his reign at 25 million francs a year (about 3 per cent of government expenditure). In addition he received the revenues from the Crown lands around Paris, known as the Domain of the Crown, which amounted to about 3 million francs a year. Although prices had risen considerably since Louis XVI had been given the same income in 1790, the Emperor's settlement was in reality extremely generous. Louis XVI had had to pay for the enormous households of his wife, children, sister and aunts out of his civil list (his brothers, like the Emperor's, received separate incomes from the government). He also had to pay for his Bodyguard, which cost 8 million francs a year. In contrast, Napoleon I's female relations had smaller and cheaper households than Louis XVI's. Most important of all, the Imperial Guard was paid for by the Ministry of War, not the civil list. The Emperor's financial position grew even stronger with the expansion of his Empire.

As the Emperor annexed Tuscany, the Papal States and Holland, he added the properties of the defeated monarchs to what he already had. As a result, by 1813 his income had grown to 36,269,019 francs. Money for the court also came from the Domaine Extraordinaire — the lands he confiscated from governments or individuals in the countries he had conquered. It was probably the greatest single accumulation of property in European history. Although much of it was used to balance the budget of the Empire, or to pay the army in time of war, it was a source of wealth which the Emperor kept under his own control. The cash was stored in the cellars of the Tuileries. The Emperor also had the Domaine Privé — his private property, and the money he saved from his French civil list, which is said to have amounted to 150 million francs in 1814. Although the cost of the court jumped from around 15,152,000 francs in 1805 to 29,233,454 in 1813, because of the increase in its

Marzocchi (after Gautherot), *Marshal Davout, Colonel-General of the Imperial Guard* *Davout was ruthless, loyal and effective on the battlefield. This portrait comes from the series of marshals' portraits, commissioned by the Emperor in 1805, which hung in the Hall of Marshals in the Tuileries.*

size and in the number and splendour of Napoleon's palaces, the civil list could cope.[20] For the first time in decades money was no problem at the court of France.

One of the reasons for the court's sound financial position was that the Emperor paid close personal attention to its budget. He drew it up himself in 1807, and wrote to Duroc: 'I crossed out what I did not want included.' He attended many meetings of the body which went through the accounts, known as the Council of Administration of the Household, fixing the expenses of each service himself. His extraordinary energy did not fade before the most mundane details. In January 1810, for example, he decided to go through 'all the objects of expense in the greatest detail' for the stables. If the Bourbon kings had devoted even a fraction of the Emperor's attention to the expenses of their court, they would have saved a fortune. When he was in exile on Elba, Napoleon even checked the number of grapes and lettuces consumed by his household.[21]

In structure the Emperor's court was rather conventional. Most other courts, including that of Louis XVI, had had the same divisions into the services of the chapel, the stables, the ceremonies and so on. However, the Emperor's court, despite its size, was not so large as that of Louis XVI. In every department, particularly in the stables, far fewer servants were employed than at Versailles. It was also less domestic than the court of Louis XVI. Its senior officials performed fewer personal duties for the monarch (see p. 49). The two independent departments devoted to Louis XVI's food and clothes, the Mouth and the Wardrobe, were, in the household of the Emperor, absorbed into the services of the palace and the chamber.

Whereas the court of Versailles had been in essence domestic, traditional and French, the Napoleonic court was élitist, military and European. Louis XVI had had many servants in his service of the chamber, but only one Grand Chamberlain and four First Gentlemen of the Chamber. Napoleon I had fewer servants, but one Grand Chamberlain, one First Chamberlain and 107 other chamberlains. Napoleon I had 26 aides-de-camp and ordonnance officers: Louis XVI had had none. The significance of these figures is that the chamberlains, equerries and aides-de-camp in Napoleon's household came from the élite of birth and wealth, which was therefore more numerous at his court than at that of Louis XVI.

Napoleon's court was more European than the court of Versailles because he was not only Emperor of the French but also King of 'Italy' (that is to say, the north-eastern quarter of present-day Italy, including Lombardy, Venetia and Romagna). As King of Italy Napoleon I had a separate Italian

Appiani, ***Napoleon crowns himself King of Italy, in Milan Cathedral, 26 May 1805*** *Napoleon is surrounded by his Italian court and is wearing his costume as King of Italy; Josephine watches from a box. Appiani was First Painter of Napoleon as King of Italy and helped organize the coronation ceremony. This scene comes from Appiani's* Triumphs of Napoleon *which adorned the throne room of the palace of Milan.*

household based in Milan, which he called 'my household of Italy'.

This household was formed by the Viceroy, his stepson Prince Eugene, in 1805-06. It observed the same etiquette as the French court, and was organized in the same way, although on a smaller scale: there were only 35 chamberlains in 1814 compared to 107 in the French household. There was a Grand Almoner, a Grand Master (the equivalent of Grand Marshal of the Palace), a Grand Chamberlain, a Grand Equerry, a Dame d'Honneur, and 26 ladies-in-waiting: there was no Grand Huntsman or Grand Master of Ceremonies.[22]

The Italian household was paid for by a separate Italian civil list. Although Prince Eugene was careful not to spend too much money on it, Duroc described the court as 'well organized'. It was much grander than the court maintained, before and after the Empire, by the Austrian Viceroys of Lombardy. It made Milan, more than at any other time in its history, a 'court city' with the atmosphere of a capital. The Italian household served the Viceroy in Milan until 1814: it only served the Emperor during his visits to Italy in 1805 and 1807, and when it sent a deputation of 53 senior officials to Paris for the Emperor's wedding to Marie-Louise in 1810. When the two courts met, Italian court officials had to give precedence to French court officials of the same rank.[23]

The Emperor's court was also more European than that of Louis XVI because many of his courtiers and servants came from the newly conquered territories of Belgium, the Rhine and Piedmont, where many of his palaces were situated. In addition, one of his models was the greatest single source of rank and honour in Europe, which had been more influential than the court of Versailles itself, namely the Holy Roman Empire. After Napoleon became Emperor of the French in 1804, he created Grand Dignitaries of the Empire, such as Cambacérès, the Arch-Chancellor (who told his old friends, 'in private do not address me as Highness, simply call me Monseigneur'), Lebrun the Arch-Treasurer and later Talleyrand the Vice-Grand Elector. These titles, which carried no effective functions, were reminiscent of those which

ABOVE **Gérard, *Prince Eugene, Viceroy of Italy*** *Prince Eugene, represented here in the official costume of a French prince, ruled the Kingdom of Italy as Viceroy for his stepfather the Emperor from 1805 to 1814.*

RIGHT **Anon, *Count Angelo Lecchi*** *The Lecchis were an ancient noble family of Brescia in Lombardy, which served Napoleon with enthusiasm and was admired by the novelist Stendhal. Angelo Lecchi was an equerry and an officer in the Italian army.*

RIGHT **Canonica, *The entry of the Emperor into Milan in 1805*** *The Emperor has come to be crowned. Wherever he went he was greeted by triumphal arches erected in his honour, which were dismantled after his departure.*

BELOW RIGHT **Anon, *The entry of the Emperor into Milan in 1807*** *The Emperor made a brief visit to Italy in November 1807, greeted by a fresh set of triumphal arches, in order to inspect his Kingdom and see his brother Lucien. Lucien, however, refused to divorce his wife and become King of Spain, as Napoleon wished.*

FAR RIGHT **Borsato, *The entry of the Emperor into Venice in 1807*** *The Emperor is about to be rowed down the Grand Canal in a state barge. A triumphal arch has been erected over the canal, and soldiers of the Italian Royal Guard line its banks. It was said that Napoleon made more changes in Venice in four days than Austria had made in four years.*

PROSPETTO DELL' ARCO TRIONFALE
ERETTO ALL' IMBOCCATVRA
DEL CANALE GRANDE IN VENEZIA
PER LA VENVTA DI S. M. I. R.
NAPOLEONE IL MASSIMO
IMPERATORE DEI FRANCESI RE D' ITALIA
A. Selva inv.
G. Borsato delin
G. Maina Sculp.

had been given to the Electors of the Holy Roman Empire. Indeed, in 1806, the year Francis I, who had already taken the title Emperor of Austria, abolished the Holy Roman Empire, Napoleon became Protector of the Confederation of the Rhine which replaced it.

But the court of Napoleon I reflected most faithfully the current monarchical practice of the day. In its structure and organization it was not substantially different from the courts of great contemporary monarchs, like the Emperors Francis I of Austria and Alexander I of Russia and King Frederick William III of Prussia. Indeed, the titles of chamberlain and Grand Marshal of the Palace, and the layout of the palaces, were European, particularly Austrian, rather than French. Under Napoleon I the court of France lost its unusual domestic features and became as élitist and institutional as the other courts of Europe. This European influence made the court more formal, and the monarch more distant, than had been the case under Louis XVI.

However, the Napoleonic court could not completely escape the influence of Versailles. Indeed it became increasingly important after Napoleon ascended the throne. Although few of the Emperor's senior court officials had served at the court of Versailles, a very large proportion of his servants had been born in the town: most of its inhabitants had been connected with the royal households, and knew the customs and traditions of the old court. The First Doctor and the Governess of the Children of France (itself a pre-1789 title) based the organization of their services, in 1804 and 1810 respectively, explicitly on the practice of the court of Louis XVI. The Emperor wrote in 1805 that mourning at his court should be based on 'the court of Versailles, whose practice I want [to follow]'. Eagerness to imitate Versailles can be detected in a note from Duroc to the Grand Master of Ceremonies, certainly written on the Emperor's instructions, at the time of the birth of the Emperor's son, the King of Rome: 'Did the Dauphin's carriage have eight or six horses?'[24] Despite its size and splendour, there was a certain lack of self-confidence at the heart of the Napoleonic court.

All the government ministries together employed about the same number of people as the Emperor's court in 1813. The question is whether the court began to rival the government in importance as well as numbers. In such an autocratic monarchy as the Empire it would have been surprising if an institution devoted to the personal service of the Emperor did not assume a significance beyond its apparent functions.

Indeed the Secretariat of State, which was officially part of the 'Household of His Majesty the Emperor and King', came to be more influential than the whole government. The Emperor used this department as an instrument of centralization and control. Its seventy officials kept records of all his decisions and issued his orders to officials. Napoleon liked to say that he could govern the entire Empire with the Minister Secretary of State and half a dozen secretaries, whether he was in Illyria or Russia.

The Minister Secretary of State for almost the entire reign was a former revolutionary politician, Maret, later created Duke de Bassano. Unlike the other ministers Maret could see the Emperor at any time of day or night. Napoleon's secretary Baron Fain said that he was Prime Minister in reality and, under any other monarch, would have been Prime Minister in name as well.

Maret hardly ever contradicted the Emperor — or, as Fain put it, in the official French of the time, he was 'less capable than anyone of openly disagreeing with the Emperor's ideas'. That a man like Maret, a member of the household, a man famous for his 'soft, conciliatory manner' and his personal devotion to the Emperor, should have been the effective Prime Minister was a symbol of what led the Empire to disaster, and hundreds of thousands of people to their deaths.[25] Napoleon had seized power by a military *coup d'état*, and consolidated it by his victories. Even more than most monarchs he liked wars; and there was no individual or institution to prevent him starting new ones.

2
The Emperor and his Court

Then, taking the almanac [the Emperor] looks at the names of the ladies-in-waiting and appears deeply moved: 'It was a fine Empire!'

Diary of Baron Gourgaud, First Ordonnance Officer, Saint-Helena, January 1817.

WHEN HE WAS FIRST CONSUL, Napoleon had been surrounded by ministers, generals and councillors of state. After 1804 they were less prominent. It was the Emperor's courtiers who were always with him. He was not like contemporary monarchs, such as the King of Bavaria or the Emperor of Austria, who walked in the streets of their capitals unaccompanied, chatting to their subjects with a minimum of formality. In contrast Napoleon I believed, correctly, 'in Paris nobody would have been able to get used to the idea of a sovereign walking in the streets'.[1] His court surrounded him wherever he went (except when, very occasionally, he went on incognito walks through Paris with Duroc).

On a journey to Holland in 1811, for example, he was accompanied by the Grand Marshal of the Palace, the Grand Equerry, the Grand Huntsman, two aides-de-camp, two equerries, four ordonnance officers, four members of his Cabinet or private office, four pages and a doctor. The Empress was accompanied by the Grand Chamberlain, four ladies-in-waiting (the court was so international that they were French, Genoese, Roman and Belgian respectively), four chamberlains, two equerries, two officials in charge of accommodation, two doctors, four pages and her First Equerry; and these figures exclude servants.

A reduced household followed the Emperor when he went on campaign. It included valets, pages, equerries, aides-de-camp and Duroc. It was ready to leave, at any time of day or night, when the Emperor said '*A cheval!*' Baron Fain wrote: 'Everything seemed to happen at once and without planning; but everything was regulated according to a clock which only told the time for Napoleon.' In the campaign of 1809 against Austria, the Emperor travelled so fast that he left his household behind, and for a few days had to live 'as a soldier'; but this was an exceptional event.[2]

His court not only surrounded the Emperor; it also provided the basic structure of his day, more than was the case with many monarchs. The Emperor spent most of the day working alone with his ministers and secretaries (he also dictated to a secretary from two to five in the morning). This was the centre of his existence, his real life and the heart of his Empire. However, the Emperor also spent part of the day with his courtiers and servants. He gossiped with his servants between seven and eight in the morning, while they bathed, shaved and dressed him, and rubbed him with eau-de-Cologne. His favourite servants were his First Valet, Constant, and Roustam, a former Georgian slave he had brought back from Egypt. Roustam slept outside the Emperor's bedroom, on a special bed which could fold into a cupboard in the daytime. Although Roustam was as unpopular with the Emperor's courtiers as Queen Victoria's Indian servant 'the Munshi' was with hers, he followed the Emperor everywhere, on campaign as well as on the journeys of the court. The sight of Roustam in his lavish oriental costume was a sure sign that the Emperor was nearby.

The Emperor received his court officials at his *lever* at 9 am and his *coucher* after 11 pm, which meant that they saw him before and after everyone else. These were relatively intimate occasions,

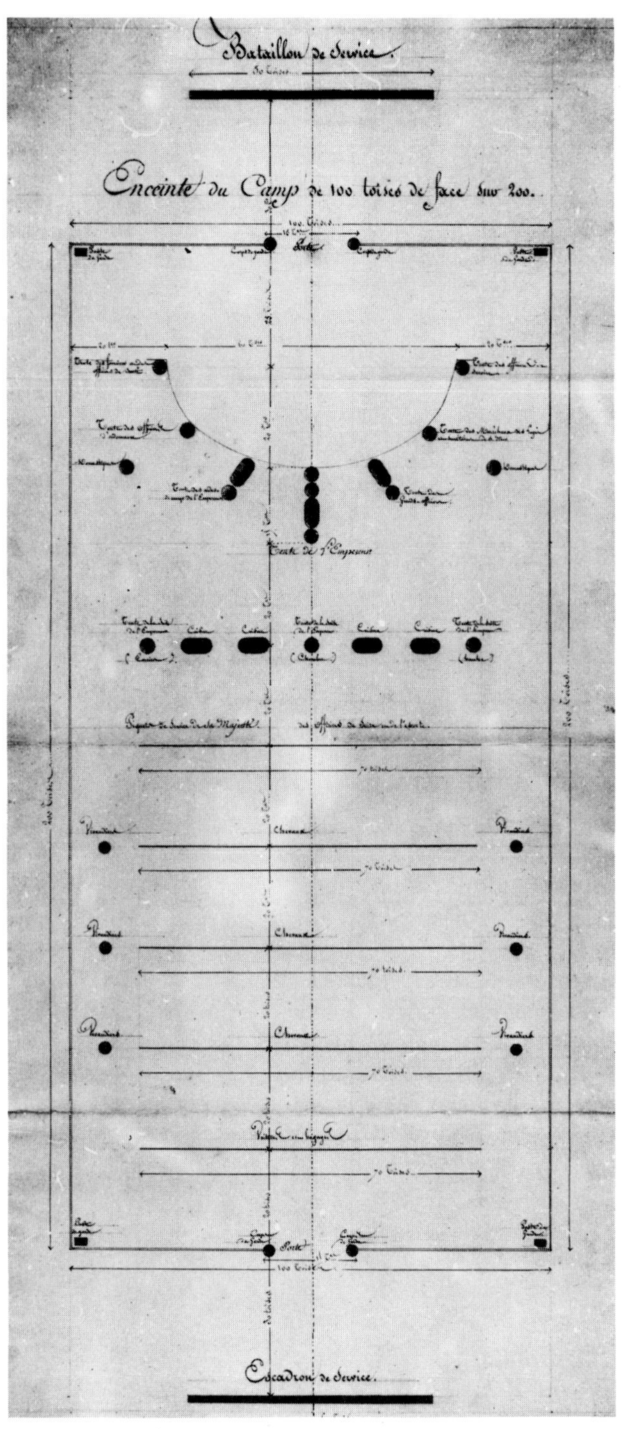

Plan of the Emperor's camp *The Emperor's tent (at the centre of the semicircle) is surrounded by those of his courtiers, doctor and servants. The Emperor's tent was in red, white and blue, the colours of the tricolour, and contained two salons, a study and a bedroom. It could be erected in half an hour.*

when there could be a real conversation between the Emperor and his courtiers. He said that he often learnt important items of news from his chamberlains; the stupidest were frequently the most informative.[3]

The most important of the courtiers admitted to the *lever* and the *coucher*, the people who really ran the Emperor's daily life, were the six Grand Officers, who were in charge of the six services of the household. The first in order of precedence, the Grand Almoner Cardinal Fesch, was half-brother of the Emperor's mother Letizia. As well as being in charge of the religious life of the Emperor and the court, he also had the right to appoint chaplains for the army, the navy and prisons, to run religious missions in France and abroad, and to direct the Emperor's official charities. Fesch was a pious, not very intelligent priest, who liked long religious ceremonies. His devotion to his religious duties did not prevent him amassing a fortune and an impressive collection of pictures.

Duroc, Grand Marshal of the Palace, was the most important court official and the person with most influence over the Emperor. Like the Emperor himself, he was a member of the lesser nobility, the *petite noblesse*, who had attended the military school of Brienne and had continued to serve in the French army during the Revolution. He was an ideal courtier, cold, polite and efficient. Since he hardly ever left the Emperor, he often directed his department from a great distance. On 4 December 1812, for example, he wrote to the secretary-general of the Tuileries from Bianitsa in western Russia, his hand trembling with cold, about the budget of the palace.

Duroc was not only the leading court official; he was also used by the Emperor to conduct delicate diplomatic negotiations, with the King of Prussia in 1801 and 1805, or the King of Spain in 1807, and to raise Polish regiments for the Imperial Guard in 1807. Duroc was liked at court: he often tried to smooth over the effects of the Emperor's outbursts of rudeness, assuring the victims that the Emperor's mood would pass. When he died in agony on the battlefield of Bautzen, in May 1813, the Emperor was distressed. He wrote, with characteristic self-centredness: 'it is the only time in twenty years that he did not guess what would please me'.[4]

Duroc was succeeded as Grand Marshal of the Palace by another of the Emperor's aides-de-camp, Count Bertrand. Bertrand followed the Emperor to Elba in 1814, back to France when he returned in triumph in 1815 and finally to Saint-Helena. When the Emperor's domains had shrunk to an Italian island, or a few battalions marching on Paris, Bertrand, in his capacity as Grand Marshal of the Palace, acted as the Emperor's chief political and military adviser — as Duroc, in their private, unrecorded conversations, had probably always done.

The Emperor's courtiers could be political figures of the greatest importance. The Emperor's personal style of government meant that he not only employed them on government business, but also chose many people already prominent in public life to serve in his household. For example, Talleyrand is best known as a devious and corrupt Minister of Foreign Affairs, but he was also Grand Chamberlain from 1804 to 1809.

He came from a noble family which believed itself to be more ancient than the Bourbons. His parents had served at the court of Versailles, and he himself had been a prominent revolutionary politician. He had the qualities of tact, experience and self-confidence necessary to set up a court department. Although there is mysteriously little trace of Talleyrand's years as Grand Chamberlain in the archives of the Household of the Emperor, he was a real, not a nominal, court official. For example, he signed the bills for the Emperor's coronation robes and the embroidery of his throne, and ensured that the stars of the Emperor's orders were sewn onto his coats in the correct manner.[5] He handed the Emperor a glass of lemonade after dinner, if the Empress was not present, and organized the *entrées* to the Emperor's private apartments. Duroc wrote to him in January 1808, about the *entrées*: 'Your Most Serene Highness can alone give orders about this matter.'

Whatever his political doubts, in his role as a courtier Talleyrand appeared to be devoted to the Emperor and the imperial family. When he was dismissed as Grand Chamberlain in 1809, as a result of a political disagreement with the Emperor (see Chapter 7), he wrote: 'Among the dignities with which [Your Majesty] had deigned to honour me, that which attached me more particularly to the service of his person was most precious to me.'[6] Such language, exalting the personal service of the Emperor above all else, was what the Emperor heard from his courtiers every day of his reign.

To his great surprise, for he had had little contact with the regime, the Count de Montesquiou was chosen by the Emperor to succeed Talleyrand as Grand Chamberlain. Montesquiou also came from an ancient noble family which claimed to be older than the Bourbons. He had known the court of Versailles, had been an ambassador of Louis XVI

Isabey and Percier, ***Cardinal Fesch, Grand Almoner*** *Cardinal Fesch was made Archbishop of both Lyons and Paris by his nephew the Emperor. This illustration, like those on pages 47 and 80, comes from the official Book of the Coronation, which took eleven years to finish. Isabey, who had designed the costumes, also drew the figures. Percier, the intimate friend of the Emperor's architect Fontaine, did the decorative borders. Here is the court as it wanted to be seen, in full official costume, and commemorated by its own artists.*

FAR LEFT **Gros, *Duroc, Grand Marshal of the Palace*** *Duroc, who had been Napoleon's aide-de-camp since 1796, was his only real friend. He is standing on a balcony of the Tuileries palace, which he ruled until his death in 1813. This portrait, like those on pages 39, 40 and 46, was part of a series of portraits of senior court officials, which was commissioned by the Emperor and hung in the palace of Compiègne.*

LEFT **Prud'hon, *Talleyrand, Grand Chamberlain*** *Talleyrand's love of luxury and sense of style made him an appropriate choice as Grand Chamberlain. He is wearing the red and silver uniform of his office, from which he was dismissed for criticism of the Emperor's policies in 1809.*

ABOVE **Sauerweid, *The Emperor's horse l'Epicurien*** *Only the best horses in the stables were designated as 'suitable for the Emperor'. In 1813 a series of portraits of these horses, of which this is one, was ordered by Caulaincourt.*

LEFT **Gérard, *Caulaincourt, Grand Equerry*** *Caulaincourt was the leading advocate of peace at court. Although lavishly rewarded with money, titles and offices, by the end of the regime he was disillusioned with the Emperor.*

and proved an ideal Grand Chamberlain. He was so discreet and so well-mannered that his years at court, miraculously, aroused almost no hostile comments. He remained loyal to the Emperor until the end.

The Grand Equerry, the Count de Caulaincourt, 'established an order and a discipline which Napoleon greatly appreciated' in the stables, largely by force of personality. Under Louis XVI the stables had been one of the most extravagant departments of the court and Caulaincourt's task was not easy. In 1805 he had to command maids and valets to be forced physically into their carriages, in order to get them to leave in time to reach Milan for the Emperor's coronation as King of Italy. When the Emperor, who was always in a hurry, ordered his coachman and postilion to drive faster, Caulaincourt's concern for his department was such that he would lean out of his carriage (which usually

Sèvres breakfast service *The stables provided the Emperor with the best carriages and horses available, and the crown factory of Sèvres with the finest porcelain. He gave presents of Sèvres every year to favoured courtiers. He sent this service, with a tray showing him out for a drive with the Empress, to his sister Caroline in 1814. It was probably for display rather than use.*

followed the Emperor's) and tell them to slow down, in order to save the horses.[7]

Like Talleyrand, Caulaincourt came from a family which had served at the court of Louis XVI. However, since he had been used by Napoleon to help kidnap a young Bourbon prince, the Duke d'Enghien (who was later executed), on neutral territory in 1804, he was loathed by many royalists. He was a noble of the old regime who became one of the most important political figures of the Empire, as Ambassador to Russia and Minister of Foreign Affairs. He was also one of the five members of the Commission of Government at the end of Napoleon's brief return in 1815 known as the Hundred Days. When he was serving as Ambassador in St Petersburg, the First Equerry, the Count de Nansouty, took charge of the stables.

The Grand Huntsman, Marshal Berthier, encouraged the Emperor to go hunting as frequently as possible. As the Emperor's indefatigable chief of staff he also had access to Napoleon whenever he wanted. Berthier helped to make the French army into an apparently invincible weapon of conquest (his absence would be one reason for the Emperor's defeat at Waterloo). His father had worked in the Ministry of War at Versailles and he was a natural monarchist, who had encouraged the First Consul to move to Saint-Cloud when the idea was first discussed.

Berthier was one of the Emperor's most important and most devoted servants. With Talleyrand, he was also one of the most lavishly rewarded. Talleyrand became Vice-Grand Elector (the only vice he did not have, a friend remarked) and Prince de Bénévent. Berthier became Vice-Constable, Prince de Neufchâtel, and later Prince of Wagram too. As a result they were sovereign princes, who signed themselves simply 'Charles-Maurice' and 'Alexandre', as if they were of royal blood. Berthier became one of the richest men in France and — much against his will, as he was in love with a beautiful *marchesa* from Milan — was married to a Wittelsbach, a princess of the dynasty which had ruled Bavaria for a thousand

Carle Vernet, ***The Emperor hunting in the forest of Compiègne*** *The Emperor, in hunting costume, is shooting a stag which has been brought to bay; he is watched by the staff of the Imperial Hunt and by Marie-Louise from her carriage. Napoleon hunted because it was a traditional royal exercise, rather than out of personal inclination.*

years. The ceremony, performed by Cardinal Fesch, took place in the chapel of the Tuileries. Berthier's aides-de-camp were the best dressed and most aristocratic young men in the army. His wife's carriage was the most elegant at the Parisians' annual fashion parade at Longchamp. His career shows that the court of Napoleon I was one of the most effective means of rapid upward mobility in the history of Europe.[8]

One of Berthier's witnesses at his marriage was the Grand Master of Ceremonies, the Count de Ségur. Formerly the Ambassador of Louis XVI to the court of Catherine II of Russia, Ségur had known the courts of Europe as well as the court of Versailles, where his father had been Minister of War. He was famous for being 'the most amiable Frenchman of the old school': for a time, ruined by the Revolution, he had lived off his pen, writing plays, verse and works of history. When he became Grand Master of Ceremonies, his brother the Viscount de Ségur began to call himself 'Ségur without ceremony'.

Ségur had the task of satisfying the paroxysms of vanity displayed by the members of institutions such as the Senate or the Council of State, desperate to obtain suitable rank at court after the proclamation of the Empire. Ségur organized the Emperor's lavish, extremely impressive coronations in Paris in December 1804 and in Milan in May 1805, and was treated as a trusted adviser and friend by the imperial family. His letters to the Emperor's sister Elisa show him to have been a graceful, practised flatterer, delighted when he had to organize the visit of a 'crowd of kings' to the Emperor's court.

Although Stendhal admired the grace with which Ségur spoke, he thought Ségur was a 'dwarf . . . one of the Emperor's weaknesses'. Stendhal sums him up by saying that he was 'consumed with chagrin at not being a duke. In his eyes it was worse than a misfortune, it was a breach of good manners'.[9] The fact that his colleagues Duroc and Caulaincourt were both made dukes (of Frioul and Vicence respectively), while Berthier and Talleyrand became princes, must

LEFT **Pajou, *Berthier, Grand Huntsman*** *Berthier points to a map of one of the Crown hunting forests, which he tried to restore to their former glory before the Revolution. Beside him is a bust of the Emperor, who showered him with honours and whom he was to desert in 1814.*

ABOVE **Isabey and Percier, *Ségur, Grand Master of Ceremonies*** *Ségur was a former ambassador who enjoyed his task of creating the rules and etiquette of the court. He was one of the few courtiers who remained loyal to Napoleon from the beginning of the Empire to the end.*

have made his title of count even more embarrassing to Ségur.

Fesch, Duroc, Talleyrand, Caulaincourt, Berthier, Ségur, Bertrand and Montesquiou were all part of the Emperor's daily life. When he was in Paris, he saw and talked to them every day at the *lever* or the *coucher*: and Berthier and Duroc (and often Caulaincourt) followed him on campaign. Another occasion for informal contact with his courtiers was in the evening, in the apartments of the Empress, when Napoleon received what were known as the *Petites Entrées* — those senior court and government officials, and certain intellectuals, who had the right to come to the Empress's apartments until she retired at about half past ten.

Most of the people with the *Petites Entrées* were court officials or their spouses. 'Going to the *entrées*' (*aller aux entrées*), as Talleyrand called it, in his elegant pre-revolutionary French, was an important part of the courtier's day. Every nuance of the Emperor and Empress's behaviour and appearance was analysed. Talleyrand, for example, wondered what it meant that on one day the Emperor addressed him as *Monsieur le Vice-Grand Electeur*, and on another as *Monsieur le Prince de Bénévent*.[10]

At Versailles senior court officials such as the Grand Officers had dressed and undressed the King every day, and had attended him when he dined in state, once or twice a week. This aspect of court life was greatly reduced, although not abolished, by Napoleon I. In keeping with the modernized, stream-lined character of the Napoleonic court, few courtiers were present at the Emperor's meals.

FAR LEFT, ABOVE *Napoleon filled his palaces with furniture, books and utensils stamped with his crown, his initial and the mark of each palace. These wine-glasses bear the mark of, left to right, the Trianon, the Tuileries and the Elysée, as well as the crown and N.*

FAR LEFT, BELOW *This teapot comes from a silver-gilt service, designed by Percier and made by the Emperor's goldsmith Biennais, which was delivered in 1810. The Emperor sometimes spent as much as half a million francs in one year on gold and silver.*

LEFT *The sword, covered in N's, bees and eagles, was made by Biennais and used by Napoleon only on the most formal occasions.*

He did not dine in state, served by his court officials, more than once or twice a year. The Emperor took his main morning meal at about ten, at a table set up in one of the rooms of his private apartments — or, when he was on campaign, in one of his tents. His favourite food was fricassee of chicken — now known, after one of his greatest victories, as chicken Marengo — lentils or haricot beans and rice. His favourite wine was a white Burgundy, Chambertin. The Prefect of the Palace in waiting supervised the serving of his morning meal by the *maîtres d'hôtel*. It rarely lasted more than ten minutes, after which his nephews and nieces, or (after 1811) his son, would be brought in to be played with and teased by the Emperor.[11]

Dinner was served by the pages. It was a slightly longer and more elaborate meal, and the Emperor always took it with one of the most important figures of the court, the Empress.

Napoleon's first Empress, born Josephine Tascher de La Pagerie, came from Martinique, and was the widow of a revolutionary noble, Alexandre de Beauharnais. She had two children by her first husband, Eugene and Hortense de Beauharnais, but none by Napoleon. He had been passionately in love with her, but she was seven years older than he was. Moreover, despite her charm and elegance, she had lost her looks. Her skin was yellow, her teeth so bad that she tried not to show them when she smiled (hence her rather tight-lipped look in portraits). She was hated by her husband's family, who had told him about her liaison — the last of many — with the handsome, charming and corrupt Lieutenant Hippolyte Charles.

By 1804 she was compensating for past adventures by a growing passion for her husband. She

David, ***The Empress Josephine with two ladies-in-waiting*** *Josephine had arranged with David to have special prominence in his picture of the coronation in Notre Dame, of which this is a detail. The lady-in-waiting on the right is Madame de Lavallette, the Mistress of the Robes, a cousin of the Empress who was so simple and good-natured that she felt out of place at court. On the left is Madame de La Rochefoucauld. While she was at court, she obtained an embassy for her husband, the hand of a Roman prince for her daughter and large sums of money for herself.*

was kind, charitable and ready to help others — except when her own interests were at stake. In 1802 she had shown her ruthlessness by arranging for her daughter Hortense to marry Napoleon's difficult, hypochondriacal younger brother Louis Bonaparte, rather than the man Hortense preferred, Duroc. Thereby Josephine's own position in the Bonaparte family was consolidated.

The proclamation of the hereditary Empire in 1804, coupled with the Emperor's adoption of a separate bedroom, as court etiquette required, meant that Josephine's position was not as strong as it appeared when the Emperor crowned her on 2 December 1804 in Notre Dame. The Emperor had to found a dynasty and she was barren. Nevertheless she was given her own household. Its most important member, the principal lady-in-waiting, was a distant cousin who had married a younger son from one of the oldest families of the French nobility, Countess Alexandre de La Rochefoucauld. The Emperor, one of the rudest monarchs of all time, called her 'a little cripple, as stupid as she is ugly' (she was so small and misshapen she was almost a dwarf).[12]

The Empress was not the only woman in Napoleon's life. For, in addition to his social contact with servants, courtiers and the people he saw at the *Petites Entrées*, the Emperor had contact of a more intimate nature with some of the female members of his wife's household. Indeed he had almost as many love affairs as Louis XIV, although he took them far less seriously. He was thirty-five and healthy in 1804, and like most men of the day treated female domestic servants as fair game. He slept with Félicité Longrois, an Ordinary Woman of the Bedchamber (who guarded the doors of the Empress's apartment and showed in her visitors) in 1805–06.

At the same time he had an affair with Madame Gazzani, a beautiful woman from Genoa whom Talleyrand had helped to become a Reader to the Empress (an attendant whose duties were to read out loud). One of the Empress's ladies-in-waiting, Madame de Rémusat, wrote that she was 'the most attractive woman in a court full of attractive women'. For a time the Emperor was so smitten that he insisted that Madame Gazzani be invited to court balls, and admitted to the room reserved for the Empress's ladies-in-waiting.

The Emperor also had a more intense affair with one of the Empress's ladies-in-waiting, Madame Duchâtel, wife of a councillor of state thirty-one years older than herself. His stepdaughter Hortense remembered that Madame Duchâtel had 'a lively face, black hair, large, appealing dark blue eyes, a long very pointed nose, a large mouth, the finest teeth in the world, and a complexion which was dull in the morning but wonderful at night'. For a time the Emperor was in love. He wrote love-letters (which have never been published), and even ran the risk of going to see her at night, accompanied by Duroc, in a private house in the middle of Paris. The importance of these love affairs lies in their effect on the Emperor's marriage. They encouraged him to believe that, contrary to Josephine's wounding allegations, he could be a father. On Saint-Helena the Emperor remembered Madame Duchâtel saying that, according to Josephine 'it is as clear as water; on the contrary I find that it is very thick'.

The Emperor also had affairs with another Reader, Mademoiselle Lacoste, and another lady-in-waiting, the Duchess de Rovigo. Thus Josephine's household served not only to add dignity to the Empress, but also to provide distractions for the Emperor. His sisters were also eager to amuse the Emperor, and to provide mistresses from their households who could prove that it was the Empress, not the Emperor, who could not have children. The Bonapartes hated the Empress and her children, who were more charming and sophisticated than they were. In February 1806 the Emperor began an affair with a former pupil of Madame Campan, now Reader to his youngest sister Princess Caroline, called Eléanore Denuelle de La Plaigne: the princess's husband, Marshal Murat, acted as intermediary. The First Valet Constant wrote that Eléanore was 'tall, well-shaped, dark with fine black eyes, lively and a great coquette'. They met in the suite of small rooms above the Emperor's private apartments in the Tuileries. If the Emperor had visitors, Constant told them he was seeing a minister. Ten months later the birth of their son was final proof that the Emperor could be a father.

Riesener, ***Madame Riesener and her sister***
Madame Riesener, born Félicité Longrois, was one of the Empress's Women of the Bedchamber. They guarded the doors of her apartments, announced visitors and were known, from the colour of their dresses, as the Red Ladies. Before her marriage, Madame Riesener had had a brief affair with the Emperor. This is one of the few full-length portraits of a servant of the court.

ABOVE **René Berthon, *Princess Pauline and Christine de Mathis*** *Christine de Mathis (right) was one of the favourite ladies-in-waiting of the princess. It was unusual for a member of a ruling family to be painted alone with a courtier. This double portrait may commemorate the princess's triumph in making her lady-in-waiting the Emperor's mistress.*

ABOVE RIGHT **Hoechle, *The betrothal of the Archduchess Marie-Louise to Napoleon in the Hofburg, Vienna, 5 March 1810*** *Marshal Berthier is asking the Emperor Francis I of Austria for the hand of the Archduchess (centre) in marriage. Metternich, the Austrian Foreign Minister who was to be one of the architects of the fall of Napoleon, is second on the right from Francis I. The clothes, the ceremonies and the setting of the Austrian court were much simpler than those of the Napoleonic court.*

Eléanore was soon discarded (she returned to Paris, three husbands and three decades later, as wife of the Bavarian Ambassador), but it was only a question of time before the Emperor divorced Josephine.[13]

Another sister delivered the *coup de grâce* to the Empress. In 1809 Princess Pauline brought with her, on the court's autumn visit to Fontainebleau, her prettiest lady-in-waiting, Christine de Mathis. In the relative informality of Fontainebleau, it was easy for her to be 'noticed' by the Emperor and she soon became his mistress. The Emperor began to spend his evenings in his sister's rather than his wife's apartments. The gulf between the Emperor and the Empress widened. They were divorced in December. The following year the Emperor made the father of Christine de Mathis a count and a chamberlain.[14]

In 1810 the Emperor chose as his second wife the Archduchess Marie-Louise of Austria, an eighteen-year-old niece of Marie-Antoinette. The wedding, organized by Ségur, showed the degree to which the court surrounded the Emperor and the Empress, and the way in which the Emperor used it to advertise the power and stability of his Empire. Marie-Louise's procession from Vienna to France was as splendid as that of Marie-Antoinette, on which it was modelled. The Emperor met her before she reached the palace of Compiègne, north of Paris, and went to bed with her on the first night, although they were not yet formally married. The court then moved to Saint-Cloud, condescending to pause for a few minutes on the outskirts of Paris to receive loyal addresses from the Mayors.

The next few days were filled with a round of ceremonies. The civil wedding at Saint-Cloud was

followed by the State Entry into Paris, and the religious wedding in the chapel of the Louvre: the young Empress was so intimidated that all she could think of was the fact that her shoes and her bodice were pinching. The procession back from the Louvre to the Tuileries, through the long gallery decorated with pictures from all over Europe and lined with cheering subjects, was a dazzling spectacle. In the following days there were a State Banquet in the Tuileries, an appearance on the Palace Balcony, receptions of loyal addresses from the Senates, ministers and senior officials of the French Empire and the Kingdom of Italy in the throne room, and a distribution of gold and silver coins by heralds to the crowds in the gardens outside.

Throughout the round of glittering ceremonies, the Emperor and Empress were surrounded by members of the imperial family and, above all, of the court. Duroc, Berthier, Montesquiou and Marshal Mortier were especially prominent, but there was also a constellation of lesser courtiers standing by the throne or walking in processions.

The court was such a powerful, seductive phenomenon that it also affected language. Addresses emphasized subjects' loyalty and deference and the monarch's glory, grandeur and condescension. The Emperor and Empress replied in court language, expressing gratitude for the Parisians' 'attachment' and affirming 'the love we bear for our peoples'. The wedding itself was primarily a court ceremony, celebrated in the chapel of one of the Emperor's palaces rather than in the cathedral of Paris. It was watched by Napoleon's court and by selected well-dressed Parisians, not by the public.[15] The ceremony showed that the court surrounded the Emperor and Empress with an aura of splendour and deference. They lived in a different world from the rest of humanity.

Benjamin Zix, ***Wedding cortège of Napoleon I***
After their religious marriage in the Louvre, the Emperor and Empress return to the Tuileries down the Grand Gallery, which is lined with pictures by Raphael and Rubens. They are cheered by thousands of spectators and escorted by courtiers and members of the imperial family. With her enormous train, which was borne by her five sisters-in-law (much against their will), the new Empress looked like a slowly advancing tortoise.

The new Empress was fat, ugly and silent. She led a more secluded life than Josephine, surrounded all day by the women of her household. Most of Josephine's ladies-in-waiting transferred shamelessly to Marie-Louise's household. However she had a different principal lady-in-waiting, the Duchess de Montebello. The widow of Marshal Lannes, one of the Emperor's most devoted marshals, she was cold, withdrawn and bad at remembering names —

qualities which did not help to make her mistress popular. Nevertheless the Empress loved her. She wrote in her diary that the Duchess was 'the most perfect woman there has ever been'.[16] The Emperor was extremely affectionate with Marie-Louise and treated her with greater respect than Josephine. Indeed, she was probably the only person to whom he was consistently polite and considerate. Food was one of her great pleasures, and he never made her wait for dinner, as he had Josephine, sometimes for as long as three hours. Napoleon continued to have mistresses, such as the beautiful Polish woman Marie Walewska, whom Talleyrand had presented to him in 1807, but he kept them as secret as possible.

The court provided most of the artists who purveyed the official image of the Emperor to the outside world, as well as a supply of mistresses. Like the Grand Officers, many of the court artists came from the world of the old regime. Indeed some had known the court of Versailles at first hand.

Denon, a former Gentleman in Ordinary of Louis XV and Louis XVI, was a member of the Emperor's Household as Director-General of the Musée Napoléon (the Louvre) and of the Imperial Mint. He was a friend of the Emperor, frequently attended the *lever* and *coucher*, and followed the Emperor's armies all over Europe in search of loot for the palaces and museums of France. He could take what he liked. A letter Duroc wrote to Denon from Moscow in October 1812 reveals the arrogant rapacity of the Napoleonic court. One crate of treasures had already been sent to Paris, wrote the Grand Marshal of the Palace, but 'Your presence would certainly have been necessary in Moscow to choose the historical monuments and treasures which should complete the numerous collections we possess in Paris.' Eight days later the retreat from Moscow began, and Duroc had other things to think about.

Denon designed the Emperor's coat of arms, an eagle facing left, and supervised artists' representations of the Emperor and his court. In 1809, for example, he was summoned to the Council of Administration of the Household to provide information about the pictures the Emperor had ordered of the principal ceremonies of his reign.[17] In 1814 he arranged the production and distribution of a print showing the Emperor's son praying 'for my father and for France'.

Under Denon the most important artist attached to the court was David, the greatest painter of the age and First Painter of the Emperor, whose coronation he immortalized on canvas. Fontaine, First Architect of the Emperor, was always busy, as the Emperor never stopped acquiring or restoring palaces. In Duroc's approving words, 'he knows the Emperor's taste and the habits of the court'. Isabey, the Dessinateur du Cabinet, or Official Draughtsman, also knew the court intimately and was a friend of both Empresses.

Denon, David, Fontaine and Isabey were part of the Emperor's life: he often talked to them during his morning meal. Other artists attached to the court included Prud'hon, a former protégé of Marie-Antoinette, who was drawing-master to the Empress Marie-Louise. Canova, the greatest sculptor of the age, was paid 40,000 francs in 1806 in order to make copies, drawings and prints of a statue of the Emperor. He later joined the Emperor's household as Director-General of the Imperial Museums in Rome.[18]

Members of the imperial family also employed their own artists. The Emperor's stepdaughter Hortense, for example, used Auguste Garneray as her 'co-ordinator of arts'. He designed costumes for her balls, chose her pictures, finished her sketches and made innumerable drawings of Hortense and her mother. The Empress Josephine employed Redouté, Prud'hon and her chamberlain Count Turpin de Crissé. The latter became very fond of the Empress, but found that he was kept so busy making drawings for her ladies' albums or designing patterns for them to embroider, that he had no time to paint the serious landscapes he preferred.[19]

One of the main tasks of the artists attached to the Emperor and the imperial family was to produce flattering pictures of their patrons and of the principal ceremonies of the reign. Compared to the simplicity of what was produced under the Consulate, these pictures — such as *The Coronation of Napoleon I* by David or Isabey's drawings of the leading figures of the court in full costume — show that the Emperor and his family were encased in splendour and formality after 1804.

The Emperor was surrounded by what a later Emperor, Franz Josef of Austria, called his nimbus. By this he meant the atmosphere generated by his court, which impressed his visitors and cut him off from reality. Napoleon believed in splendour and formality. He wrote to Ségur in January 1805, about the ceremony at which he was to be offered the crown of the Kingdom of Italy: 'I will be on my throne, surrounded by the Grand Officers of the Empire, the officers of my household and some councillors of state all in full dress.' With the help of Ségur, he personally supervised the increasingly elaborate structure of court etiquette. The book in which Ségur codified it, *Etiquette du Palais Impérial*, is an extraordinary document, as important for an understanding of the nature of the Napoleonic Empire as the Code Napoléon.

Some of its provisions describe the etiquette to be followed 'when Their Majesties eat in public. The Grand Chamberlain holds a basin for the Emperor to wash in; the Grand Equerry offers him his armchair; the Grand Marshal of the Palace takes a napkin and presents it to HM. The First Prefect, the First Equerry and the First Chamberlain of the Empress perform the same functions for HM; the Grand Almoner goes to the front of the table, blesses the dinner and retires. During the meal the Colonel-General in waiting stands behind the armchair of the Emperor; the Grand Chamberlain stands on the right of the Colonel-General in waiting, the Grand Equerry on his left.'

Other articles state that officials and their wives are notified by the chamberlain-in-waiting of the day and time that they should go to the palace to present their respects on the occasion of a birth or marriage in the imperial family. Princes and princesses sit on stools on either side of Their Majesties' thrones. The Grand Officers stand behind. There was a strict order of precedence for presentation by the chamberlain on duty. The ladies-in-waiting of the Empress and the princesses were followed by the wives of the Grand Officers and Senators, and so on, down to the wives of colonels and *les dames présentées* — women who had been presented at court. The same order, with court officials first of all, was followed for men: 'All these persons make a bow as they enter the throne room; they then salute the Emperor, then the Empress and withdraw. The Grand Chamberlain, standing beside the Emperor, at one pace from the lowest step of the throne, names them to HM. The principal lady-in-waiting, placed in the same way on the other side, names them to HM the Empress.'[20]

Etiquette at Napoleon's court was extremely strict. He never mixed with the crowd at balls (unless they were masked balls). There was always a 'respectable distance' between him and his guests, so that he was the object of every glance and the centre of attention. In contrast, at court balls during the Congress of Vienna in 1814–15, the Emperors of Austria and Russia and the King of Prussia mixed with the guests and danced like ordinary people.

Napoleon I insisted that the formal ritual of

Gérard, ***The Empress Marie-Louise and the King of Rome*** *The birth of the King of Rome seemed to assure the future of the dynasty. This picture hung in the Emperor's study in the Tuileries. Gérard was more popular with the court than David, who charged too much.*

court life should be maintained when he was away from Paris. He wrote to the Empress Josephine in 1807 from Poland that she should be surrounded by 'an appropriate splendour' in Paris. If she went to the opera she should always use the imperial box. 'Grandeur has its drawbacks: an Empress cannot go where a private person can.'[21]

For the Emperor, having a court, and holding court, were almost as important a part of being Emperor as having an army or a treasury — as the remark quoted at the head of this chapter implies. Even in adversity the court continued to surround him like a cloak.

He was accompanied into exile not by ministers or marshals, but by courtiers and servants. On the minuscule island of Elba the Emperor had a household of 78 courtiers and servants, including 4 chamberlains and 6 ordonnance officers, selected from the most prominent local inhabitants. Even on Elba there was, in the words of his devoted First Valet Marchand, 'a ceremonial as at the Tuileries, but on a lesser scale: presentations, *entrées*, receptions, and *cercles*'. Many families on Elba were ruined by the cost of buying suitable clothes in which to go to the Emperor's court.

Twenty-five courtiers and servants followed the Emperor to Saint-Helena, including Bertrand, Grand Marshal of the Palace (who ran the household at Longwood as he had done at the Tuileries). Although a prisoner, the Emperor maintained as much state as was possible — more than his Bourbon rival Louis XVIII had done in exile in England. His insistence on using the title of Emperor was the main cause of his quarrels with the governor of the island, Sir Hudson Lowe.

His courtiers were kept standing in his presence, even while he played chess: on occasion Bertrand came close to fainting. The Emperor was furious if his footmen did not wear green and gold livery and silver shoe-buckles in his presence, and if his courtiers failed to put on full-dress uniforms.

Clearly the man who created such a splendid and élitist court was not the culmination of the Revolution. In fact, as he told his chamberlain Montholon on Saint-Helena, Napoleon I believed that 'A revolution is, whatever people say, one of the greatest disasters which divine wrath can inflict on a nation.'[22] He was prepared to uphold certain aspects of the Revolution, in particular the principle of equality between nobles and non-nobles which was one of its most treasured reforms. He also defended former revolutionaries' material interests, and furthered the careers of those who were willing to serve him obediently.

But he had little interest in the other principles of the Revolution, except in so far as they increased the power of the French government. His court shows that Napoleon I was neither the culmination of the Revolution nor, in the words of a German philosopher, 'the world-soul on horseback'. Napoleon I was a monarch, whose principal concerns were the power of his throne, the splendour of his court and the future of his dynasty.

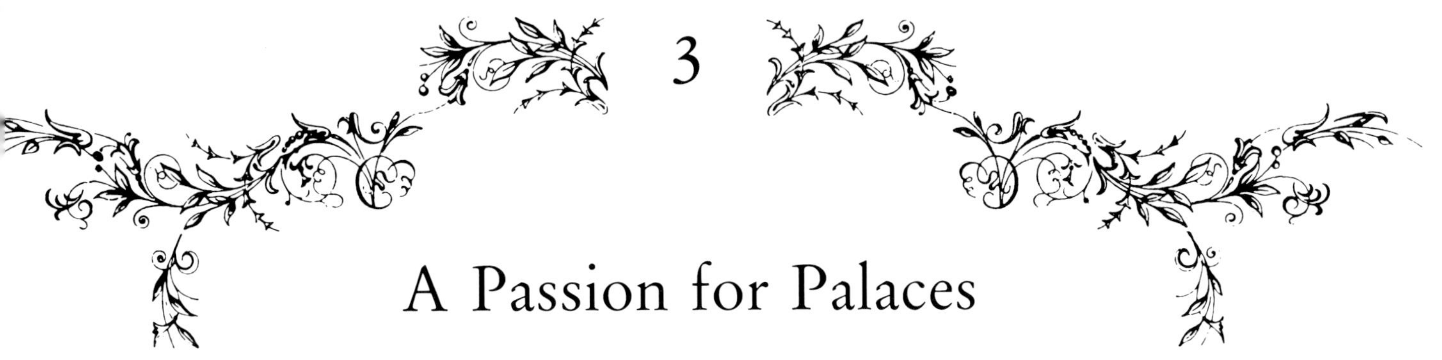

3
A Passion for Palaces

'How can the descendant of so many Emperors live in this garret?'
Napoleon I on the Hofburg, palace of the Emperor Francis I of Austria, 1805.

THE EMPEROR'S PALACES provided a setting of incomparable grandeur and luxury for his court. After 1802 his principal residences were the Tuileries in winter and Saint-Cloud in summer: it was still the custom for rich people to leave the heat and germs of a city during the summer, and the court was no exception. In 1804, when Napoleon became Emperor, he also inherited the legendary palaces of the kings of France, set in the forests around Paris, such as Fontainebleau and Compiègne.

Fontainebleau is a huge Renaissance palace built on the edge of a hunting forest south-east of Paris. It was one of the Emperor's favourite palaces, perhaps because it had been built by the kings of the House of Valois rather than by his rivals the Bourbons. 'This is the real house of kings, the residence of the ages', he declared and he spent over 3 million francs on furnishing it during his reign.[1] He used Fontainebleau, as the kings of France had done before him, for hunting and spent four to eight weeks there in the autumns of 1807, 1809 and 1810. The entire court, the Minister Secretary of State and the Ministers of Foreign Affairs of the French Empire and the Kingdom of Italy moved to Fontainebleau. The princes and princesses competed to have the most splendid household and hospitable table. People flocked from Paris to attend Sunday Mass or the theatre. The court was at its most relaxed and enjoyable.

Compiègne is a beautiful classical palace built on the edge of another hunting forest, north of Paris, by Louis XV and Louis XVI. It was used by the Emperor in 1810 for Marie-Louise's reception and honeymoon (the Empress's boudoir, draped with white cashmere shawls, is one of the most voluptuous of all Empire interiors), and in the autumn of 1811 for hunting.

The Emperor loved palaces, more than most legitimate monarchs. Indeed he was the first ruler of France since Charlemagne a thousand years before to own palaces outside the Ile-de-France and the valley of the Loire. He acquired the former archbishops' palaces at Strasbourg and Bordeaux in 1805 and 1808 and a house at Marrac near the Pyrenees (built for a Queen of Spain) in 1808: they were useful half-way halts when the Emperor was going to fight in Germany or Spain. In addition, since the French Empire included what had been Belgium, Piedmont and Parma, the Emperor inherited the former rulers' palaces at Laeken outside Brussels, and in and around Turin and Parma. As King of Italy he also acquired palaces in Milan, Monza, Modena, Bologna, Brescia, Venice and Stra. By 1812 the Emperor had forty-four palaces, more than any contemporary monarch.

The Emperor's palaces were distinguished by their exaggeratedly monarchical and authoritarian layout and decoration. From the end of 1804 the main room in the state apartments of the Tuileries, looking east over the Cour du Carrousel, was the throne room: the throne, with a rounded back and a globe at the end of each arm, visible in many pictures of the Napoleonic court, appears to symbolize the global scope of the Emperor's ambitions. The Emperor preferred this style of throne and introduced it in other palaces, such as Saint-Cloud, Fontainebleau and Turin.

The throne room was preceded by two ante-

Bouhot, *The palace and garden of the Tuileries* *The palace was the principal residence of the court, the garden the main meeting-place of the rich. On the horizon are the mills of Montmartre (known during the Empire as Mont Napoléon), grinding flour for the Parisians' bread. The carriage on the left, since it is drawn by eight horses, and escorted by soldiers of the Imperial Guard, contains either the Emperor or the Empress.*

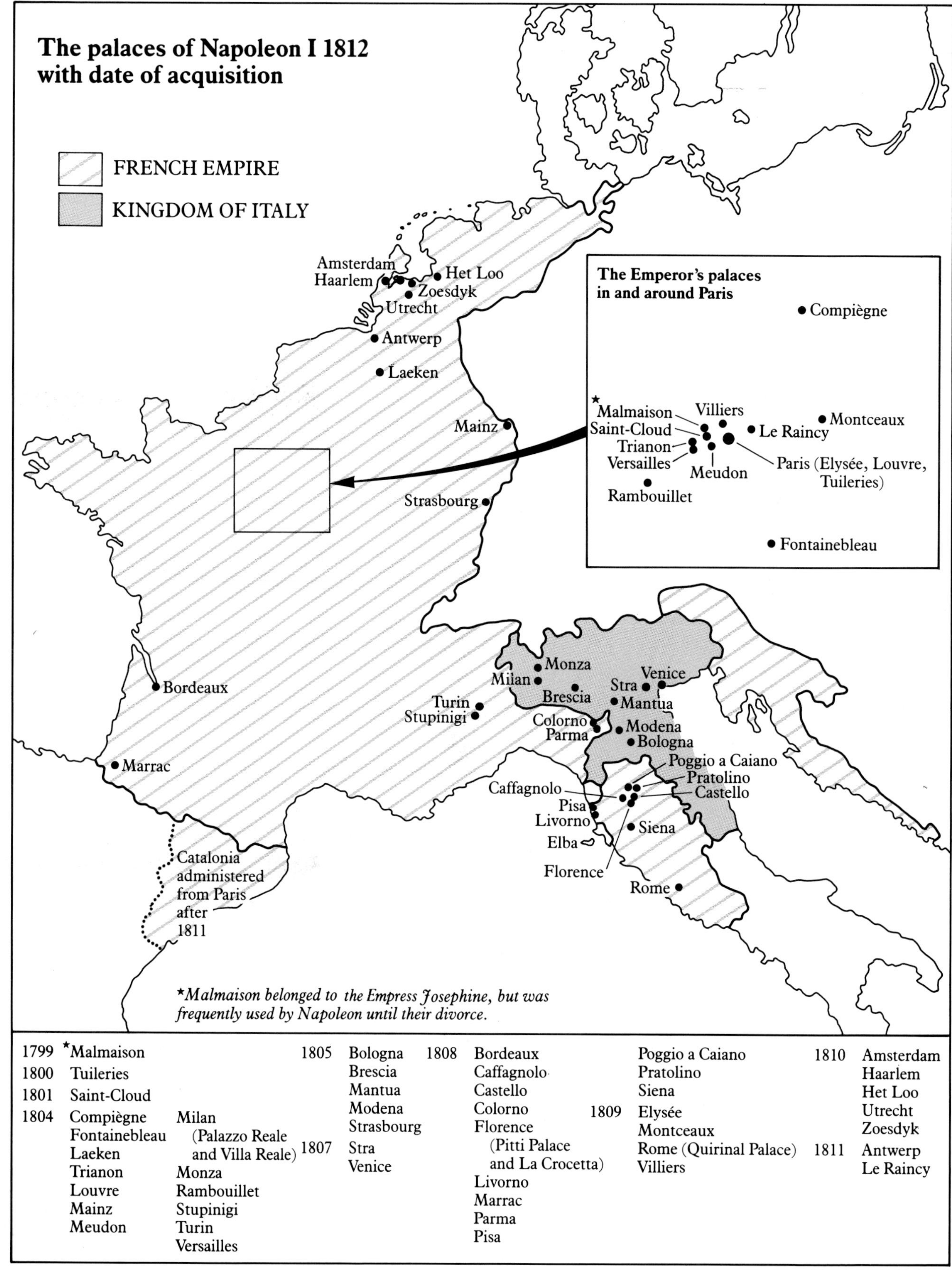

Year	Palaces
1799	*Malmaison
1800	Tuileries
1801	Saint-Cloud
1804	Compiègne, Fontainebleau, Laeken, Trianon, Louvre, Mainz, Meudon, Milan (Palazzo Reale and Villa Reale), Monza, Rambouillet, Stupinigi, Turin, Versailles
1805	Bologna, Brescia, Mantua, Modena, Strasbourg
1807	Stra, Venice
1808	Bordeaux, Caffagnolo, Castello, Colorno, Florence (Pitti Palace and La Crocetta), Livorno, Marrac, Parma, Pisa, Poggio a Caiano, Pratolino, Siena
1809	Elysée, Montceaux, Rome (Quirinal Palace), Villiers
1810	Amsterdam, Haarlem, Het Loo, Utrecht, Zoesdyk
1811	Antwerp, Le Raincy

Bidault and Carle Vernet, *Departure of the Emperor and Empress for the hunt from Compiègne*
Compiègne, north-east of Paris, was used by Napoleon in 1810 and 1811 and still contains the finest suite of Empire rooms in existence. This picture comes from a series of scenes of the Emperor's daily life which were painted for the château of Marshal Davout.

chambers, the Hall of Peace and the Blue Hall, and by the large central hall of the Tuileries, the Hall of Marshals. As under the Consulate, each of these four rooms, and the Emperor's Grand Cabinet beyond the throne room, was reserved for officers and officials of a certain rank, from captains and sub-prefects in the Hall of Marshals to princes, marshals and cardinals in the Grand Cabinet. This brought the French court into line with other European courts, and broke with the traditions of Versailles.

Life at the court of Versailles had revolved around the King's person. He ate in public and dressed and undressed in the King's bedroom before a circle of courtiers who were admitted according to a strict timetable depending on rank. This bedroom was the centre of the state apartments and of court life.

Napoleon I changed all that. The new importance of the throne room, and its preceding hierarchy of antechambers, showed that the court of France now glorified the official position of the monarch rather than his physical person. This difference in character was shown by the fact that Napoleon's throne rooms were installed in what had been the king's bedroom in both Fontainebleau and the Tuileries. Rank was now revealed by space not time. People of a certain rank at court were no longer admitted at a certain time into the king's bedroom. Now they had the right to enter a particular room of the state apartments with everyone else of similar position. In this way the official hierarchy of the French Empire was made plain for all to see, with the Emperor on his throne at the head. No longer was there the confusion between the public and private lives of the royal family which had been deplored by the Emperor's architects, Percier and Fontaine, as hemming in royalty. The ruling family was now liberated from public scrutiny of its private life.

The Emperor's private apartments, on the garden side of the first floor of the Tuileries, were quite separate from the state apartments, although both were under the authority of the Grand Chamberlain and run by the service of the chamber. They consisted of a guard-room, a room for the pages, one for the courtiers in waiting (known as the

Cagnola, ***The Milan Civic Guard defends the Royal Palace, 21 April 1814*** *Prince Eugene held court in this palace as Viceroy of Italy from 1805 to 1814. After the fall of the Empire in 1814 a hostile mob tried to sack it. On the left is the cathedral where Napoleon crowned himself King of Italy in 1805.*

TOP **Anon, *The Royal Palace of Monza*** *Monza, which had been built for a brother of Marie-Antoinette, was set in a magnificent park outside Milan. The Vicereine Augusta, wife of Eugene, liked it so much she referred to it as 'beloved Monza'.*

ABOVE **Antonelli, *The Royal Palace of Venice*** *From 1807 this side of St Mark's Square served as a royal palace. A new staircase and ballroom were installed and a church was destroyed to improve the view.*

RIGHT **Percier and Fontaine, *The Emperor and the Empress receiving homage on their thrones in the Tuileries the day after their marriage, 3 April 1810*** *The ceiling is decorated with eagles and mythological scenes, the canopy with bees and more eagles. This is a rare representation of the physical act of paying court: the officials in front of the throne are half-way through their bows.*

Dessiné par Percier et Fontaine. Gravé par C. Normand.

L'Empereur et l'Impératrice, recevant sur leur Trone, les hommages et les félicitations, de tous les Corps de l'Etat; le lendemain de leur Mariage.

salon de service, it was the best place to find out what was going on at court), a series of studies and his bedroom. There was a private staircase connecting his apartments with the Empress's on the floor below. Their private apartments were where the Emperor and Empress lived, where they slept, ate, worked and in the evening received the *Petites Entrées*.

The Emperor greatly valued the distinction between state and private apartments, and the hierarchy of antechambers preceding the throne room. He insisted on the introduction of a similar layout in all his major palaces, in Milan and Turin as well as the Tuileries and Saint-Cloud.[2] This insistence was for political rather than personal reasons. He often praised relatively small unpretentious residences with direct access to a garden, such as Malmaison or Frederick the Great's villa at Sans-Souci. The Tuileries was draughty and uncomfortable and, since its garden was open to anyone decently dressed, far too public. After 1809 he often deserted it for the smaller and more secluded palace of the Elysée.[3]

However, it was more important to him that his palaces should enhance his glory than that they should ensure his comfort. His view of monarchy, and the insecurity of his regime, meant that he wanted to inhabit palaces which were as magnificent as possible. As the French royal palaces had suffered terribly during the Revolution, a massive programme of restoration and redecoration was necessary. It was supervised by Duroc, Fontaine and the officials of the Buildings and Furniture Offices of the Crown.

When Fontaine visited Fontainebleau in 1803 he found it in a 'state of extreme degradation and abandon'. Revolutionaries' cannon and bullet-marks were still visible on the façade of the Tuileries. Those indispensable props of court life, a chapel and a theatre, were not restored to proper working order in the Tuileries until 1806 and 1808 respectively. In 1810 Duroc admitted that, of the palaces, 'except Versailles and the Tuileries . . . all lack decoration and all show outward signs of the recent devastation'.[4]

The problem was made worse by the fact that, in addition to neglecting the royal palaces, the government of the Republic had sold the royal furniture (at absurdly low prices). A celebrated remark by a court official refusing to buy some of it back — 'His Majesty wishes to create the new, not to order the old' — shows that there was a conscious policy to refurnish Napoleon's palaces in a new imperial style.

One of the main differences between the court of France and other courts before the fall of the monarchy had been the all-embracing luxury of its setting. Whereas other courts had had magnificent palaces, paintings or furniture, only at the court of France was everything of the highest quality — and usually produced by the King's own artists and craftsmen, working in factories belonging to the Crown. In comparison the furniture and china of the Habsburg Emperors was second-rate. Moreover the beauty and luxury of the court of France were not confined to the King's principal palaces, but were displayed in all his residences, from Versailles to the smallest hunting pavilion. Napoleon I continued this tradition of ubiquitous and pervasive luxury, using the Empire style which now epitomizes his reign. Thanks to his generous civil list, and help from other sources, he had a lot of money to spend. In 1807, for example, the Minister of the Interior could write to Fontaine that 3 million francs were available to be spent on orders to Crown factories for the furnishing of the palaces, particularly Compiègne and Versailles.

The Emperor's insistence on magnificence in his palaces also had a certain economic justification. Such lavish expenditure helped what the *Gazette de France* called 'a number of branches of industry fallen with the monarchy' — in other words the silk, tapestry, embroidery, furniture and china industries. In 1810 the Emperor wrote to Duroc: 'I would like to increase in my palaces the amount of furniture made of long-lasting materials, in order to use primary products from France and to give encouragement to industries which need it.' These immense furnishing projects kept workmen in jobs and factories in business — a great advantage for any government in charge of Paris.

By 1813 the Emperor had redecorated and refurnished all his residences throughout his dominions. The furnishings used were nearly always supplied by the Crown factories, or by craftsmen with imperial warrants, such as Biennais the goldsmith, or Jacob-Desmalter the furniture-maker, 'of His Majesty the Emperor and King'. From the Trianon to Turin, and from Marrac to Milan, all his palaces were filled with Jacob furniture, Gobelins tapestries, Savonnerie carpets, Sèvres china, Thomire bronzes and Biennais silver.[5]

Laeken in Belgium, for example, was restored and refurnished at a cost of 721,215 francs. By 1807 court officials reported that it was 'very well furnished and perfectly ready to receive Their Majesties'. A hierarchy of antechambers preceding a throne room had been created, in addition to

For the sake of its secluded garden, Napoleon sometimes preferred the Elysée to the Tuileries. This chair comes from a set ordered by Murat for the royal palaces of Naples, and shows the Tuileries and the Elysée.

separate sets of private apartments for the Emperor and the Empress. Pictures or allegories of the Emperor's triumphs adorned the walls and ceilings of his palaces. On the ceiling of the Hall of the Council of State in the Tuileries was a scene from the Battle of Austerlitz; on a wall of the Royal Palace of Mantua was a bas-relief depicting *Italy swearing on an altar fidelity to Napoleon, while Fame spreads the news of the Oath, which History engraves on its tables.* Louis XIV's one-storey

Appiani, *Sketch for the apotheosis of Napoleon I*
Napoleon was depicted as Jupiter in a fresco above the throne in his palace in Milan. The throne is supported by Justice, Force, Prudence and Temperance. The Iron Crown of Lombardy is held by an angel and Napoleon grasps the globe in his hand. This is one of the last European representations of a monarch as a god.

pavilion in the park of Versailles, the Grand Trianon, was also luxuriously refurnished. Napoleon first used it on 16 December 1809, the day after he was divorced from Josephine. He also spent Christmas there that year; Josephine came over from Malmaison for what must have been a rather strained Christmas lunch. Count Clary wrote of Trianon: 'I do not think that the Orient has ever known anything finer in bronzes, embroidered velvets, porcelain, pictures, parquet, fireplaces and everything which good taste can produce.' The Emperor was so pleased that he said 'Trianon is from now on my spring house'; and he used it again for short periods in 1810 and 1813. The relatively small château of Rambouillet south-west of Paris, which he visited for hunting trips in 1806 and 1807, was refurnished with such speed that on one day in April 1805 427 packets weighing 8982 kilos arrived.[6]

The best surviving examples of Napoleonic interiors are the throne room of Fontainebleau and the Emperor's and Empress's apartments at Compiègne. The dominant colours are red, gold and white, and the effect is one of startling splendour and luxury. The furniture is heavier, more rigid and gilded than that of Versailles, or of contemporary palaces in Potsdam and St Petersburg.

Like the walls and ceilings, it was covered with the symbols of the Empire — N's, eagles and Bonaparte bees — revealing the Emperor's determination to give visual expression to his imperial status. Perhaps for that reason, unlike the more relaxed furniture of the reigns of Louis XV and Louis XVI, furniture in the Empire style has found few subsequent imitators. It has not been adapted to the twentieth century, in contrast to the 'Louis style' so popular in Cairo and Los Angeles. Empire furniture is too grand.

The way in which furniture was used to reveal and determine status is shown by the extraordinary game of musical chairs played by members of the imperial family over who had the right to sit in an armchair. Most courtiers stood at ceremonies; the old proverb of the court of France, 'Sit down when you can, pee when you can and ask for any job going', was equally true of the Napoleonic court. Courtiers of the highest rank had the right to sit on a stool or tabouret. Princes and princesses had the right to sit on chairs without arms. In principle only the Emperor and Empress sat in armchairs. In January 1806, however, Duroc wrote to the concierge of the Tuileries that extra armchairs should be available for Madame Mère and for visiting sovereigns. When members of the imperial family were subsequently raised to foreign thrones, this posed a difficult problem of court etiquette. Should they be treated as French princes or foreign sovereigns?

In August 1807 the Emperor wrote to Ségur that 'for this voyage only' Julie, Queen of Naples — the wife of his elder brother Joseph, King of Naples — should have an armchair.[7] In 1809, when many foreign sovereigns came to pay court to the Emperor in Paris, Duroc admitted that they all had the right to an armchair: 'but at the same time the

Napoleon's palaces were filled with magnificent Sèvres vases depicting events in his reign. This vase, showing the Emperor's arrival at Laeken outside Brussels in 1804, was delivered to the Grand Trianon in 1810 and is still there.

Emperor will have a more distinguished one . . . it seems to me that the shape of the throne in the Tuileries pleases him'. In 1811, however, when the Emperor was at the height of his power, he complained that there were too many armchairs in his apartments. He ordered that they should be available only for the Emperor, the Empress and, as a special favour, Madame Mère. All other members of the family, even pregnant princesses, had to use chairs without arms.

This decision infuriated his family. Both Madame Mère and Queen Julie, whose husband was now King of Spain, refused to attend the ceremonies for the baptism of the King of Rome later that year, because they were not given the right to have an armchair. As one courtier remarked: 'few family celebrations will have given rise to more quarrels than this baptism'.[8] If the Bonapartes' preoccupation with armchairs seems childish, it should be recalled that their interest was shared by many other people. Nor is it extinct today: at modern British cabinet meetings only the Prime Minister has an armchair.

The lack of privacy, comfort and space in the Tuileries remained a source of annoyance to the Emperor. In 1808 Duroc wrote to the indispensable Fontaine: 'Everything that could be done in the Tuileries to have some apartments has been done; but the result is a dismal and mediocre residence. HM has visited the Royal Palace of Madrid built by Charles III [into which his brother Joseph had just moved]. The apartments of the Tuileries cannot be compared to those of that palace, neither for grandeur, nor for decoration, nor for convenience of layout.'

The Emperor had no intention of letting his brother live better than he did; and from 1808 his taste for grandeur became almost uncontrollable. In September 1808, when he met Tsar Alexander I of Russia in Erfurt, Napoleon insisted that he should have the largest palace, on the grounds that he had brought the largest suite. The Tsar was so impressed by the French court and by Fontaine's work that he arranged to receive a monthly bulletin of the government building programme in Paris.[9]

The same year the Emperor began to plan the restoration of Versailles. A throne room and antechambers were to be installed in the state apartments; a new neoclassical facade was to be built on the side facing Paris; 'masses of granite' would replace the statues in the garden. The Emperor planned to move in in the summer of 1811: Duroc wrote that the Emperor intended to inhabit Versailles 'as Louis XVI did'.[10] If he had, he would have shown that the Revolution had been merely an interlude in the history of the French monarchy.

The splendour of the Emperor's palaces took precedence over the needs of his museums. Whereas other monarchs (including his own brothers) were by now allowing pictures to be taken out of their palaces and displayed to the public in museums, Napoleon I did the reverse. The contents of French museums should, Duroc wrote, 'serve for the decoration of the palaces'; and from 1802 the Tuileries, Saint-Cloud, Compiègne, Fontainebleau, Bordeaux and Strasbourg were hung with pictures from French museums. Protests from dismayed curators were ignored. Admittedly the Musée Napoléon (the Louvre) had received so much loot from all over Europe that it had enough pictures to decorate a hundred palaces.[11]

The Emperor's appetite for large palaces grew with the expansion of his Empire. Laeken had been built for a sister and brother-in-law of Marie-Antoinette in the 1780s and restored for Napoleon I. It is a large and elegant château, which is today the principal residence of the King of the Belgians. But soon it was not good enough for Napoleon I. In 1810 he complained: 'What an idea of the Archduchess to build such an uncomfortable château here! The layout is ridiculous. There are not enough salons.'

When he annexed Holland from his brother Louis in 1810, he also took over five royal palaces. 'I want to keep this palace for myself', he wrote of the Royal Palace of Amsterdam. 'I am in no hurry to give' he added, refusing to let a general live in the main country palace at Het Loo.[12] In 1811 he acquired new palaces, at Antwerp, Le Raincy and Turin. There were plans to buy the Château d'Eu in Normandy and the castle of Castelgandolfo near Rome. Work began on a huge palace for the King of Rome (known as the *Palais de Rome*), above the Seine where the Trocadéro now is; and there was a project to build a palace on an island in the Rhône, in the middle of Lyons.

The largest palace in Florence, the Pitti, former residence of the Grand Dukes of Tuscany, was completely redecorated in 1810–13 in order to make it worthy of the Emperor. (Stendhal, on one of his tours as Inspector of Crown Furniture, called it *Palais de l'Empereur, ancien Palais Pitti.*) The Hall of Apollo and the Hall of Mars, named after gods of Olympus, were transformed into the antechamber of the princes and the throne room. The influence of Napoleon I was bringing the monarchies of Europe down from the clouds, and was making their palaces more visibly authoritarian and hierarchical. Separate private apartments for the Emperor and Empress were installed. The Crown Furniture Office in Paris despatched Gobelins tapestries, silk wall-hangings, Thomire bronzes, Sèvres china and Savonnerie carpets to Florence (including a carpet decorated with the insignia of the Légion d'Honneur, like the one in the Emperor's Grand Cabinet in Saint-Cloud). Only the furniture and the frescoes were entrusted to local talent. By early 1813 the palace was ready to receive the Emperor and his court.[13]

At the same time an even more lavish scheme of

The palace of Saint-Cloud, shown on this vase, was one of Napoleon's favourite palaces, and the principal residence of the court in summer.

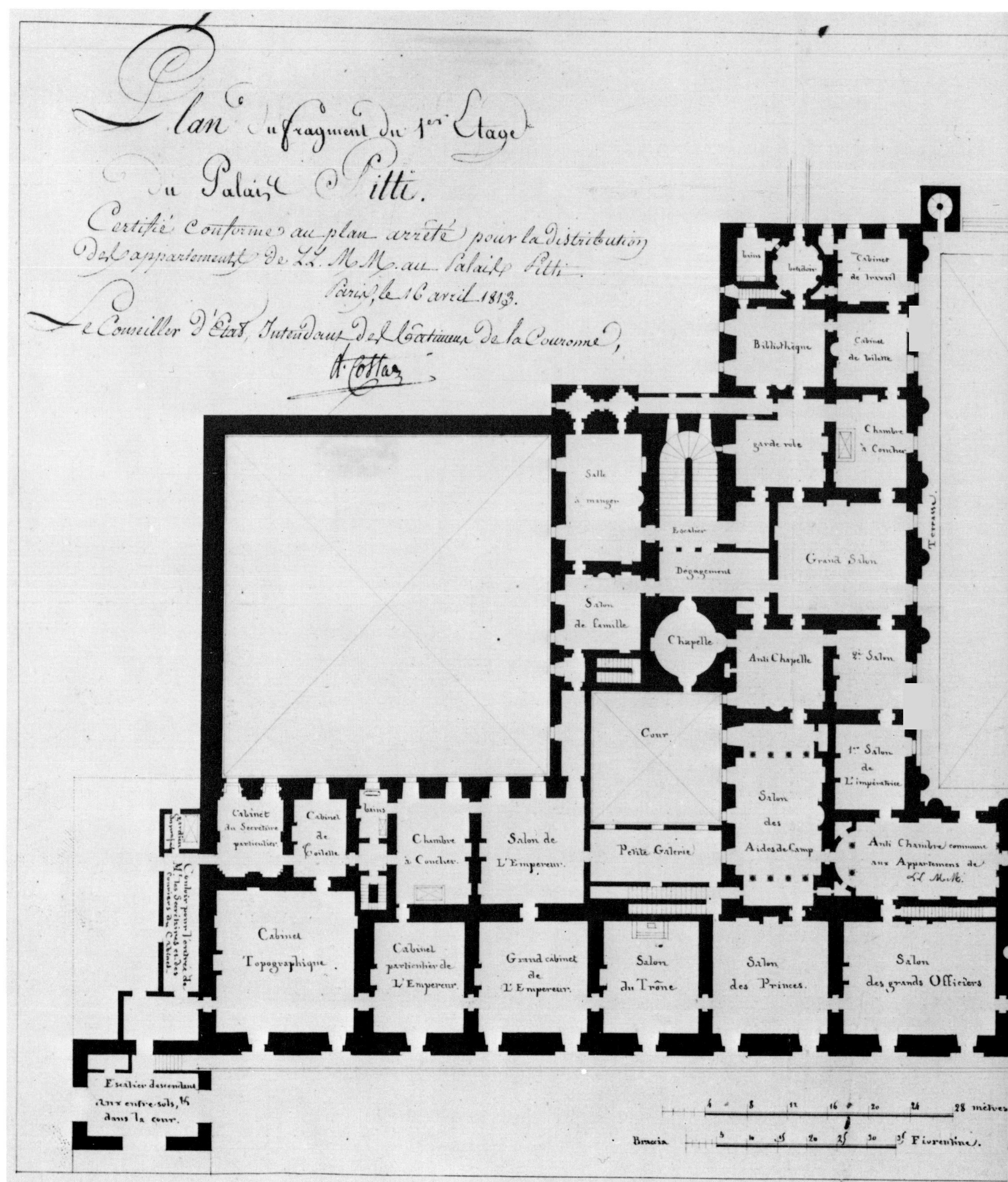
Plan du fragment du 1er Etage du Palais Pitti.
Certifié conforme au plan arrêté pour la distribution des appartements de LL. MM. au Palais Pitti.
Paris, le 16 avril 1813.
Le Conseiller d'Etat, Intendant des Bâtimens de la Couronne,
Costaz
bains
boudoir
Cabinet de travail
Bibliothèque
Cabinet de toilette
garde robe
Chambre à Coucher
Salle à manger
Escalier
Dégagement
Grand Salon
Terrasse
Salon de famille
Chapelle
Anti Chapelle
2e Salon
Cour
1er Salon de L'impératrice
Salon des Aides de Camp
Anti Chambre commune aux Appartemens de LL. MM.
Cabinet du Secrétaire particulier
Cabinet de Toilette
bains
Chambre à Coucher
Salon de L'Empereur
Petite Galerie
Cabinet Topographique
Cabinet particulier de L'Empereur
Grand cabinet de L'Empereur
Salon du Trône
Salon des Princes
Salon des grands Officiers
Escalier descendant aux entre-sols, et dans la cour.
28 mètres
Braccia
Fiorentine.

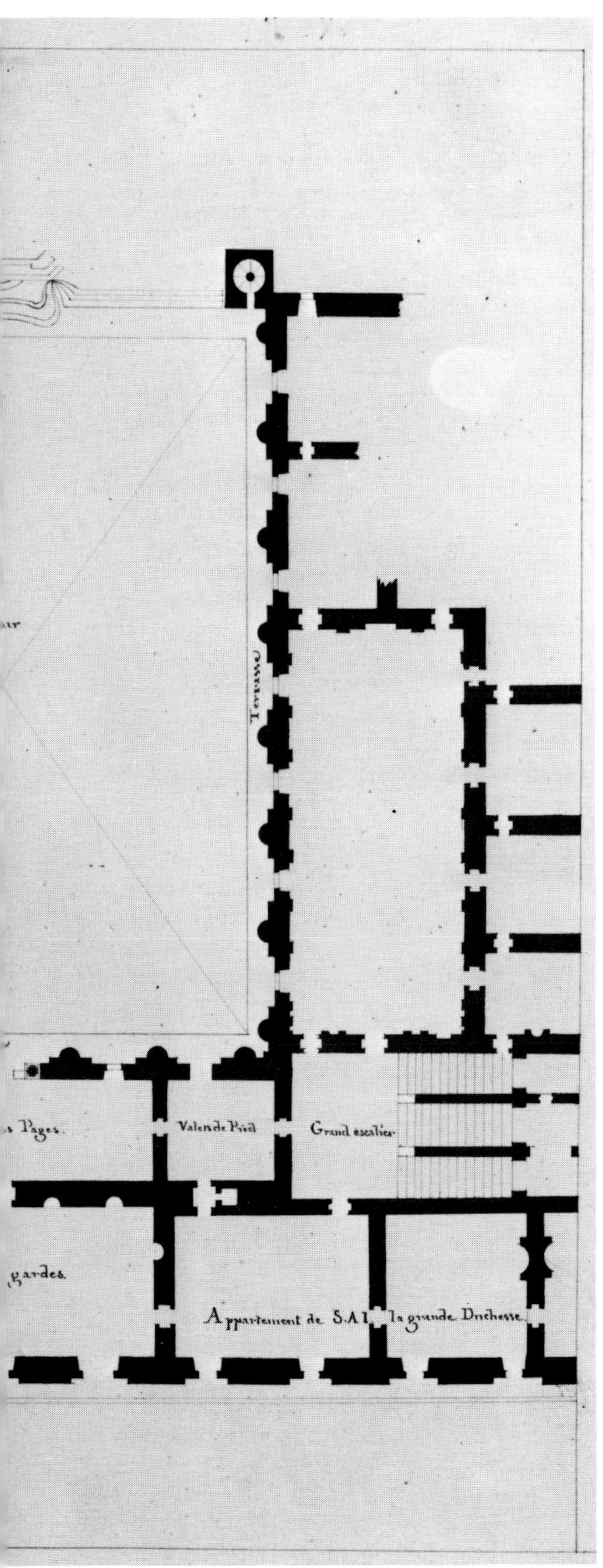

redecoration was going on in the massive seventeenth-century Quirinal Palace in Rome. It had been the Pope's official residence, and is the largest palace in the city after the Vatican. With its gardens and dependencies it is bigger than many villages. Nevertheless, according to the Emperor's architect in Rome, it was 'not large enough for HM and it lacks everything: the apartments are very small and it is merely a skeleton'. There was a plan to enlarge it by connecting it to the Barberini Palace, half a kilometre away, and over a million francs was spent on redecoration.

A throne room, a Hall of the Marshals and antechambers were created. The palace was refurnished with the standard tapestries, silver, furniture and china from Paris. Ingres painted a massive mythological scene for the Second Salon of the Empress: *Romulus carrying to the Temple of Jupiter the weapons of his enemy Acironius.* Thorwaldsen executed a frieze depicting the entry of Alexander the Great into Babylon for the Third Salon of the Emperor (it is still there).

The Quirinal would have been occupied during a long state visit planned for the summer of 1813. St Peter's would have been the scene of the Emperor's third coronation, even grander than those already performed in Paris and Milan. However, his determination to imitate Alexander in real life, and to conquer the East, deprived him of the chance of enjoying his Tuscan and Roman palaces. He spent 1813 fighting rather than holding court. It was the Pope who benefited from the modernization of the Quirinal.[14]

The grandest architectural scheme of all, however, was never realized. Like the kings of France before him, Napoleon dreamt of uniting the Tuileries and the Louvre and creating the largest palace in the world. All the buildings between them would be demolished. A winter garden, an opera-house, an imperial library and an imperial stables would be constructed as part of the palace complex. Fontaine produced many different plans but, despite the

Baron Costaz, *Plan of the imperial apartments in the Pitti Palace, Florence* *The Emperor and his architects reorganized the layout of all his palaces to emphasize his grandeur and aloofness. He planned to occupy a far larger area in the Pitti Palace than the former Grand Dukes of Tuscany.*

Emperor's interest, they were never put into effect. It was his nephew Napoleon III who finally made this ancient dream a reality for a few years in the 1860s, until the Tuileries was destroyed by the Commune and the Third Republic.[15]

Even when the Empire itself was threatened, the Emperor did not lose interest in his palaces. As the French armies retreated in 1813, he was concerned not to lose what he regarded as personal possessions. In November 1813 Caulaincourt was ordered to ensure that silver, linen and china were taken from the palaces of Amsterdam to Antwerp, and from those of Parma to Turin. Soon, however, Turin and Antwerp had also fallen to the enemy. By April 1814 the only palace the Emperor could call his own was Fontainebleau, which he had to leave for Elba on 20 April 1814.[16]

After the fall of the Empire and the revival of tourism, the splendour of the Emperor's palaces overwhelmed visitors from England. The Duke d'Orléans, a cousin of Louis XVIII and a connoisseur of royal palaces, wrote enviously of the Tuileries: 'What grandeur! What splendour! What magnificence!' English travellers were particularly impressed with Saint-Cloud: 'The interior presents a scene of astonishing elegance and splendour. . . . The style of furnishing and ornamenting within is very princely and magnificent and the furniture is superb . . . the Graces themselves might not scorn to repose upon the sofas.'[17] The artist Benjamin Haydon wrote of Fontainebleau: 'No palace of any Sultan of Baghdad or monarch of India ever exceeded the voluptuous magnificence of these apartments.'

Anon, ***The Emperor's villa on Elba in 1815***
Napoleon bought the villa of San Martino on Elba for 180,000 francs in 1814. Since it was his main country residence, his courtiers called it 'Saint-Cloud'.

All visitors were amazed by the profusion of the Emperor's dynastic symbols. The kings of France, particularly Louis XIV, had traditionally scattered their initials and emblems throughout their palaces. However Louis XV and Louis XVI had begun to abandon this practice, which had no parallel in contemporary monarchs' palaces. The Georges of England did not adorn Windsor and St James's with G's; and the Fredericks of Prussia refrained from covering their palaces in Berlin and Potsdam with a rash of F's. But the Duchess of Rutland, who visited the Tuileries in 1814, noticed that: 'At every corner is a large N; the draperies are covered with bees and each piece of furniture is surmounted with an imperial eagle.'[18] There were even N's on the glasses. No other monarch in history, not even Henry VIII or Louis XIV, stamped his personality, literally as well as figuratively, on the art of his reign to the same extent as Napoleon I.

His acquisition of five separate residences on the island of Elba, after he arrived there on 3 May 1814, is even more revealing of the Emperor's passion for palaces than his forty-four palaces on the mainland. Most important were I Mulini in the 'capital' of Portoferraio and San Martino in the country. He at once began to enlarge and modernize these 'palaces' (as they were officially designated), acting as his own architect and engineer, and giving orders to the workmen in person. He had not lost his interest in furniture. He seized furniture from the palace of his sister Elisa in Piombino and from a boat loaded with the pieces his brother-in-law Prince Borghese was taking from Turin. 'Thereby it does not leave the family', he laughed. He also ordered furniture from Naples, Genoa and Rome. In October one of his servants wrote: 'He is furnishing and building three palaces at the moment; it is he who supervises everything.'[19]

Nevertheless, as he later told Fontaine, he felt cramped on Elba. However much work he put into them, his dwellings consisted of a few small, low-ceilinged rooms, and could not be compared with the golden splendour of his palaces in the Ile de France. After the silence he was used to, the fact that I Mulini faced directly onto a noisy public street was a shock. Perhaps the inadequacy of the accommodation was a minor factor in the Emperor's decision to leave Elba and sail for France on 26 February 1815.

4 The Courtiers

'All the men were young, all the women were beautiful.'

Count de Sainte-Aulaire, a former chamberlain of the Emperor, 1817.

THE MOST UNUSUAL ASPECT of the court of Napoleon I was its courtiers. It was the first court in European history at which senior positions were held by non-nobles. At Versailles, all senior court offices had been held by members of what was known as the *noblesse présentée* — that section of the French nobility which was ancient or well-connected enough to have been presented at court more than once. Not only the middle classes, but also large sections of the nobility were excluded, including the *petite noblesse* from which the Emperor and Duroc came, and the *noblesse de robe* which traditionally filled most legal offices.

This exclusion, and the old festering divisions within the nobility, had been one of the great weaknesses of the French monarchy: it had no ruling class united in the service of the monarch and the defence of its interests. However, the Revolution had weakened many of the barriers within the élite of birth and wealth. Non-nobles could now reach the highest positions in the service of the state, such as marshal or minister. Marshals Bessières, Soult and Mortier, for example, sons of a surgeon, a lawyer and a farmer respectively, were all Colonels-General of the Imperial Guard; Maret, son of a Dijon doctor, was Minister Secretary of State.

In addition to successful non-nobles, the ruling class of the French Empire also included nobles, even as early as 1804. The Revolution had been a disaster for the French nobility, but not a complete catastrophe. Although many nobles had lost their lives and property, others had stayed quietly on their estates — and had sometimes been able to expand them. Many nobles, such as Duroc, Caulaincourt, Berthier and the Emperor himself, had spent the Revolution fighting in the French army.

Even some nobles who had opposed the Revolution were prepared to serve the Emperor after 1804. The execution of the Duke d'Enghien shocked many French people and horrified the royal families of Europe. But a noble dining with Joseph Bonaparte told his host, 'The First Consul is making a mistake if he thinks that the nobility which did not emigrate, and above all the historic nobility, is deeply committed to the Bourbons.'[1]

Many nobles, like the Bonapartes themselves, blamed the Bourbons for the disaster of the Revolution. They felt that Louis XVI and his brothers, the Counts of Provence (in 1804 pretender to the French throne as Louis XVIII) and Artois, had let down the cause of monarchy and aristocracy. Napoleon I was a monarch committed to the defence of property and the maintenance of law and order. He offered money and status to those who entered his service. His court was enormously attractive for nobles and non-nobles, supporters and opponents of the Revolution alike.

A look at the backgrounds and careers of nine different court officials of the Empire will reveal the special character of the Napoleonic court. The Count and Countess de Rémusat, born in 1763 and 1780 respectively, were members of the court from its earliest days until 1814. After two years as a Prefect of the Palace, the Count de Rémusat became First Chamberlain, Master of the Wardrobe in 1804, and was also made responsible for the theatres of Paris. Napoleon I was in the habit of using court officials as personal servants, although to a lesser extent than the kings of France. As Master of the Wardrobe Rémusat was in charge of the Emperor's clothes, until in 1811 certain discrepancies in the accounts lost him the job.

Madame de Rémusat, a friend and confidante of the Empress Josephine, was one of the few ladies-in-waiting who condescended to remain in her household after her divorce. Josephine's daughter Hortense later wrote that Madame de Rémusat was 'one of the people in whom the Empress had most confidence'.[2] Both the Rémusats came from magisterial or ministerial families which had been excluded from court office before 1792. Count de Rémusat's father was an official of the Parlement of Provence; Countess de Rémusat was a niece of Vergennes, the great foreign secretary of Louis XVI. Both the Rémusats were devoted to Talleyrand and, like many of his allies and many of the Emperor's earliest and most disillusioned servants, rallied to Louis XVIII with enthusiasm in 1814.

In contrast the career of the Duchess de Bassano is an example of the ease with which some French men and women from the bourgeoisie took to court life under the Empire. Born Mademoiselle Lejeas, daughter of a mayor of Dijon, in 1780, she was the wife of the Emperor's favourite minister, Maret, Duke de Bassano, and one of the most beautiful and fashionable ladies-in-waiting, first of the Empress Josephine and then of the Empress Marie-Louise. For non-noble court officials of the Empire such as the Duchess de Bassano, it was enough to have ambition, self-assurance, good manners and above all a taste for court life, and they could be as polished and decorative as the noblest court official of Versailles. The ladies-in-waiting were helped by being unusually attractive. During the upheaval of the Revolution, many men had, for once, chosen wives for their looks rather than their dowry.

After the Emperor's marriage to the Archduchess Marie-Louise in 1810, many ladies-in-waiting from the old nobility had expected the new Habsburg Empress to make a distinction between them and non-nobles such as the Duchess de Bassano. However, to their fury, she never did. As the Emperor remarked of Marie-Louise, 'It was the same thing to her.' Other people's ancestry made little impact on a Habsburg.

The Duchess de Bassano remained one of the most prominent ladies of the court. Indeed, thanks to her husband's high positions and her own beauty and cleverness, her salon became 'the centre and the perfection of the court' — and a source of constant

Isabey and Percier, ***The Countess de Rémusat***
Madame de Rémusat was Josephine's favourite lady-in-waiting. In 1804 she received diamonds and a dress allowance of 10,000 francs in order to appear suitably splendid for the coronation, as she is shown here.

The Emperor was so proud of his wife's ladies-in-waiting that in 1812 he ordered a set of Sèvres cups to commemorate them. Madame de Montmorency, portrayed here, was famous for the number of her lovers and the sharpness of her tongue.

LEFT **David,** ***Countess de Vilain XIIII and her daughter*** *Madame de Vilain XIIII was a lady-in-waiting who came from an ancient Belgian noble family (which had had XIIII added to its name as an obscure pun on its motto). She remained attached to the Emperor after his fall and chose his exiled First Painter David to paint her portrait in 1816.*

ABOVE **Prud'hon,** ***Countess Edmond de Périgord*** *Stendhal particularly admired her 'pure features' at the New Year reception in 1811. She is better known by the title of Duchess of Dino, which she acquired after the fall of the Empire, when she was the mistress and hostess of her uncle Talleyrand.*

LEFT **Adèle de Broc, *Maréchale Ney*** *Maréchale Ney was a niece of Madame Campan, a friend of Queen Hortense and a lady-in-waiting of the Empress. She was socially ambitious and gave a ball for Tsar Alexander I a few days after the Russian army entered Paris in 1814.*

ABOVE **Isabey, *Countess de Luçay*** *Countess de Luçay served at court from the beginning to the end, first as lady-in-waiting to Josephine and then as Mistress of the Robes to Marie-Louise. She never lost her fervent admiration for the Emperor.*

annoyance to her husband's enemy, Talleyrand. She was so fashionable that most diplomats posted to Paris and even 'the Queens' — the Emperor's sisters-in-law, the Queens of Spain, Holland and Westphalia — attended her receptions.

When she accompanied the Empress Marie-Louise on a visit to Prague in 1812, the Duchess de Bassano captivated the Prince de Ligne, the greatest connoisseur of good manners and female beauty of the day. Comparing her to the Empress's beloved principal lady-in-waiting, the Duchess de Montebello, he wrote: 'She is even more beautiful, with much finer and more sparkling eyes, the Duchess de Bassano! She is more amiable, more amusing and charmingly malicious. They both appear to me just as perfect for style, grace and manners as the real Duchesses of the past, and the latter were much less attractive. Of the four ladies-in-waiting of the Empress, the one who is least noble by birth has the noblest air and vice versa.'[3] From a prince of the Holy Roman Empire, a European *grand seigneur* who had been a frequent visitor to the court of Marie-Antoinette, this was praise indeed.

For Napoleon one of the main purposes of his courts was to provide a vehicle through which he could win over opponents of his regime. In 1805, for example, Prince Eugene appointed a member of the noble family of Cicogna to the position of chamberlain at the Italian court because 'he belongs to a family which has always been listed among the enemies of our government'. Other people were also chosen to be chamberlains because they were part of what was optimistically called 'the former opposition', or came from recently annexed regions.

An example is Count de Mercy-Argenteau, a member of an old Belgian noble family, who was appointed chamberlain in 1804. He was nephew and heir of the former Austrian Ambassador at the court of Versailles, who had mysteriously managed to combine his role as adviser of Marie-Antoinette with that of confidant of revolutionary politicians such as Mirabeau. His nephew liked the Emperor and enjoyed the relaxed atmosphere when the court was at Malmaison. His position at court enabled him to join first the army and then the diplomatic service under particularly favourable circumstances. If the Empire had lasted, he had expected to become French ambassador in Vienna — a complement to his uncle's career as Austrian ambassador at Versailles.[4]

Mercy-Argenteau is also interesting as a representative of what had been called 'the Queen's party' before 1789. This was a group of politicians and courtiers distinguished, like Mercy-Argenteau's uncle, by enthusiasm for alliance with Austria and the power of the Austrian Queen Marie-Antoinette, and by lack of enthusiasm for the Bourbons. Many of them rallied to the Emperor, including the Baron de Breteuil, a powerful minister in the 1780s who was Marie-Antoinette's principal representative in the years 1790–4. On Saint-Helena, Napoleon remembered that Breteuil had tried to persuade many nobles to serve the Emperor 'and as he was in the Queen's party, people paid great attention to him'. Breteuil's granddaughter Madame de Montmorency, wife of the head of one of the oldest and most famous families in the French nobility, became a lady-in-waiting in 1805, and her son was one of the Emperor's chamberlains.

Napoleon's court was a vehicle for taking over the aristocracies of Europe as well as for rallying the opposition. Among his chamberlains, aides-de-camp and ordonnance officers were members of the Salm-Kyrburg, Corsini and Monaco families, some of the grandest in Europe. The future King Leopold I of the Belgians, when he was simply Prince Leopold of Saxe-Coburg, and one of the handsomest princes in Europe, aspired to be one of the Emperor's aides-de-camp. The Emperor was so eager that his court should be European that he appointed five Poles as chamberlains, although he was never the legal sovereign of Poland. Among them were a Radziwill, a Sapieha and Count Krasinski of the Imperial Guard.

The most interesting was Prince Alexander Sapieha, head of an ancient noble family which had, long before its annexation by Russia, once aspired to the throne of Lithuania. Like many members of the European nobility, the prince, born in 1773, had been attracted to the French Revolution when young — although he had not gone so far as the Emperor's future brother-in-law, Prince Borghese, who made a bonfire of his family's genealogies and coats of arms when French troops entered Rome.

Sapieha travelled extensively. He knew Paris well, became a friend of Napoleon (and of the great actress Mademoiselle Georges) during the Consulate and frequented the salon of the Duchess de Bassano. Although he was so fond of Paris, he was

Gérard, *The Duchess de Bassano* *The Duchess de Bassano loved her position as wife of the Emperor's most important minister, and helped to keep him in power by her intrigues at court.*

able to help the Emperor to organize Lithuania on behalf of the French war effort against Russia in 1807. In 1812 he was President of the Military Commission of the Provisional Government of Lithuania, and his death in September of that year was felt to be a serious blow to the Emperor. The Duke de Bassano wrote that he had been 'a good citizen and a faithful servant of Your Majesty'.[5]

Although Napoleon preferred servants with historic names and polished manners, particularly at court, this never led him to exclude people with poor backgrounds. He had used the Revolution, and revolutionaries, as a means to attain supreme power, and he was not going to alienate his earliest power-base. Count Defrance was a typical example of the non-nobles from poor backgrounds who served at court. He showed that extreme Republican antecedents were by no means incompatible with a strong appetite for court life.

Defrance was born in the Haute Marne, near Lorraine, in 1776. He was the son of an apothecary who had been a member of the Convention, the Assembly which turned France into a Republic in 1792 and endorsed the Reign of Terror in 1793–4. Defrance fought his way up to the rank of general in the armies of the Republic. The Emperor made him a count and an equerry and gave him land worth 30,000 francs a year. As equerry in waiting, Defrance was sent to Joseph Bonaparte in Spain with the news of the birth of the King of Rome. He was so fond of court life that after 1820 he became an equerry again, this time to Louis XVIII.

There was always a place for non-nobles like Defrance at court. The Duchess de Montebello, appointed principal lady-in-waiting of the Empress in 1810, was non-noble by birth. Nevertheless, as the following figures show, there was a dramatic rise in the proportion of nobles at court, and the proportion of non-nobles fell by almost a half.

Géricault (?), *Count Krasinski* *Count Krasinski was one of the many Polish nobles who served Napoleon with enthusiasm. He was a chamberlain and commanded one of the Polish regiments of the Imperial Guard (although he never served in the regiment whose uniform he is wearing in this portrait). He later became a favourite aide-de-camp of Tsar Nicholas I of Russia.*

Senior court officials in the households of the Emperor, the Empress and the King of Rome

	1804 83	1814 217
Proportion from the *noblesse présentée*	22.5%	32 %
Proportion from the *noblesse non-présentée*	33.5%	23.5%
Proportion of non-nobles	35 %	18.5%
Proportion of foreign nobles	8.5%	26 %

Even at the start, there were more nobles than non-nobles at the court of Napoleon I. A large proportion came from the old *noblesse présentée*, as was natural in a court whose leading figures had names like Talleyrand, Ségur and Caulaincourt.

The Emperor liked noble birth for itself. Madame de La Tour du Pin, wife of the Prefect of Brussels (himself a member of an ancient noble family) relates the 'magic effect' the phrase 'his ancestor Constable under Saint Louis' had on the Emperor when her husband presented a Belgian noble, the Marquis de Trazegnies. Such ancient lineage, combined with a willingness to be presented, entranced the Emperor. A few months later Madame de Trazegnies was appointed a lady-in-waiting to the Empress.

Another reason why the Emperor liked having nobles in his households was because he felt that they made excellent servants. On Saint-Helena he told his First Ordonnance Officer, Baron Gourgaud: 'I was better served, I mean served, by Madame de Mortemart than by bourgeois. The latter were afraid of appearing to be maidservants.'[6] Nobles intoxicated with the antiquity of their own lineage had no such fears. They were perfectly prepared, if the opportunity arose, to act as the Emperor or Empress's personal servants, picking up handkerchiefs, or waiting at table. The rewards were so great . . . (see Chapter 5).

After the nomination of over a hundred chamberlains, equerries and ladies-in-waiting in 1810, the year of the Emperor's marriage to Marie-Louise, the court was even more aristocratic. Families of the old *noblesse présentée* now colonized the court of Napoleon I as they had done the court of Versailles. One example is the Montesquiou family.

LEFT **Anon, *Count Rapp*** *Rapp was an aide-de-camp of Napoleon from 1800, and later rose to be a general and chamberlain. This portrait reveals that Rapp's pride in his career was greater than his concern for historical accuracy. He is shown at the siege of Danzig (in the background) in 1813, wearing both the insignia of an aide-de-camp of the Emperor and the decorations he received from Louis XVIII after 1814. (Musée d'Unterlinden, Colmar, photo O. Zimmermann)*

ABOVE **Gérard, *Count de Flahault*** *Flahault was a brilliant officer who was the Emperor's favourite aide-de-camp in 1813–15. He may have helped prepare Napoleon's return from Elba.*

L. David
1816

Count de Montesquiou was Grand Chamberlain and his wife was Governess of the Children of France — two of the most important and best paid posts at court. His brother and two of his sons were chamberlains, and another of his sons was an ordonnance officer. Montesquiou would not have been out of place at Versailles where, indeed, his father had been First Equerry of the Count de Provence. Montesquiou is described as being hostile to the Revolution and 'of aristocratic manners and habits'.[7] He was devoted to the Emperor, bringing him glasses of lemonade and helping him on with his clothes. If the Montesquiou are compared to the great favourites of Louis XVI and Marie-Antoinette, the Polignac, it is clear that a family of the old *noblesse présentée* could rise to a position of outstanding favour and success at court just as easily after the Revolution as before. Only the favourites' names had changed.

Apart from the Montesquiou family, many other members of the old nobility became part of the Emperor's daily life. A chamberlain particularly devoted to the Emperor came from one of the oldest and grandest families of Lorraine. Count de Beauvau, born in 1773, was one of the chamberlains most frequently on duty, during the Hundred Days as well as before. He was a nephew of a Captain of the Guard of Louis XV and XVI, who had passed the Revolution on his estates; he amused his friends by the air of special knowledge and awareness which he suddenly adopted after he became a chamberlain, and started meeting ministers and councillors of state. His wife was a lady-in-waiting and his two sons fought in the French army. After the Emperor died, Bertrand sent Beauvau a piece from the weeping willow beside the Emperor's tomb on Saint-Helena, a sacred relic still displayed at the family château at Haroué.[8]

Other important courtiers who came from Lorraine were Counts d'Haussonville and de Choiseul, who were also chamberlains, and Duroc himself, the Grand Marshal of the Palace. Their presence at court, like that of the members of the former 'Queen's party', emphasized its 'Austrian' character. Lorraine was an eastern province which had only been part of France since 1766, and its dukes had long been enemies of the Bourbons. The last hereditary Duke of Lorraine had gone to live in Vienna, and was grandfather of the Emperor Francis I of Austria. The nobles of Lorraine had little reason to love the Bourbons, and those who did not go to serve the descendants of their dukes in Vienna rallied with enthusiasm to the Emperor Napoleon I.

Another chamberlain who became part of the Emperor's life was the Count de Rambuteau. Born in Burgundy in 1781, he is an example of a member of the old provincial nobility who became a courtier. Although so many members of his family had been guillotined that his father refused to go to Paris ever again, Rambuteau had no difficulty in adapting to the new France of the Empire. In 1806, through the influence of friends at court, he was presented to the Emperor — an act which, for members of the old nobility, implied commitment to the regime and hopes of subsequent promotion. In 1809 he became a chamberlain. A remark in his memoirs reveals the extraordinary world of power and privilege, far removed from the lives of most French people, in which the courtiers moved. It relates to the Emperor's journey to Cherbourg in 1811, during which Rambuteau was in waiting: 'I always had two or three rolls of gold for distribution [to people lining the Emperor's route]: when they were exhausted I simply gave my note to Méneval [one of the Emperor's secretaries] and obtained a fresh supply.'

Rambuteau enjoyed his service at court. It gave him opportunities to talk to ministers, princes and ambassadors, and in the evening to the Emperor himself (when the *Petites Entrées* were admitted). In his memoirs he wrote that he liked the Emperor, whom (unlike many other courtiers) he found polite and 'really good-natured'. He felt at home at court. His father-in-law, the Count de Narbonne, a court official and Minister of War under Louis XVI, was one of the Emperor's favourite aides-de-camp. His sister, Madame de Mesgrigny, was an Under-Governess of the King of Rome. Her husband was an equerry; and they were often all in waiting at the same time. In 1813 he realized an ambition of many other chamberlains and became a Prefect. After the fall of the Empire he remained, in his words, 'attached at heart to the dynasty of the Emperor'.[9]

David, ***Count de Turenne*** *Turenne was rich, aristocratic and Master of the Wardrobe from 1811. The Emperor liked his jokes and entrusted valuable personal effects to him in 1814. (His son returned them to Napoleon III forty years later.) This portrait was painted by David in 1816, while they were both in exile in Brussels for their attachment to the Emperor.*

Anon, ***Visit of the Emperor to Cherbourg, 1811*** *On the left footmen prepare to serve a picnic. On the right Napoleon, Marie-Louise and their courtiers watch French ships sail by. In reality the Emperor's power stopped at the sea, which was still controlled by Britain. Courtiers had distributed money to spectators along the Emperor's route from Paris.*

The court was administered by a large bureaucracy under the Intendant-General of the Crown — from 1805 to 1809 Count Daru, and from 1810 to 1814 the Duke de Cadore. The Intendant-General was in charge of those aspects of the administration and finance of the court not directly controlled by the Emperor and Duroc. Stendhal was a typical court bureaucrat in his role as Inspector of the Furniture and Buildings of the Crown from 1810 to 1814. He obtained his job at the age of twenty-eight through the influence of his cousin Daru. Although Stendhal had written that the Emperor was a tyrant in 1804, he was one of Napoleon's most enthusiastic admirers after he obtained an official position. He enjoyed going to court and watching the ladies-in-waiting, or the Emperor himself; and he liked impressing Italians with his conversation about the court when he travelled through Italy inspecting the furniture in the Emperor's palaces.

In his way he was as much part of the court as Count de Beauvau or the Duchess de Bassano, whose balls he admired. Indeed he knew the court so well that he believed that it was 'the contaminated air of the court' which had corrupted the Emperor and, after 1810, 'raised his vanity to the level of a disease'.[10] Stendhal despised the Bourbon restoration which succeeded the Empire, and he glorified the Emperor in his novels *The Red and the Black* and *The Charterhouse of Parma*, published in 1830 and 1839.

It is clear that Count de Sainte-Aulaire was hardly exaggerating when he wrote that, at the court of Napoleon I, 'all the men were young and all the women were beautiful': the Duchess de Bassano, Madame de Rémusat and Mercy-Argenteau were all under twenty-five when they received their court appointments. Whatever their background, whether they were members of the *noblesse présentée*, the *petite noblesse*, the foreign nobility or not noble at all, the Emperor's courtiers were united by the fact that they were of high official rank and relatively rich. In their own opinion they were all aristocrats, whose presence made the Emperor's court the equal of any in Europe.

The popularity, or inevitability, of Napoleon's court is shown by the fact that it was revived under the Consulate, long before the Emperor dared to create an aristocracy. Because it was seen as an inevitable aspect of supreme political power, a court was more acceptable to public opinion than an aristocracy which might have old regime associations. However, after 1808 the Emperor began to award the titles of duke, count, baron and chevalier (those of marquis and viscount were thought to be too closely associated with the old regime). Everyone connected with the court and the government received a title, even those who had one already (22.5 per cent of Napoleonic titles went to members of the old nobility). The Emperor did not recognize titles which he had not himself awarded.

To show that all the new aristocrats were Napoleon's own creation, the titles he conferred on members of the old nobility were always different from those they had inherited. Thus, among the courtiers, the Prince de Beauvau became Count de Beauvau, the Prince de Monaco the Baron de Monaco and the Duke de Montmorency the Baron de Montmorency. This led to endless jokes. One duke of the old regime (perhaps Cossé-Brissac or Clermont-Tonnerre, both of whom were courtiers of the Bonapartes) met Talleyrand just after he had been made a count. The Grand Chamberlain congratulated him and expressed the hope that the new count would soon be promoted to be a baron.

Although most of them were not of noble birth, the Empire aristocracy was profoundly élitist. This was understood by two particularly acute observers. Metternich, at that time Austrian ambassador to Napoleon I, saw the creation of the aristocracy as a stroke of genius. In this way, he wrote, the Emperor succeeded in tying 'private interest, that most powerful motive' to his person, his dynasty and — by awarding the new aristocrats estates in Germany, Poland and Italy — his conquests.

One of the most sensitive of all social analysts, Marcel Proust, was also impressed by the Empire aristocracy. He pointed out the contrast between its real wealth, its experience of 'high positions where it is necessary to command great numbers of men and to know how to do so', its 'air of cold dignity' and 'reserve full of grandeur', and the powerlessness and exaggerated affability of the royalist nobility.[11] Most aristocratic families had been founded on military success or money: the Emperor had plenty of both with which to create new ones.

Members of the old nobility came to dominate

Quenedey, *Stendhal* *The novelist Stendhal knew both the glory and the misery of the court at first hand. He often went to court and inspected the palace furniture. He also accompanied the army during the retreat from Moscow.*

the social circle of the court, which included everyone presented at court and invited to court entertainments, as well as the members of the imperial households. The people on the Grand Chamberlain's *Liste Générale d'Invitations au Cercle de la Cour*, or *Registre de la Cour*, were almost always court officials and their spouses; members of the Senate, the Council of State, the Legislative Body and their wives; distinguished foreigners; and men and women who had been presented at court. Surprisingly few army officers were on the list. Between *c.* 1807 and *c.* 1812 the number of court officials and their spouses on the list rose from 213 to 418, and the number of men and women presented at court from 96 to 585.[12] Since the court officials were predominantly noble, as were over three-quarters of those presented at court, nobles were clearly beginning to dominate the guest-list. The former general of the Republic had become a monarch surrounded by nobles.

The bourgeois of Paris were once invited to a court ball, on 20 April 1806. Otherwise their only access to court entertainments was by service in the army or administration, or as spectators from the balconies in the state apartments. Because the course of the Revolution had brought many non-nobles into senior positions in the army and the administration, the court was not yet exclusively noble. But how long would this last?[13]

The increasingly aloof nature of the court pleased the Emperor. At the banquet held in the Paris Hôtel de Ville to celebrate his victory over Austria in December 1809, the ceremonial was stricter, and Paris mayors played a less prominent part, than at Louis XVI's visit to the Hôtel de Ville in 1782. At the ball afterwards, Jerome Bonaparte, King of Westphalia, sent a chamberlain to forbid his wife Catherine from dancing with a Paris bourgeois. There was an unpleasant scene in front of the other dancers. In the end her father, the King of Württemberg, insisted that she carry on: legitimate dynasties like the Bourbons and the Württembergs were usually less arrogant, or more socially secure, than the Bonapartes. In 1811 the Emperor was furious with the Duke d'Ursel, member of one of the oldest noble families in Belgium, for putting the wife of a merchant on the list of people to be presented at Laeken.

The Emperor's distaste for trade, his preference for aristocracy, whether it was founded on birth or official rank, his refusal to have 'men without anything' as his chamberlains, and the growing predominance of nobles at his court, shows the nature of his regime.[14] It was one of the most élitist, as well as the most monarchical, regimes in recent European history.

5

Ends and Means

'... this court devoured by ambition.'

Stendhal

IN 1811, WHEN THE EMPRESS MARIE-LOUISE was expecting a child, the woman she had replaced, the Empress Josephine, was living in a château in Normandy. Nevertheless, members of Josephine's household were determined not to miss what was going on at the centre of events. They wrote to Marie-Louise's principal lady-in-waiting, the Duchess de Montebello, asking 'to be included among those who will be summoned [to the Tuileries] at the moment when Her Majesty the Empress enters into labour'. In theory court life was an end in itself: court officials were meant to add dignity and comfort to the life of the monarch or prince they had the privilege to serve. In practice, as the shameless letter from Josephine's courtiers reveals, court life was a means to an end. With almost no exceptions, courtiers were more interested in advancing themselves and their families than in serving their masters.

Josephine knew this as well as anyone. She was kindness itself to her courtiers. She arranged their marriages and advanced their careers. She wrote to her son Prince Eugene of her desire to 'do something for the people who surround me and who contribute every day to making my life agreeable', and she put her words into practice. Nevertheless, she was abandoned by most of her household when the Emperor divorced her. Those who did continue to serve her wanted to witness her rival's triumph in childbirth. And in 1811, when she wanted to go to Milan to visit Prince Eugene, none of her courtiers would accompany her.[1] Like the courtiers of Louis XIV, those of Napoleon I and his family could not bear to leave the court.

Life at the court of Napoleon I was even stranger than life at other courts. Just as the Emperor's palaces were distinguished by their size and luxury, so life at his court was unusually dramatic and intoxicating. There were far greater risks and opportunities than in private life. One chamberlain wrote after his appointment: 'The peace and charm of my private life have vanished. From now on it will be public, varied, agitated, lost in the whirlwind of titles, ministerial receptions, the drama of high politics.'[2]

Indeed a courtier's life was so varied that it could change from one day to the next, depending on his feelings, and the state of his own and the Emperor's fortunes. From the outside life at the court appeared extremely glamorous. As every courtier knew, the Emperor was a military genius, and he lived in an age which valued military success above almost anything else. War had been the origin of Napoleon's fame and power, and it was one of his favourite methods of conducting foreign policy. He was bent on conquests — more to satisfy his own drive for glory than for any other reason.

In 1802 Napoleon added Piedmont and Parma to French territory, and in 1805 Liguria. In 1803 he was appointed 'Mediator of the Helvetic Confederation', which meant that Switzerland became a French satellite. Britain, Austria, Prussia and Russia were powerful states which saw no reason why France should continue to expand at will. War was inevitable. Britain (which was also at fault, since it had refused to give up Malta as it had promised) was at war with France from 1803 and eager to subsidize other countries' war efforts. Opportu-

Gérard, ***Count Rapp bringing the banners of the defeated Russian Imperial Guard to Napoleon on the battlefield of Austerlitz, December 1805*** *Behind the Emperor are Duroc, Bessières, Marshal Junot (with a crested helmet) and the Mameluke Roustam; Berthier is on his right. They were deliberately painted with 'the calm appropriate to the habit of victory', and the splendour of their uniforms was designed to set off the simplicity of the Emperor's. This picture was painted for Rapp. A larger version was on the ceiling of the Hall of the Council of State in the Tuileries.*

nities to do so soon presented themselves. Austria was at war with the French Empire in 1805–06 and 1809, Russia in 1805–07, Prussia in 1806–07 and Spain from 1808. Their efforts were unsuccessful. Much of the glamour of life at court came from the military glory won by the Emperor and his army from their defeat of Austria and Russia at Austerlitz in 1805, Prussia at Jena in 1806 and Austria at Wagram in 1809.

When not on campaign, the Emperor reviewed his guard — the best troops of the age — in front of his palace every Sunday, or every other Sunday, after the weekly court reception. Napoleon himself usually wore the uniform of the Grenadiers of the Guard. Even a mocking Austrian visitor, Count Clary, wrote in 1810 that it was 'the finest military spectacle it is possible to see'. To be guarded by the Imperial Guard, to have antechambers filled with marshals such as Murat, Ney and Davout, who were legends in their own lifetime, to serve the greatest genius of the age, gave the Napoleonic court a unique aura of splendour and success.

The splendour of the court was also civilian. A series of dazzling ceremonies included the Coronation, the weddings of Princess Stephanie (a cousin of the Empress adopted by the Emperor) in 1806, the Emperor's youngest brother Prince Jerome in 1807, and the Emperor himself in 1810, and the baptism of the King of Rome in 1811. The palaces were overwhelming, while the courtiers' coats glittered with gold and silver embroidery, and all the orders of Europe (except, Stendhal noted, the Garter). As one Russian visitor remarked, orders were now so common that they were no longer a distinction, but simply a form of clothing.[3] Men such as

Ménageot, ***Wedding of Prince Eugene to Princess Augusta of Bavaria in the Residenz in Munich, 14 January 1806*** *The Emperor later said to the Elector of Bavaria: 'If you had not let Princess Augusta marry Beauharnais, I would have had her carried off by a regiment of Cuirassiers.' Napoleon and Josephine, with the Elector and Electress, sit under the canopy. Murat sits on the left. Eugene and Augusta hold hands in the middle; Duroc, Caulaincourt and Bessières face the Emperor on the right. The presence of farmers in peasant costume (back) would have been unthinkable in the Tuileries.*

Talleyrand, Berthier, Junot and Bessières had been transformed into the Prince de Bénévent, the Prince de Neufchâtel, the Duke d'Abrantès and the Duke d'Istrie — titles which, however pompous and grandiloquent, undoubtedly have a certain allure. The sound as well as the sight of the court was intoxicating. The military marches played in the palace courtyards were almost as impressive as the terrified silence which fell on each room the Emperor entered.

To serve at such a court must have been exhilarating. The Emperor's court officials shared, however remotely, in his incomparable glamour and prestige. Indeed one chamberlain, the Count d'Haussonville, records how gratifying it was to share the same antechamber, before the Emperor's *lever*, with the Kings of Bavaria, Saxony and Würtemberg — polite old gentlemen who did not push or shove when the Emperor came through.[4]

The excitement of life at the Napoleonic court was enhanced by its role as a centre of entertainment. The Emperor and Empress frequently gave balls and concerts, and there were command performances of plays and operas in the palace theatres — sometimes twice a week when the court was at Fontainebleau, Saint-Cloud or Compiègne. The Emperor insisted that his court be the social centre of Paris. During the carnival of 1811, for example, he ordered his sister-in-law Queen Hortense, his beautiful sister Princess Pauline, Marshal Berthier and six ministers to give balls, some of which he himself attended: 'all the court and the *étrangers présentés* will be invited'.[5]

One of the most splendid balls of all was given to mark the beginning of the carnival of 1812. It was held in the theatre of the Tuileries, which was transformed into a ballroom for the occasion. The first quadrille was composed of ladies-in-waiting dressed as peasants from different parts of Europe. The Empress was dressed as a woman from Normandy, the Emperor's sister Caroline, now Queen of Naples, *en Provençale*, the Duchess de Montebello *en Romaine*, the Duchess de Bassano *en Tyrolienne*, Madame de Montmorency *en Hambourgeoise*. Their dresses were paid for by the Empress. Princess Pauline led a second quadrille, whose dancers wore costumes from southern Italy and danced the tarantella to the sound of tambourines and castanets.

The finest quadrille of all was devised by Queen Hortense, who entered the ballroom leading a group of courtiers dressed as Incas. They then enacted a scene from the days of the Spanish conquest: Queen Hortense, as the Grand Priestess of the Sun, was dressed in gold-embroidered muslin covered in pearls and diamonds. She danced so well that, despite the presence of the Emperor, which normally inhibited any reaction from an audience, the spectators broke into applause.

Her sister-in-law and great friend, the Queen of Naples, was furious. Her own quadrille a few weeks earlier, representing the union of Rome and France, had not been so well received. The Emperor, disguised in a domino and mask, went around the ballroom after the quadrilles. His disguise made it easier than usual for him to indulge his favourite habit of making rude or disconcerting remarks to his guests. He left at 2.30 am. A year later the quadrille of the Incas was repeated. But the atmosphere was no longer the same. There were too many wounded dancers whose steps were not so nimble as the year before: fear and death, not power and pleasure, now dominated the court of Napoleon I.[6]

Many guests claimed to be bored by the entertainments at court — and women were always afraid that the Emperor would criticize the number of their lovers or the quality of their clothes. There could be terrible crowds — 2500 were invited to the ball held at the Tuileries for Princess Stephanie's marriage.

Nevertheless, people went to these entertainments because they were pleased to be important enough to be asked, and because they liked to observe who was there. The other guests included the most prominent people in the government, whose wives were often extraordinarily attractive. At the ball for the marriage of Princess Stephanie, for example, a guest observed of Princess Caroline (not yet promoted to be Queen of Naples) that 'the splendour of her diamonds could not efface that of her complexion'.[7] The Duchess d'Abrantès, in memoirs written twenty years later to pay her debts, praised 'the really fantastic sight provided by the Hall of Marshals the night of a grand concert, when both sides were lined with three rows of women, nearly all young and pretty, covered with

Percier and Fontaine, ***The Emperor and Empress receive the homage of the troops on the day of their wedding from the balcony of the Tuileries*** *The army files past to the sound of trumpets. This is one of the few occasions when the Emperor used the accessibility of the Tuileries to lower the barriers between himself and the world beyond his court.*

Dessiné par Percier et Fontaine. — Gravé par Pauquet et C. Normand.

L'Empereur et l'Impératrice recevant sur le Grand Balcon des Tuileries les Hommages des Troupes qui défilent devant elles, le jour de la Cérémonie de leur Mariage.

flowers, diamonds and waving feathers'. Behind them were courtiers and generals 'all wearing rich costumes, their chests covered in the stars and ribbons which Europe offered us on bended knee'.[8]

If an occasion involved music, there was also the pleasure of listening. Frédéric Masson, a late nineteenth-century historian who is still the greatest authority on the Napoleonic court, wrote that: 'No sovereign has ever spent so much money for his private orchestra as Napoleon.' Madame Grassini, the most famous singer in Europe, who had briefly been the Emperor's mistress, received the title of First Singer of the Chamber for her performances at court. The celebrated composer Paër was lured from the court of Dresden to be 'Composer and Director of the Music and the Theatres of the Court': his music, although now long forgotten, was extremely popular in his lifetime. The greatest violinist of the day, Kreutzer (to whom Beethoven dedicated the Kreutzer Sonata), was first violin in the court orchestra. The excellence of the music at Sunday Mass was one of the compensations for the wasted time and crowds at the subsequent reception.[9] Presumably the music on such occasions was more appealing than the only Napoleonic ceremonial music now on record, Le Sueur's Coronation March and Paisiello's Coronation Mass and Te Deum, whose hysterical pomposity quickly palls.

The entertainments and receptions were so impressive that an experienced foreign judge, like Countess Potocka, agreed that the court was 'magnificent'. A Dutch officer in the Imperial Guard, who went to a New Year reception in the Tuileries, wrote that the sight of the Emperor on his throne, surrounded by his court, was 'so dazzling that I was overwhelmed and could not distinguish anybody'.[10]

A particularly unequivocal tribute came from Metternich, when he arrived in Paris as Austrian Ambassador in 1806. After presenting his credentials to the Emperor, he wrote that: 'The whole court together presents a very imposing spectacle and the richness of the costumes is less astonishing than the air of permanence it has acquired: the household functions as if everybody had been doing the same job for a hundred years.'[11]

Clearly an air of confidence, as well as outward magnificence, characterized the court of Napoleon I. This can still be seen today in the innumerable portraits of court officials, usually in full uniform, the very existence of which is a tribute to their pride in their rank and achievements. They appear free of doubts or uncertainty. They were rich, successful and the personal servants of the greatest monarch of the age. Their confidence and panache, displayed in the swirl of Duroc's cloak, the prance of Rapp's horse or Caulaincourt's assured smile, helped to enhance the appeal of the regime, and have attracted admirers ever since.

The impression conveyed by the portraits was true to life. People at court could be ludicrously condescending. The Emperor's sister Caroline wrote to her sister-in-law Hortense in December 1805, only a year after they had become princesses, to complain that the court of Bavaria was very dull: 'Do not have an exaggerated idea of this court, for they are all like *de bons bourgeois*.' From a young woman who a year before had been plain Madame Murat, such arrogance towards one of the oldest dynasties and most splendid courts in Europe is staggering: it shows what other monarchs had to endure from the court and family of Napoleon I. It also shows the crude competitiveness of the Napoleonic court, since Princess Caroline may have adopted this attitude in order to annoy Hortense, whose brother Eugene was about to marry a Bavarian princess.[12]

The Emperor himself was extremely condescending. No palace in Europe, except perhaps the Royal Palace of Madrid, was grand enough for Napoleon I. When he met other monarchs, whether on his own territory or abroad, he insisted that he was host: his court officials arranged the accommodation and entertainment, and regulated the ceremonial. He thought himself superior to other monarchs, and had himself depicted as Jupiter on the ceiling of the throne room of the Royal Palace of Milan. Such grandeur and self-assertion naturally infected his courtiers: one Frenchman who met them on Elba wrote that, even there, they all behaved as if they were 'little Napoleons'.[13] Stendhal, so quick to laugh at French pretension and artificiality, went through Italy complaining about the Emperor's Italian palaces, and planned to refurnish them with modern French furniture. The courtiers of the Empire were as brash and grandiose as its music and furniture. Restraint, modesty or understatement were rarely apparent.

One reason for the courtiers' behaviour was that their service at court was a sign of success and a guarantee of wealth. The Emperor was extremely generous. He could afford to be, since he had as many sources of income as a modern businessman has bank accounts: his generous civil lists in France and Italy, the Domaine Extraordinaire and the Domaine Privé. From these resources, and from the funds of the different government ministries,

Napoleon was able to reward his followers on a scale unprecedented in the history of European monarchies.

At the lowest level of the court hierarchy he constantly gave presents to his most intimate servants, such as Constant, Roustam and his coachman, César.[14] The sums involved were 2000 or 3000 francs a time — sometimes 10,000 or 25,000 francs. In addition Caulaincourt received large sums of money to distribute to spectators when the Emperor's coach went past. Combined with the sight of the footmen's green and gold livery, the Emperor appeared to be surrounded by a halo of gold.

Court officials also participated in the imperial bounty. Count and Countess de Rémusat, for example, received 380,000 francs between 1804 and 1810 in addition to their salaries, in order to entertain in a style fitting to the First Chamberlain of the Emperor. To mark the birth of the King of Rome in 1811, Madame de Montesquiou, who was his Governess, received an annuity of 50,000 francs a year from the Domaine Extraordinaire.

By 1810 lands and annuities worth 18 million francs a year from the Domaine Extraordinaire had been distributed among 4035 recipients, ranging from Berthier, who received over 1.2 million francs a year from this source (in addition to his salaries and the Emperor's personal gifts), to invalided officers who were given a few hundred francs a year. Essentially this was a revival of the feudal system since the lands and income were rewards for service to the monarch and had special conditions attached.[15] Although it was difficult for courtiers to collect the income due to them from their foreign estates, it is safe to assume that none of them grew poorer by serving at court.

The Emperor's generosity, like most of his acts, had a political rather than a personal motive. By giving his followers land or income from the Domaine Extraordinaire he gave them a personal stake in his conquests, and so bound them more closely to his own authority and empire. As he told Gourgaud on Saint-Helena, with the frankness which could make him such good company, 'it was in my interests to enrich everyone around me, to have them for myself'.[16] If his calculation had been correct, however, he would not have been on Saint-Helena talking to Gourgaud.

Service at the court of Napoleon I not only brought financial rewards, but could also have a startling effect on court officials' careers. Most courtiers were only *de service* (in waiting) for a few weeks or months in the year. For the rest of the time they were free to pursue military or political careers. The end of the old regime meant the end of the formal barriers between the legal nobility (see p. 79), the *petite noblesse* and the *noblesse présentée*, which had prevented some sections of the nobility from enjoying military, legal or administrative careers before 1789. Moreover, the upheaval of the Revolution meant that they often needed such careers to repair the damage done to the family fortunes. Service at court was particularly attractive because it gave access to the Emperor, and the opportunity to ask for jobs or promotion 'without any difficulty'.

The Emperor felt that it was in his own interests to further his courtiers' careers. If his ablest courtiers entered the army or the administration, perhaps they would bring an extra edge of personal devotion and loyalty to their jobs. As a result over a fifth of the Emperor's senior diplomats came from his household.[17] Even the Grand Officers and court officials often in waiting, such as Rambuteau and Mercy-Argenteau, pursued careers outside the court. Talleyrand was Minister of Foreign Affairs as well as Grand Chamberlain. Ségur, the Grand Master of Ceremonies, served in the Council of State.

The Emperor's aides-de-camp had especially brilliant careers. Savary became Minister of Police and Duke de Rovigo. The Emperor trusted another aide-de-camp, General Mouton, Count de Lobau, to such an extent that after 1810 he was given the job of organizing military personnel and checking the reports of the Minister of War. As the Minister complained, 'an aide-de-camp of the Emperor is independent of the Minister of War and far more important than he is'. Another aide-de-camp, the Count de Flahault, was put 'in charge of all matters concerning military personnel' during the Hundred Days. Marshal Davout, the Minister of War, never forgave him.[18]

Perhaps the most successful was General Bertrand. After being appointed an aide-de-camp in 1805, he was sent on repeated missions of inspection of ports and armies, received estates from the Domaine Extraordinaire and the title of count, was made Governor-General of the Illyrian Provinces in 1811 and Grand Marshal of the Palace in 1813. For any Frenchman, let alone the son of a minor government official in Bourges as Bertrand was, this was a brilliant career: clearly it paid to be a personal servant of the Emperor. Not everyone, however, felt that an aide-de-camp of the Emperor was sufficiently grand. A relation of the Empress Josephine, when told that she was going to marry

Bertrand rather than a German prince or the King of Spain, exclaimed: 'Bertrand, Sire! Bertrand! Why not the Pope's monkey?'[19]

The ordonnance officers also benefited by serving at court. After the Emperor's marriage in 1810 they were all given regiments. In 1813, Monsieur de Caraman, an old regime noble who had just become an ordonnance officer, received an estate on the Domaine Extraordinaire, the cross of the Légion d'Honneur and the title of baron. Even more important, Caraman felt that he had made contacts in the army through his functions as ordonnance officer which would be very useful in furthering his career. The Emperor called Caraman by his name, an unusual favour, and at the end of 1813 corresponded directly with him during his mission of inspection in the Rhineland and Holland.[20]

Spectacular civilian careers were open to the chamberlains. By 1813 ten, including Rambuteau, had become Prefects — one of the most coveted posts in the administration. Moreover, they received some of the most important Prefectures, based in Lyons, Versailles and Bremen. Mercy-Argenteau was appointed minister to Bavaria in 1811 although, as a Russian diplomat pointed out, 'he is very young and has been attached only to the service of the court'.[21] Even the almoners did well. The abbé de Pradt, a cousin of Duroc and a notoriously irreligious priest, became an almoner in ordinary in 1804. He was a great favourite of the Emperor, who often talked with him at the *lever*. As Bishop of Poitiers, he acted as the Emperor's spy on priests in the royalist west of France. He was promoted to Archbishop of Malines in Belgium in 1808, and in 1812 received the key post of ambassador in Warsaw — the last priest to receive a diplomatic position in European history (with the exception of those appointed to or from Rome).[22]

For both priests and laymen, therefore, the court of Napoleon I was an excellent employment bureau. It could catapult chamberlains or aides-de-camp into senior positions before they were forty. Flahault was thirty when he was put in charge of army personnel, Mercy-Argenteau thirty-one when he became minister to Bavaria.

The fact that positions at court enabled their holders to leap ahead of rivals who had had earlier starts was extremely important. Many members of the élite had been prevented from entering public service by their families' opposition to the French Republic before 1804. Having been unable to start their careers in their late teens, as was normal, they were unwilling to begin at the bottom, serving under officers or officials who, although higher in rank, were often younger than themselves.[23] Through the court they could hope to obtain those positions to which, in their own and the Emperor's opinion, they were entitled.

Monsieur de Bondy was a typical example of a court official who knew how to use the court. A financial official before 1789, he had, like many non-nobles as well as nobles, lost money during the Revolution. From his correspondence with his wife it is clear that he regarded his position as chamberlain primarily as a means to obtain money and jobs for himself and his family. In the first letter he wrote during his journey to Milan for the Emperor's coronation as King of Italy, he said: 'I must create a stable existence for us and our relations and I must profit with energy from the opportunity with which providence has provided me' — a classic statement of courtier ambition. During this journey he even learned to like the Emperor and praised his admirable 'patience' and 'gentleness'. He found that his service as chamberlain gave him the opportunity to talk often, and at length, with the Emperor, particularly about his brother-in-law's desire to be an official of the Ministry of War: 'the Emperor does not like people to recommend but he welcomes those who advance their families'.

Bondy's service at court bore fruit. In 1808 a relation received a prefecture, and in 1809 Bondy himself received the title of baron and an income of 4000 francs a year from the Domaine Extraordinaire. He was then in waiting at the palace of Schönbrunn outside Vienna, during the Emperor's second campaign against Austria. He wrote in ecstasy: 'My family is now bound for all eternity to serve the Emperor and his family.' In 1810 he became Prefect of the Rhône and during the Hundred Days, as Prefect of the Seine, he was in charge of Paris. He remained attached to the Bonaparte dynasty after 1815 and, as a liberal deputy, voted against the government of the Bourbons.[24]

Bondy's career shows that courtiers tried to help their relations as well as themselves. The Emperor approved, on the principle that the entire family would then (in theory) be committed to his regime. Thus, although officials could not influence senior

Anon, *Count Bertrand* *Loyal and honest, Bertrand was chosen to hold the most important post at court, Grand Marshal of the Palace, in 1813.*

court appointments, all of which were decided by the Emperor himself, some families, such as the Montesquiou, and Rambuteau and his relations, were able to establish themselves at court on an impressive scale.

Senior court officials could be very effective in helping — or hindering — their friends' careers. It was an age when there were few exams or tests for jobs, and contacts were even more important than they are now. Stendhal wrote in 1809, 'you will only get on by the salons', and the court was the greatest salon of all. Even the footmen went to the palace with their pockets full of petitions.

The Emperor was amazed at the devotion displayed by Monsieur de Viry, a former Piedmontese ambassador at Versailles, who was sixty-eight when he was appointed a chamberlain in 1804. De Viry explained that service at court was his sole remaining pleasure: 'here I learn the news; I do something, I think that I am still useful to somebody; when I stay at home my friends come to see me . . . for in fact I have helped and can still help several of them, whereas if I was not at court I would die of boredom and would be good for nothing.'[25] The court was an enormous employment bureau.

The letter-book of the Count de Ségur is primarily concerned with recommendations for jobs. On a typical day in 1810 he wrote to the heads of the army commissariat, the customs and the military administration to recommend protégés. The recommendations were often successful. A letter written in 1811 suggests that he could easily obtain either promotion or a pension for a cousin from the Minister of War.[26]

Although the court of Napoleon I was a spectacular employment bureau, and possessed a unique combination of splendour and panache, there was a void at its heart. The motor that drives most courts is love and respect for the monarch, and his or her family. These feelings are the necessary basis of a

Isabey, *The birth of the King of Rome, 20 March 1811* *Servants (far left and right) are, for once, as prominent in the picture as courtiers. Madame de Montesquiou holds the cushion, her enemy the Duchess de Montebello is at the Empress's bedside. The Emperor is the only man in the room, as other males were normally forbidden access to the Empress's private apartments. The furniture on the right was a present from the City of Paris.*

system that glorifies the personal service of the monarch, and they were hard to find at the Napoleonic court.

The Emperor was a genius, but he was not a lovable master. The expressions of affection and respect made by Mercy-Argenteau, Rambuteau and de Bondy are unrepresentative. They are tributes to a passing mood, to a career that was going well, or to a desire to defend the Emperor after his fall. There is far more contemporary evidence that, for most of the time, the Emperor was heartless and rude.

There are innumerable examples of his unpleasantness. In September 1805, during dinner at Saint-Cloud, the Emperor attacked his wife's ladies 'in the most violent way'. He told them that in Paris they had the reputation of being 'quick and good': Madame de Rémusat could not believe her ears. At a *lever* in 1806 he embarrassed the Crown Prince of Bavaria by asking:

'Who is your mistress?'

'No-one, Sire.'

'Nonsense, tell me.'

The Crown Prince thereafter disliked the Emperor; he said Napoleon had 'a green laugh'. If the Emperor behaved in such a way to the son of an important German monarch whose alliance he valued, one can imagine how he treated his own courtiers. The Emperor's behaviour to the people around him did indeed amaze another of his German allies, the King of Saxony.[27]

The Emperor liked to attack, in conversation as well as on the battlefield. One of his favourite tricks was to suggest to courtiers that their wives (or husbands) were unfaithful. He did not care about his courtiers' happiness: he prevented Berthier and Caulaincourt from marrying the women they loved, and tried to turn Duroc and Caulaincourt against each other. His servants also suffered from his taunts and onslaughts. Roustam wrote that the Emperor was 'rather violent' and that only the intervention of the Empress prevented him from being dismissed on several occasions.

During the advance on Moscow in 1812 he was so offensive to Berthier that, for the first time, his devoted Chief of Staff and Grand Huntsman took his meals separately from the Emperor. At the same time the Emperor was taunting Caulaincourt for being 'Russian', because Caulaincourt had advised against the war. This so infuriated the Grand Equerry that he almost lost his self-control. Bessières and Berthier had to hold on to his coattails to prevent him assaulting the Emperor.[28] Talleyrand, Cardinal Fesch and countless other courtiers also endured vicious personal attacks by the Emperor. They were made worse by the fact that they were delivered in front of the whole court rather than in the privacy of his study.

The Emperor did not spare foreign ambassadors, behaving to them with what Lord Whitworth (British ambassador in 1803) called a 'total want of dignity as well as of decency'. He attacked the British and Russian ambassadors in 1803, the Austrian ambassador in 1808 and the Russian ambassador in 1811. At a court reception in 1813 he was so angry with a deputy of Hamburg (a city which, he claimed, with characteristic lack of realism, could only be 'Danish or French') that 'his face seemed on fire and one saw that he was very incensed'.[29] The same year he became so angry with the Pope that he almost seized the Pope by his robes.

The Emperor's rudeness was particularly significant in an age when people made a religion of good manners and studied them as a science. Individuals were judged by their manners as much as by their birth, wealth or personal ability. One of the most popular contemporary manuals of behaviour, Lord Chesterfield's *Letters to His Son*, advised its readers to 'cultivate the graces'. 'The graces' were a passport to success, even in the ruthless world of the Empire.

One of the Emperor's most dangerous military rivals was Marshal Bernadotte, a former friend of General Moreau. In 1810 the Swedish Estates chose him as heir to the throne of Sweden in order to avoid having a Danish prince, and in the mistaken belief — in part based on the fact that Bernadotte still went to court — that his designation would please the Emperor. Bernadotte was astonishingly successful in Sweden, to the extent that (unlike the Bonapartes) the Bernadottes are still on the throne today; and his manners were an essential ingredient in his success. A French general in Swedish service wrote that Bernadotte had 'the ease, the politeness, even the gallantry of the courtier', and that, 'so great is the sway of outward appearances', Bernadotte 'seduced' both the King and the people. The Queen of Sweden wrote in her diary in December 1810: 'His whole manner of behaviour, as much with the King as with me and with all his entourage, is such that it is bound to win him the affection of the people, and he is already beginning to be liked.'[30] Indeed he became one of the most popular of all kings of Sweden — although he never mastered the language.

Other monarchs, especially the Bourbons, also used good manners as an instrument of government. They were part of the civilizing process

ABOVE ***A hunt in the forest of Compiègne*** *The Emperor is wearing the green and gold coat of the Imperial Hunt. Roustam is behind him. This Sèvres tray comes from a set originally destined for Madame Mère, which was given to Wellington in 1814.*

LEFT ***The throne room in Fontainebleau*** *Napoleon installed this throne room in what had been Louis XVI's bedroom. The throne and the canopy are new and covered in Bonaparte symbols. The stools for the use of high officials were inherited from the old regime.*

ABOVE ***The Empress's bedroom in Compiègne*** *This is one of the most sumptuous of all Empire rooms and was furnished for the arrival of the Empress Marie-Louise in 1810.*

LEFT ***The Emperor's library in Compiègne*** *In such surroundings the Emperor worked with his secretaries and ministers. Only the most senior court officials were allowed to enter his study and library. The Emperor also had a travelling library. He would throw the books out of the carriage window as he finished them.*

LEFT **Appiani, *General Fontanelli*** *Fontanelli is wearing the costume of a Grand Officer of the Kingdom of Italy. He was devoted to Napoleon and was in turn an aide-de-camp, Commander of the Italian Royal Guard and Minister of War for Italy. In 1814 he tried to keep the Kingdom of Italy for Prince Eugene.*

BELOW **Borsato, *Aquatic regatta in Venice*** *In 1807 Napoleon was received with enthusiasm in Venice, despite the collapse of its maritime commerce because of his war with England in the Mediterranean.*

ABOVE **Goubaud**, ***Reception of a deputation of the Senate of Rome in the Tuileries, 16 November 1809*** *The Emperor, on his throne, has announced that he has 'reunited' Rome to his Empire. Cambacérès, Bessières and Cardinal Fesch stand on the left of the throne; Lebrun, Talleyrand and Berthier immediately to the right, and King Jerome in front of them on the top step. Ségur, holding his wand of office, is in the middle. It had been hard to find Roman nobles willing to join the deputation: the government had to pay for their journey and costumes.*

ABOVE RIGHT **Garnier**, ***Entry of the Emperor and Empress into the Tuileries, 2 April 1810*** *Pages cling to the carriage which takes the Emperor and Empress from their civil marriage in Saint-Cloud to their religious marriage in the Louvre.*

ABOVE **Casanova,** ***State banquet in the theatre of the Tuileries, 6 April 1810*** *Members of the imperial family surround the Emperor. The silver-gilt service presented by the City of Paris is on the table: courtiers watch and serve. Selected Parisians watch from behind a balustrade, segregated from the court. The meal proceeded in silence, while piles of linen mounted behind each chair, as the Emperor and his guests tossed aside a napkin each time it was used.*

ABOVE RIGHT **Schmidt,** ***King Joachim at the siege of Capri*** *Murat is giving one of his aides-de-camp, Prince Strongoli-Pignatelli, the order to take Capri, which was occupied by English troops under Sir Hudson Lowe, the future Governor of Saint-Helena. Behind the King are the Duke of Gallo, the Minister of Foreign Affairs, General Reynier, the Minister of War, and Saliceti, Minister of Police.*

RIGHT **Benvenuti,** ***The Grand Duchess Elisa and her court*** *On the left are the princess's ladies-in-waiting. Count degli Alessandri, her First Chamberlain, stands to the left of the princess, Bartolomeo Cenami, her lover, and Napoleone, her daughter, to the right. On the right her husband Felix points to a bust of the princess held by Canova, the Bonapartes' favourite sculptor. Between them is the Grand Master of the court, Lucchesini. Two artists, Benvenuti and Fabre, are painting the princess. This is the only picture of a ruler surrounded by the artists and officials of her court.*

Gérard, ***King Joseph*** *The King is wearing his official costume as King of Spain. His position in Spain was so difficult that he often wished he was back in Naples or France.*

which was one of the *raisons d'être* of court life; and they helped to make monarchical power more acceptable.

In contrast the Emperor's rudeness was unlikely to be forgiven or forgotten. It revealed the Emperor's true character: he was ruthless, infuriated by disagreement or disobedience, and had very little self-control. The Emperor's outbursts poisoned life at his court and weakened his hold over his followers: Caulaincourt wrote that 'he would have turned all heads' if only he had had a little 'French courtesy'.

To a certain extent the Emperor's rudeness was mitigated, before 1810, by the tact and charm of the Empress Josephine. Although the court was full of malice and intrigue, she never made an enemy apart from her husband's family, which always hated her. Count Turpin de Crissé wrote a tribute to her character which is all the more convincing because it was made after the fall of the Empire, when few other courtiers found time to defend the imperial family. In his words, after her divorce she held a court 'where dignity, grace, wit, talents and good conversation made a seat of exile into a place of enchantment and a queen without a crown into a woman surrounded by real friends'.[31]

Indeed Josephine's solitude in the first months after her divorce was soon a thing of the past. She came back into fashion, particularly when she returned to Malmaison. She was so kind and charming, and the food and the music at Malmaison were so good, that even courtiers in waiting at Saint-Cloud or the Tuileries visited and dined with her. In contrast the Emperor had no friends apart from Duroc. Duroc's successor as Grand Marshal of the Palace, Bertrand, had unrivalled opportunities to get to know the Emperor at court and on the battlefield, in France and in exile. On Saint-Helena he concluded that: 'It is because of the Emperor's character that he has no friends, that he has so many enemies, and indeed that we are at Saint-Helena.'[32]

Josephine's replacement, the Empress Marie-Louise, although neither stupid nor unpleasant, lacked her charm. Being born an Archduchess, she may not have felt the same desire to please. When the Emperor sent her to Cherbourg in 1813, to raise morale and launch a ship, the Minister of Police wrote a revealing letter to the commander of the contingent of the Imperial Guard which was escorting her. He begged Count Caffarelli to ensure that the Empress would be punctual, that she would smile, that she would speak kindly to those who were presented to her, and that she would show confidence. 'For God's sake, my friend, no ice . . . you understand', he added. The Minister did not write to the Duchess de Montebello, because he knew it would be a waste of time.[33]

The Emperor's rudeness and the reserve of the Empress Marie-Louise helped give the court its exceptionally tense and uneasy atmosphere. It was not improved by the fact that many courtiers came from different backgrounds or different countries. With the best will in the world, members of ancient noble families such as Count de Beauvau and Prince Sapieha found conversation with self-made men such as Count Defrance and Count Rapp a little difficult.

Before the proclamation of the Empire the court had been quite relaxed. But already in 1805 Madame de Rémusat noted that 'every day people are more reserved and distrustful. They hardly dare talk about the most harmless matters.' From her letters it seems that Madame de Rémusat's life at court was composed of anxiety, argument and attempts to further her ambitions. Any feeling of love or warmth for the Emperor or Empress is absent. 'Pleasure does not inhabit palaces', she wrote in 1805. The same year, Princess Hortense wrote to her brother Eugene, the Viceroy of Italy: 'The court is as you remember it, just as sad; nothing much happens.'[34]

Talleyrand's letters to Caulaincourt also present a grim picture of court life, even when the Emperor was away fighting. In 1807 he wrote that the Empress's salon was 'sad', in 1808 that 'the palace is not very agreeable; the women do not get on very well. I do not think that Madame de La Rochefoucauld has all the tact necessary when one is at the head of a court service.'[35] A sure sign of the Napoleonic court's lack of appeal was the fact that Madame de La Rochefoucauld did not occupy the apartment allotted to her in the Tuileries as principal lady-in-waiting of the Empress. The Duchess de Montebello did only because the Emperor ordered her to; and Corvisart, the First Doctor of the Emperor, also refused an apartment in the Tuileries.

Like many courtiers, Corvisart and the Duchess de Montebello (when she could get away from the Tuileries) lived in splendid *hôtels* which they acquired in the most aristocratic quarter of Paris, the Faubourg Saint-Germain. The *hôtel* of the Duchess de Montebello, 61 Rue de Varenne, was filled with magnificent Jacob furniture, portraits and busts of the imperial family and the dignitaries of the Empire, and pieces of Sèvres given by the Empress.[36] Talleyrand, Berthier and Ségur also had their own *hôtels*, acquired with the help of the

LEFT **Isabey and Marie-Louise, *Visit of the Duchess de Montebello to the Empress*** *As she often was, the Empress is ill in bed. She liked the company of her intimate friends Baron Corvisart (left, holding a bust of the King of Rome) and the Duchess de Montebello, to whom she gave this drawing in 1813. Isabey 'finished' the drawings which the Empress began.*

ABOVE **Menjaud, *The Emperor with the King of Rome*** *At the end of his morning meal, Napoleon liked to relax for a few minutes with his wife and son. They are watched by de Bausset, a Prefect of the Palace who has just supervised the serving of the meal, Madame de Montesquiou and an under-governess. Other courtiers rarely obtained such an intimate view of the Emperor and Empress.*

Emperor. Caulaincourt lived opposite the Tuileries, near the imperial stables. The only senior court official who lived in the Tuileries was the Grand Marshal of the Palace, who entertained in his magnificent apartment on the ground floor, looking on to the courtyard. Court officials in waiting automatically ate at his table.

When compared with the desperate scramble for even the corner of an attic at Versailles, this reluctance to inhabit the Tuileries makes it clear that the Napoleonic court was less agreeable than its predecessor. It was also quite different in character from its chief political and social rival, the court of Vienna, as a remark by the Prince de Ligne reveals. When Berthier and his staff went to Vienna in 1810 to ask for the hand of the Archduchess Marie-Louise in marriage, they criticized the Austrian court to the Prince on the grounds that 'people made too much noise, they did not show enough respect for the imperial family'.[37] In other words the courtiers knew each other so well, and were so relaxed, that they actually talked to each other. At the same time the Habsburgs were so sure of their courtiers' loyalty that they did not require the exaggerated forms of deference prevalent at the court of Napoleon I, such as silence, bowing and pushing.

Life at court was also poisoned by the insecurity caused by the Emperor's endless wars. The courtiers could not be sure that the Emperor would always return victorious. Even his magnificent armies received occasional checks — at Eylau in Russia in 1807, Baylen in Spain in 1808 and Aspern in Austria in 1809. Before each final victory there was an agonizing period of doubt. What would happen if the Emperor was killed or defeated? The courtiers' panache and dash hid the fact that there was little real confidence in the duration of the regime. One reason why the Emperor called Madame de La Rochefoucauld 'a little cripple, as stupid as she is ugly' in 1807 was that he knew that she had been spreading fear and despondency at court before his victory over the Prussians at Jena.

On the other hand, the atmosphere at court was not always unpleasant. The Emperor was a genius who could illuminate any subject he chose. What he said about the French Revolution on Saint-Helena, for example, is far more perceptive and interesting than the analyses of most participants and historians. The secret of his appeal was described by his second Empress. She wrote to her father, soon after her marriage, that 'there is something very forceful and captivating about him which it is impossible to resist'.[38] Some courtiers and servants always remained under the spell of his personality, such as the Ségur and Montesquiou families, and Marchand, who replaced Constant as First Valet in 1814. For them the Emperor's genius excused his behaviour. Harsh words and endless wars did not stop them keeping their oaths and doing their duty.

Moreover, when it suited him, the Emperor could be affectionate, generous and charming. Even on Saint-Helena he could enchant anyone he met, as the representative of his rival Louis XVIII admitted. When he was still on the throne his powers of seduction are likely to have been even greater. The Magravine of Baden-Baden wrote to a princess of Hesse-Darmstadt in 1806 that the Emperor had been 'so friendly and so attentive to me that in a tête-à-tête of an hour I talked to him frankly'. Napoleon was able to remove her objections to her son's marriage to Princess Stephanie.

Napoleon's outbreaks of charm were calculated and rare and were exaggerated in retrospect. One of his aides-de-camp, Count van Hogendorp, wrote in exile that, 'I was sincerely attached to Napoleon, who treated me with great kindness.' Of his service at Saint-Cloud in the summer of 1811 he wrote: 'I have never passed a more agreeable time in my life. Above all I was charmed to see the intimacy and the gentleness of his marriage with his wife.'[39] On the other hand, when the Emperor was in a good mood, he had a way of showing favour that was unlikely to appeal to everyone. He would tweak the favourite's ear — and in one case his Empress's nose. Sometimes Napoleon squeezed a courtier's ear or cheeks so hard that he cried, and kept the bruises for days.[40]

Towards the end of the Empire, the court acquired a certain poise and dignity, partly through the influence of Queen Hortense. She was the most charming of the Bonaparte princesses. At the Emperor's wedding to Marie-Louise, when the princesses were forced to carry the Empress's train (the Emperor's sisters were outraged), it was said that the only one who performed her part with dignity

Anon, *Marchand, First Valet of the Emperor* *From 1814, Marchand was Napoleon's most important personal servant. He was well educated, wrote valuable memoirs and, by a deliberate misreading of Napoleon's will, assumed the title of count on Napoleon's death.*

was Queen Hortense, 'because she has tact and intelligence'. After 1810, separated from her husband, she was consoled by one of the great charmers of the age, Charles de Flahault: by brilliant planning, she bore his son (the future Duke de Morny) in 1812 without anyone finding out. Her salon in the Rue Cérutti became one of the social centres of Paris. She boasts in her memoirs, with that vanity which characterized even the most elegant members of the Napoleonic court: 'Despite my big receptions and my balls, everyone wanted to come to my *petites soirées*.' She was helped by the fact that she was the mother of the Emperor's senior nephew, who would be heir if anything happened to the King of Rome. At her *petites soirées*, for the first time in Paris, guests sat round a table and talked, read and sewed. They also sang songs glorifying feats of chivalry, often composed by the Queen herself, with the same fervour which had been displayed for Liberty and Equality during the Revolution.[41]

The increasing poise and confidence of the Emperor's court towards the end of the regime became apparent in the palace itself, particularly when the Emperor was away. The Empress's procession to mass at Saint-Cloud, escorted by her ladies, was described by Talleyrand in 1812 as having 'the greatest elegance imaginable'. The letters that a lady-in-waiting, Madame de Montmorency, wrote to an equerry, Count Charles de La Grange, in 1812–14, show that the court was beginning to create its own atmosphere and generate its own gossip. In 1812, for example, she wrote of other ladies-in-waiting: 'Madame de Dalberg is pregnant — Madame de Bouillé is spitting blood — Madame de Duchâtel has a bilious fever — Princess Aldobrandini has had a daughter.' Clearly she had become accustomed to colleagues from a variety of countries and backgrounds, and other letters contain news of Anatole de Montesquiou, the Duchess d'Elchingen (Maréchale Ney), Princess Pauline, General Lariboissière and the Duchess de Bassano. Such an extraordinary combination of names, from the old nobility, the bourgeoisie, Corsica, Germany and Rome, could only have existed at the court of Napoleon I.[42]

Some chamberlains were sufficiently relaxed in conversation at court to tell stories which made the ladies-in-waiting blush. Since morals at court were not strict, there was much to tell. When the Empress Josephine had surprised the Emperor in bed with a lady-in-waiting, she made such a scene that the lady in question, Madame de Vaudey, had had to leave. The Emperor flew into a rage, smashed the furniture and threatened a divorce. Another lady-in-waiting, Madame Octave de Ségur, one of the Priestesses of the Sun in the Quadrille of the Incas, had aroused the jealousy of her husband, a son of the Grand Master of Ceremonies, when he found an anonymous love letter addressed to her. He was so angry that he left at once, enlisted in the army as an ordinary soldier and did not return for eight years. There was a brief reconciliation. But soon his jealousy, not without reason, revived. He threw himself into the Seine and drowned.[43] The Empress's ladies-in-waiting could arouse strong feelings. Caulaincourt was in love with another lady-in-waiting, Madame de Canisy. She was one of the most beautiful women of the age, and had been married to her aged uncle, one of the Emperor's favourite equerries. Despite the Canisys' divorce, and Caulaincourt's eminent services, the Emperor refused to allow Madame de Canisy and Caulaincourt to marry. He only gave permission after his abdication.

In addition to generating their own gossip, the courtiers were also beginning to marry among each other, even when they came from different backgrounds. Count Philippe de Ségur, a member of the old *noblesse présentée* and the elder son of the Grand Master of Ceremonies, was Governor of the School of Pages. He married Mademoiselle de Luçay, from a family of pre-1789 tax officials, and the daughter of one of the Empress's ladies-in-waiting, in 1806. One Montesquiou married a daughter of a minister, Mademoiselle Clarke de Feltre, in 1809, another married a cousin of the Emperor, Mademoiselle de Padoue, in 1812. At the end of the regime the Napoleonic court was beginning to acquire a momentum of its own. With time and a different monarch, it might have rivalled Versailles.

6

The Family Courts

'The true place of a monarch is neither in the fields nor in the forests; it is in his court, at the heart of his government, where he can best control those who administer in his name.'

Stanislas de Girardin, First Equerry of King Joseph-Napoleon, 1807.

FOR CENTURIES EUROPE had been dominated by a few ruling families. In 1800 the most powerful were the Bourbons of Spain and Naples, the Habsburgs of Austria, the Romanovs of Russia and the Hohenzollerns of Prussia. The ambitions and evolution of these dynasties were as important in shaping events as the forces of geography, demography or economics. By becoming Emperor of the French, with the power to found his own dynasty, Napoleon I was acknowledging that dynastic monarchy was still the accepted norm. In Europe in the early nineteenth century most politicians believed that the events of the Revolution had confirmed that 'monarchical government is the only one suitable to large associations of men'.[1]

Napoleon I needed a dynasty which would rival the other dynasties of Europe in power and splendour, help maintain his authority, and guarantee the future of his regime. In 1804 his family consisted of his elder brother Joseph, his younger brothers Lucien, Louis and Jerome, his sisters Elisa, Pauline and Caroline, his widowed mother Letizia and Josephine's children by her first marriage, Eugene and Hortense. Like their brother's courtiers, the Bonapartes were extraordinarily youthful: they were all under thirty-six at the beginning of the Empire in 1804. Even their mother was only fifty-four and still beautiful.

The Bonapartes were also passionate and devoured by ambition. Napoleon's ablest brother Lucien left France in 1804, as a result of political and personal disagreements with the First Consul. When Napoleon reproached him for marrying a woman with a disreputable past, Lucien replied: 'At least mine is pretty.' Until the fall of the Empire in 1814, Lucien lived in exile, opposed to his brother, first in Rome and then in England.

The youngest Bonaparte brother, Jerome, served in the navy until he disgraced himself by marrying an American (Napoleon soon had the marriage dissolved). However, the other brothers, Joseph and Louis, were useful allies who had held high positions under the Consulate. In May 1804 they became Imperial Highnesses with the right to succeed their brother and were given one million francs a year each and households of their own.

Prince Joseph was the brother to whom the Emperor was most attached and in the years 1800–06 he had considerable political influence. He was able and liberal and his household was distinguished by its 'constitutional' character. His most important courtier was Monsieur de Jaucourt, a former liberal deputy during the Revolution and friend of Talleyrand, who became First Chamberlain; Stanislas de Girardin, another liberal, was made First Equerry. Girardin's father had been a patron of Rousseau, who is buried in the Girardins' park at Ermenonville. One of the distinguishing features of the Napoleonic courts, which emphasized their artificiality, was their recruitment from men who had once been devotees of the Revolution. Members of other courts were content to be personal servants of the monarch and his family, without pretending to be liberals as well.

Joseph lived in the palace of the Luxembourg, former residence of the senior brother of Louis XVI, the Count de Provence, while Louis presided over his large household in his house in the Rue

Cérutti. They also had country houses north of Paris, at Mortefontaine and Saint-Leu respectively. The Emperor's sisters Elisa, Pauline and Caroline also became Imperial Highnesses in May 1804. Their mother Letizia, however, was not given the title *Son Altesse Impériale Madame, Mère de l'Empereur* (she was known as Madame Mère for short) until March 1805: the delay may have been due to the Emperor's resentment that she sympathized with her favourite son Lucien. Napoleon's sisters and mother also received households, although they were mainly composed of insignificant distant relations or acquaintances of the Empress Josephine, the only member of the family who knew many French people. Nevertheless there were some brilliant acquisitions. Perhaps because they were impoverished by the Revolution, the heads of two of the oldest families of the French nobility, Counts (Dukes before 1790) de Cossé-Brissac and de Clermont-Tonnerre, consented to be chamberlains of Madame Mère and Princess Pauline respectively: Princess Pauline also secured a Cardinal, the Archbishop of Genoa, as her First Almoner.[2]

Even though it transformed every aspect of their existence, the Bonapartes easily adapted to their new rank. All the members of the family, even Lucien, believed that the genius of the Emperor and the plebiscites of 1802 and 1804 gave them every right to the throne of France, and they were determined to exploit and enjoy their imperial status. As Lord Roseberry wrote, 'No Bourbons or Habsburgs were so imbued with their royal prerogatives as these princes of an hour.' Indeed some of the family thought that they were not receiving their due, and began to behave in ways which gave new meaning to the words *parvenu* and *nouveau riche*.

As early as November 1804 Prince Joseph quarrelled bitterly with the Emperor and Ségur over whether his wife Princess Julie should or should not carry the Empress's train at the coronation. Such a role seemed intolerably demeaning to her husband. At the coronation of Queen Marie de Médicis two hundred years earlier, he reminded them, the princesses had not *carried* the Queen's train. They had merely *accompanied* her in the procession. In early 1805 Prince Joseph refused the offer of the throne of Italy as he did not want to lose the chance of succeeding to the throne of the French Empire.

Madame Mère had as sharp an appetite for status and possessions as any of her children. Within a year of becoming an Imperial Highness, she was complaining about the quality of the rooms and the furniture in the Grand Trianon. On 9 May 1806 she wrote a revealing letter to the Emperor. She complained that her income of 450,000 francs a year was not enough to cover the cost of setting up her household and buying suitable linen, silver and furniture. She felt that her income should not come from the Emperor's civil list, but should be fixed by a special law passed by the Senate, based on what had 'always' been allotted to the mothers of French monarchs. She also asked for what she called 'a state of splendour worthy of you and me . . . . She must have an increase in her household of honour and her officials must have advantages which raise the status of their functions and which show the world that, by their services about her person, they have acquired special claims to the favour of the Emperor.'[3]

This letter reveals some of the basic assumptions of the Bonapartes. Their overriding ambition was to raise their own status, to have more money and to live in greater splendour. A particularly effective way to realize this ambition was to increase the grandeur of their households. As a result the Bonapartes' households were often more lavish and more important than other royal households of the early nineteenth century.

Madame Mère's complaints did not go unheeded, and by 1807 she had an income of one million francs a year. She was able to buy an *hôtel* in the Faubourg Saint-Germain, and the Emperor gave her a house in the country, at Pont south-east of Paris. Since Italian was her mother tongue, and she never mastered French, she could not establish close relations with the members of her household. She was very pious and led a retired life, surrounded by priests. She was happiest spending the day with her beloved brother the Grand Almoner, Cardinal Fesch. She never had enough money for her own liking, and was celebrated for her meanness. In 1809 she charged her own son Louis for his living expenses when he came to stay for a few weeks.

By 1805, in giving his brothers, sisters and mother the titles of Imperial Highnesses, the Emperor had created a large imperial family for himself. He even had a semi-official heir in Prince Napoleon-Charles, eldest son of Louis Bonaparte and Hortense. He was the first Bonaparte to be born a prince, and he was christened by the Pope himself at Saint-Cloud

Robert Lefèvre, *Madame Mère* *Napoleon's mother was famous for her meanness and her bad French. After the fall of the Empire she helped to support her children out of the money she had saved.*

in 1805. His was one of the first names entered in the Register of the Imperial Family.

Most ruling families have been sufficiently modest, or confident, to record their births, deaths and marriages in parish registers, beside their subjects. Even at the height of their power and splendour the Bourbons had recorded these events in the register of their parish church at Versailles. When the future Louis XVI and his brother were baptised (several years after they were born), their father showed them their names inscribed below that of the son of a poor workman and said: 'You see, my children, in the eyes of God, conditions are equal and the only distinction comes from faith and virtue. One day you will be greater than this child in the opinion of the people, but he himself will be greater before God if he is more virtuous.'

For the Bonapartes, however, a parish register was not good enough, and the Emperor ordered the creation of the Register of the Imperial Family. This is a magnificent volume bound in crimson velvet, with a gold-embossed N surrounded by stars in the centre of the cover, and laurels and wands of Mercury in the corners. It is a visible symbol of the fact that the Emperor and his family considered themselves to be raised above the rest of humanity. Count Regnault de Saint-Jean d'Angély was in charge of the register, with the title Secretary of State of the Imperial Family.[4]

In addition to giving the members of his family titles and households, the Emperor tried to raise their status by marrying them into other ruling families. The Bourbons and the Habsburgs had always pursued this policy, more often to maintain their own status than to cement an alliance or acquire an inheritance. Therefore the Bonapartes would too. The first member of *la famille*, as Napoleon I called it, to marry into the royal families of Europe was his adopted son Prince Eugene, the Viceroy of Italy. He married the ravishing Princess Augusta-Amalia of Bavaria in her parents' palace in Munich on 14 January 1806 (see pp. 102–03).

They were extremely happy and Princess Augusta proved a dignified and decorative Vicereine. It was fortunate that she never had to spend much time with the Bonapartes, for she wrote to her brother, on her only visit to Paris in 1810: 'when one has known them at close quarters one can only despise them. I could never conceive anything so abominable as their ill-breeding. It is torture for me to have to go about with such people.'[5] She was probably thinking of the Emperor's sisters Pauline and Caroline.

The Emperor had an expansionist attitude to his family. Perhaps because his dynasty was so new, and did not have many members in comparison with the prolific Bourbons or Habsburgs, he annexed many relations by marriage to *la famille*, despite their lack of a blood connection with the Bonapartes. Even the mother of the Empress Josephine, a kind old woman living peacefully on the island of Martinique, shared in the family's rise in status. She received a twenty-one gun salute and sat under a canopy when she went to church to celebrate the proclamation of the Empire; and her body lay in state, as if she were a princess, when she died in 1807.[6]

In 1806 the Emperor adopted one of the Empress's cousins, the charming fifteen-year-old Stephanie de Beauharnais, with whom he was a little in love. She became a Princess and an Imperial Highness and was married to the Electoral Prince of Baden-Baden. In 1807 the Emperor's youngest brother Jerome married Princess Catherine of Württemberg: she found the Bonapartes less objectionable than Augusta-Amalia of Bavaria and was happy to call Madame Mère *maman*. In 1808 one of Caroline's nieces by marriage, Marie-Antoinette Murat, and another of the Empress's cousins, Stephanie Tascher de La Pagerie, were made princesses and were married to a Prince of Hohenzollern-Sigmaringen and a Prince of Arenberg respectively (the first marriage was a success; the second, owing to Princess Stephanie's horror at the sight of her husband, was never consummated). In 1810, the same year that the Emperor himself married the Archduchess Marie-Louise of Austria, Louis Tascher de La Pagerie married Princess Amalia-Theodora von der Leyen and Flaminia de' Rossi, a niece of the husband of Princess Elisa, married a Prince of Salm-Salm. Other grand dynastic marriages would have been arranged for the children of Lucien Bonaparte, if he had allowed it.

The Emperor provided his family with thrones as well as titles, households and dynastic marriages. The establishment of his dynasty outside France was in fact almost inevitable. The Emperor believed that he was a new Charlemagne, the overlord of Europe with the right to dispose of its thrones as he pleased. He was able to do so because, with a population of about 30 million (compared with about 15 million in both Spain and Italy), a strong army and administration, and an exceptionally able ruling class, France was bound to be the leading power in Europe, except in unusually unfavourable circumstances.[7] Louis XIV and Louis XV had used their power and their hereditary claims to install

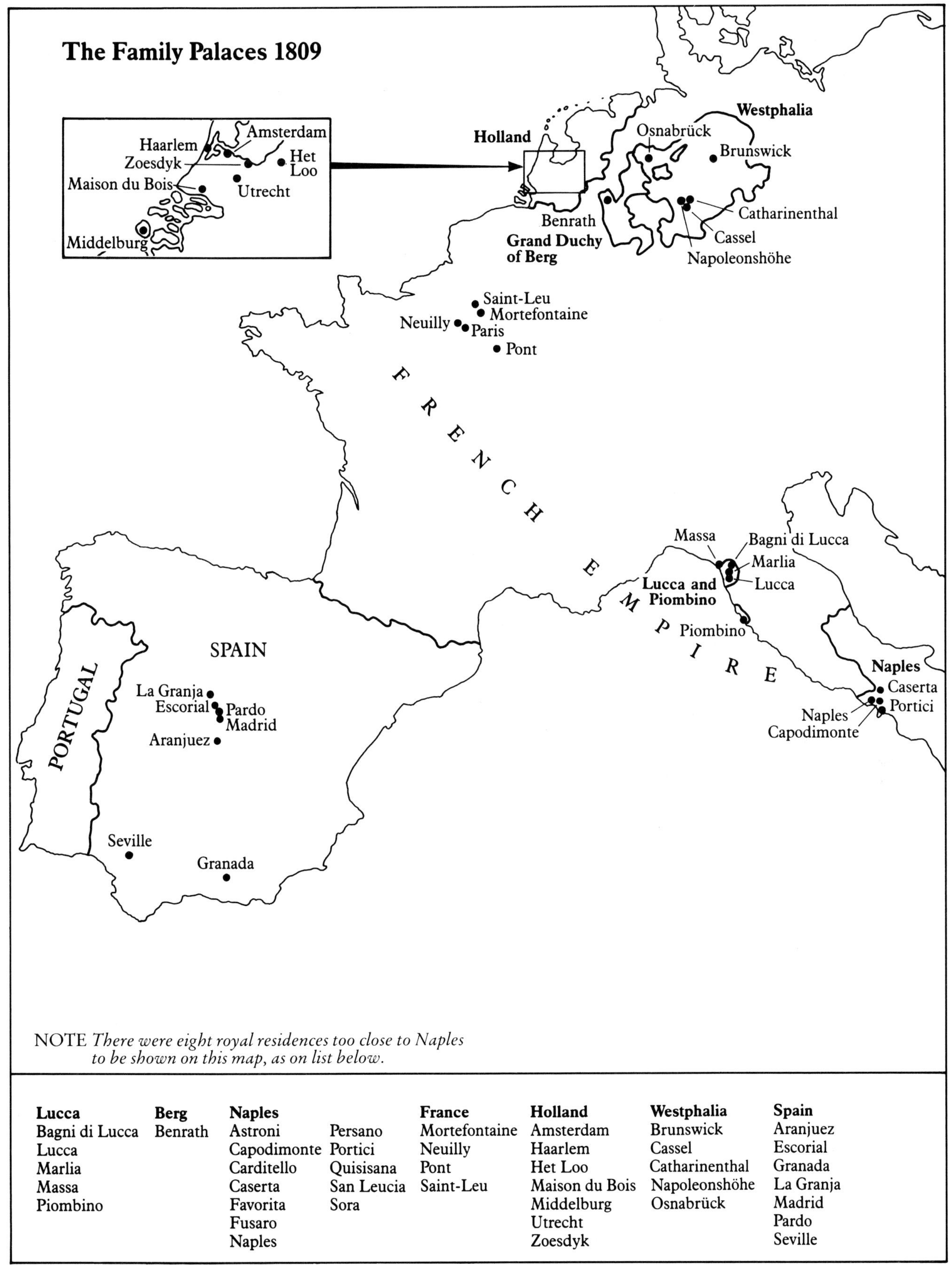

NOTE *There were eight royal residences too close to Naples to be shown on this map, as on list below.*

Lucca	Berg	Naples		France	Holland	Westphalia	Spain
Bagni di Lucca	Benrath	Astroni	Persano	Mortefontaine	Amsterdam	Brunswick	Aranjuez
Lucca		Capodimonte	Portici	Neuilly	Haarlem	Cassel	Escorial
Marlia		Carditello	Quisisana	Pont	Het Loo	Catharinenthal	Granada
Massa		Caserta	San Leucia	Saint-Leu	Maison du Bois	Napoleonshöhe	La Granja
Piombino		Favorita	Sora		Middelburg	Osnabrück	Madrid
		Fusaro			Utrecht		Pardo
		Naples			Zoesdyk		Seville

members of the Bourbon dynasty on the thrones of Spain, Naples and Parma. At the same time French had become the language of the courts and ruling classes of Europe — a victory confirmed when thousands of French nobles entered the service of foreign monarchs during the Revolution.

When Napoleon I became Emperor of the French in 1804, most of western Europe was under his influence and, both politically and culturally, was more French than it had ever been. The family was still a vital power unit in politics, as the expansion of the Bourbons and the elevation of the Bonapartes had shown. It seemed natural that the Emperor should choose to rule the states under France's influence, and new acquisitions, through his brothers and sisters.

Although they were never very good at languages, the Bonapartes were adaptable and self-confident. Indeed they showed confidence worthy of the Emperor himself when they ascended foreign thrones. (This promotion was always marked by the addition of the suffix -Napoleon to their names, hence Princess Elisa-Napoleon, King Joseph-Napoleon and so on.) Like the Emperor's courts, the 'family courts' (*les cours de famille*), as they were known to contemporaries, were a sustained attempt to take the aristocracies and palaces of Europe into the service of *la famille*. However, because the Bonapartes were at least human beings, whereas the Emperor tried to make himself into a demi-god, the family courts had more life and charm than the court of Napoleon I.

The first Bonaparte to be given a foreign throne was the Emperor's eldest sister Elisa. Tall, plain and passionate, Elisa was an intellectual with a taste for power. In 1797 she had married a dim Corsican noble, Felix Baciocchi, whom she could dominate without difficulty. The Emperor made her Princess of Piombino, on the coast of Tuscany opposite Elba, in March 1805. At the same time one of the last surviving republics in Europe, the small city-state of Lucca near Pisa, was induced to appoint Felix as its prince. He was installed as Felix I at a lavish ceremony in Lucca cathedral on 14 July 1805, organized by Talleyrand on the model of the Emperor's coronation in Milan. The new prince received a hand of justice, coronation rings and a sword of state. At the end the heralds cried 'Long live their Most Serene, and Imperial, Highnesses!' Felix I was a Most Serene Highness, but only Elisa was Imperial: Elisa's husband was her inferior in rank, as well as in power and in strength of personality.[8] Indeed Elisa was so masterful that she was known as *la Sémiramis de Lucques* after the Assyrian warrior-queen of the eighth century BC.

In the next few months a court was organized through the combined efforts of Elisa, Felix, the Lucca government and the French minister. The nobles of Lucca, for so long proud of their republican and commercial traditions, now transformed themselves into a court nobility. They began to wear swords for the first time in their history, and a French diplomat reported to Talleyrand that: 'The most distinguished families have solicited these places [at court] with an eagerness which will please Their Highnesses.' Talleyrand stated the principle on which this court was organized. Since 'the authority of the Prince is greater', there must be 'more pomp in the ceremonial'.[9] In other words, since the Bonapartes' governments had more direct power than their predecessors, the Bonapartes should have grander courts.

This principle was certainly put into practice in Lucca. Although the combined population of the principalities of Lucca and Piombino was only 150,000, they soon found themselves supporting a court even more elaborate in structure than Napoleon's Italian court. A Grand Almoner, Grand Chamberlain, Grand Equerry, Grand Master of the Court, Grand Master of Ceremonies and Captain Commandant of the Bodyguard supervised an army of ladies-in-waiting, chamberlains, equerries, pages, and aides-de-camp.

Elisa's small French household had been left behind in France, and the court was almost entirely Lucchese. The ancient patrician family of Mansi did particularly well. Camilla Mansi was principal lady-in-waiting, Raffaello Mansi was lord-in-waiting and Ascanio Mansi was Grand Chamberlain, Secretary of State, and Mayor of Lucca by 1807. The Bonapartes were passionate as well as ambitious, and believed in using their households to supply, or shelter, their lovers. Elisa's Grand Equerry, Bartolomeo Cenami, was her principal lover. His brother Tommaso was Captain Commandant of the Bodyguard and married the governess of Elisa's daughter.

Anon, *Ascanio Mansi* *Mansi was one of Elisa's most important courtiers and ministers in Lucca, as he later was of her Bourbon replacement the Duchess Maria Luigia, whose orders he is wearing. Most of the Bonapartes' courtiers were equally ready to serve other dynasties.*

The Grand Master of the Court from 1809 was the Marchese Lucchesini. A native of Lucca, he had been a favourite chamberlain of Frederick the Great — he had excelled at guiding the King onto agreeable subjects of conversation. He had later been Prussian Ambassador in Paris where, like many foreign ambassadors (even, to a certain extent, Metternich himself), he had admired Napoleon I's power and glamour. After the defeat of Prussia at Jena in 1806, Lucchesini was offered what he called 'a port in the storm' by Elisa. He was a typical courtier, charming, cosmopolitan and unreliable. In the words of another admirer of the Empire, the Saxon Ambassador to Paris, Count von Senfft, he combined 'a friendliness which, in all his social and domestic relationships, rendered him particularly gentle and sympathetic' with 'a complete lack of dignity and honesty in his character'.[10] (Indeed Lucchesini attacked the Bonapartes in print after their fall.) Despite, or because of, these defects Lucchesini acted as Elisa's Duroc: he was in charge of the court and the furnishing of the palaces, and wrote to Ségur for instructions in court etiquette, calling him 'our Great Apollo'.[11]

Elisa had five palaces, at Lucca, Marlia, the fashionable mountain spa of Bagni di Lucca, Massa (which she acquired in 1806) and Piombino. All were refurnished in the lavish monarchical style preferred by the Bonapartes. Marlia, set in a superb park a few miles from Lucca, was her principal residence. The palace of Lucca was used for formal receptions. Like the Tuileries and Saint-Cloud, it contained state apartments, consisting of a guardroom, a first and second salon, a throne room, the salon of Their Highnesses and a gallery, to each of which officials and courtiers of a certain rank could be admitted. The *Etiquette du Palais de Leurs Altesses* regulated the ceremonial of the court of Lucca in 253 articles. There was a reception after Sunday Mass, which 'only those persons who have had the honour to be presented to Their Highnesses' could attend.

Despite the fact that court life was as much of a novelty to the city of Lucca as it was to Princess Elisa-Napoleon, her court functioned from the start with considerable panache. 'My small court is gay, I maintain little etiquette', wrote the Princess happily to her brother Louis in September 1805. A few days later she wrote to Ségur with that tone of imperial condescension which came so easily to the Bonapartes: 'I have the best composed court it is possible to have and, I regret to say it, the French whom I had brought (except Madame de La Place) were far inferior in quality to the least of my [present] court.'[12]

The court, with the guard, cost more to run than the entire administration before Elisa's arrival. Its cost was met partly out of the proceeds of the sale of church property (one former monastery in Lucca was used as the Princess's stables), and partly out of public funds. There was no distinction between court and government expenditure.

The French Minister wrote in his memoirs: 'Princess Elisa liked fetes and receptions, as well as plays. She herself organized everything with remarkable enthusiasm. The costumes and dresses were very brilliant at the court.' She often gave her courtiers presents of jewels and clothes 'to add to the luxury of her receptions'. The court made solemn progresses to her palace at Piombino: she told Ségur 'I was very happy there and I had much good to do.' There may have been other reasons for her happiness: a native of Piombino, when asked later by the Emperor *'ce que faisait la Grande Duchesse à Piombino?'*, replied, *'qu'elle faisait l'amour.'*[13]

Elisa was a patron of the arts. Her architect Bienaimé transformed Marlia from 1810 to 1814, and the palace in Lucca was also modernized. Under her direction the marble works at Carrara were devoted to the mass production of busts and statues of the Emperor. Over 12,000 busts of Napoleon I were sold to municipalities throughout the Empire at a huge profit (for the princess, not the sculptors). A Lucca artist, Tofanelli, painted the princess and many of her courtiers; unfortunately his vast canvas of *The Inauguration of Felix I* was destroyed during the rejoicings over the prince's departure in 1814. The most famous violinist of the day, Paganini, was the princess's Virtuoso of the Chamber and probably also her lover. In order to give him the entrée to court receptions, he was made a captain in the bodyguard. However, he fell from favour when he insisted on conducting the court orchestra in his military uniform — an extreme example of the uniform mania which affected all Europe in the early nineteenth century.[14] In common with the other family courts, Elisa's was

Pietro Nocchi, *Olimpia Cenami* *Olimpia Cenami was a lady-in-waiting of Elisa; her brother Bartolomeo, whose bust is on the left, was the princess's Grand Equerry, confidential political agent and lover.*

Ingres Del.
roma 1819.
ML
LB

large, expensive, aristocratic, immoral, ceremonious and 'official'. It was written into the constitution, which served as a mask for Elisa's ruthless absolutism. The fact that it was accepted in the former Republic of Lucca reveals the strength of the swing towards monarchy in nineteenth-century Europe.

Like those of the other family courts, Elisa's officials were often used as trusted political agents. Elisa's lover Bartolomeo Cenami, the Grand Equerry, was put in charge of economic affairs and of frontier negotiations in Paris in 1807, and was made Director-General of Public Instruction and Vice-President of the Accademia Napoleone.

The Princess's name was as ubiquitous in Lucca as the letter N in her brother's palaces. The town contained not only the Accademia Napoleone and the Piazza Napoleone (with a colossal statue of the Emperor), but also the Collegio Felice, the Istituto Elisa, the Via Elisa, the Porta Elisa, the Quartiere Elisa and the Banca Elisiana. Clearly she believed in self-assertion.

Elisa was also ambitious: for her Lucca was not enough. She wrote to her brother's Foreign Minister in 1807 that, 'being the Emperor's sister, I should desire and claim more than the 150,000 inhabitants who form the principality of Lucca.' Later that year, without any justification, French troops marched into Tuscany and deposed its Bourbon ruler. In 1809 Elisa's ambitions were realized and the Emperor appointed her Grand Duchess of Tuscany.

As Grand Duchess she was a viceroy for her brother the Emperor rather than, like Felix I in Lucca, a theoretically independent sovereign. The palaces and the Crown lands belonged not to her but to her brother — although she tried to take them over surreptitiously. The Emperor wrote to Elisa: 'There is no more court to be held at Lucca' and appointed a large Tuscan household for her. It consisted of 12 ladies-in-waiting, including members of the powerful noble families of Corsini and Torrigiani, 9 chamberlains, 5 equerries and 19 pages.[15] As in all the family courts, the ceremonial, liveries and structure were based on the practice of the Emperor's court in Paris.

Elisa was less popular in Tuscany than in Lucca. In Lucca she was the effective sovereign and, most important of all, the guardian of the country's independence from the French Empire and conscription. In Tuscany she was the symbol of the region's subjection to the French Empire; and many of the best jobs in the administration were given to Frenchmen.

The result was that Elisa's arrival in Florence in April 1809 was a fiasco. She complained to her friend Fouché, the Emperor's Minister of Police, that there was no guard of honour to welcome her to Florence. Only a few courtiers appeared, 'in a costume so indecent that I refused their services'. At the ball given that evening 'except for the household, the other guests consisted of prostitutes and people of the lower middle class whose name nobody knew. I stayed for less than half an hour and left.' Her tone of snobbish outrage seems hardly appropriate in a letter to a former revolutionary like Fouché. But Fouché had become a minister and a duke, and as aristocratic in outlook as other followers of the Emperor. In the next four years Elisa's popularity in Florence did not increase.[16] She frequently returned to Lucca and continued to maintain her Lucchese household.

Other members of *la famille* also held court for the Emperor in Italy, in addition to Prince Eugene in Milan. In March 1808, a year before the Emperor appointed Elisa Grand Duchess of Tuscany, he named his brother-in-law Prince Borghese, husband of his sister Pauline, Governor-General of 'the Departments beyond the Alps', in other words of Piedmont, Parma and Liguria.

In theory Princess Pauline (previously suggested as a possible Queen of Portugal) was intended to assist her husband to hold court in Turin. In practice the Princess went her own way. She was not prepared to subordinate herself to anyone, least of all to her inadequate husband, and preferred to remain in France. She lived either in Paris or at spas: her health was bad because, her doctors told her, she made love too often. She was imperious and miserly: when she gave a party costing 80,000 francs, she wrote to her Intendant that she wanted the public to think that it had cost her 120,000. She drew up a list of regulations for her household, and signed each of its thousand paragraphs herself. Even more than most members of a ruling family, she treated her court officials as servants. Two different witnesses swear that she used the neck and other areas of her favourite lady-in-waiting, Madame de Chambaudoin, as a foot-stool.[17]

According to Metternich, Princess Pauline was 'as beautiful as it is possible to be'. She was more

Ingres, *Paganini* *Paganini was known as 'the Emperor of the violin'. He played twice a week at Elisa's court and composed the* Napoleon Sonata *for St Napoleon's Day in 1807.*

Joseph Franque, ***Salon of the Grand Duchess Elisa in the Pitti Palace*** *Most members of the imperial family held informal parties in the evening as well as formal receptions in the morning.*

interested in love than power, and her household was used to supply her (and occasionally the Emperor) with lovers. One of her chamberlains, Count de Forbin, was her lover from 1806 to 1810. When Chateaubriand met him in 1807, Forbin seemed to be living in paradise: his feet hardly touched the ground. The princess was probably equally happy. A contemporary wrote of Forbin, 'He combined a charming appearance with the most amiable character I have ever known.'[18]

Pauline only visited Turin once, in 1808. Nevertheless her household, like that of her husband, was used to rally the Piedmontese nobility to the Empire. Stanislas de Girardin described the court in Turin in 1808 as 'extremely brilliant'. The Piedmontese nobility was happy to serve there, perhaps because its military tradition made it more sympathetic to the Empire than the Tuscan. The Prince had 6 chamberlains, 4 equerries and 4 aides-de-camp, the Princess 7 chamberlains, 4 equerries, 10 pages and 10 ladies-in-waiting. Many had typically Piedmontese names, such as Cavour, La Cisterna, or La Marmora.

The Cavours were the family who committed themselves furthest to the Bonapartes, partly because they had bought lands confiscated from the legitimate ruler of Piedmont, the exiled King of Sardinia. In 1808 the Baron de Cavour, father of the future hero of the Risorgimento and first Prime Minister of Italy, became First Chamberlain 'in charge of the service of the Chamber, Fetes and Concerts'; his uncle was governor of the imperial palace of Turin; and his mother Philippine was principal lady-in-waiting of Princess Pauline.

Philippine de Cavour was a forceful lady, described as 'knowing the court perfectly' and enjoying 'great personal respect'. She believed in the Empire and wrote, 'We owe everything to the Emperor . . . it is a great good fortune to witness such a historic epoch.'[19] Despite her age and experience she was completely captivated by Princess Pauline, who treated her as a servant.

After 1809, Princess Pauline rarely attended the Emperor's court. Although she arranged a dazzling 'Austrian' evening for Marie-Louise in 1810 at her house in Neuilly full of waltzing Tyroleans and servants in Habsburg livery, she liked the new Empress no more than the old one. Pauline never forgave her for the humiliation of being made to carry her train at the wedding in the Louvre. She spent most of her time in the country with her lovers. Forbin was replaced by one of the Princess's musicians, Blangini, who was succeeded by a dashing young hussar, de Canouville, and subsequently by the great actor Talma. Her husband Prince Borghese remained in Turin, happy, he wrote to a friend, that he depended directly on 'the Greatest Man in the World'.[20]

There was a web of Bonaparte courts in Italy. In addition to those in Turin, Florence, Lucca and Milan, the Emperor's favourite brother Joseph held court in Naples. For although Joseph claimed, in conversation with the Prussian Ambassador, that he deplored the Emperor's love of conquest, he was prepared to benefit from it. In 1805 the Bourbon King Ferdinand IV of Naples had joined in a war against the French Empire, and had fled to Sicily when his army was defeated. Joseph was appointed King of Naples in Ferdinand's place and made his entry into Naples on 14 February 1806.

The court of King Joseph-Napoleon shows the monarchical and aristocratic instincts of his family with particular clarity. Unlike Ferdinand IV who, as Girardin wrote in reproof, preferred living in 'the fields and the woods',[21] in villas and hunting-lodges, King Joseph-Napoleon was happy to use the magnificent royal palaces in and around Naples: Capodimonte, on a hill overlooking the Bay of Naples, was his favourite. He complained that Ferdinand IV had taken everything, even the firewood, but he soon refurnished the palaces.

It was easy for the new king to find courtiers to fill his palaces. For a few months in 1799 there had been a 'democratic' and pro-French Republic, which had been supported by much of the Neapolitan nobility, and opposed by most of the poor. It was said that joining the revolution in Naples was as sure a sign of aristocratic birth as being guillotined during the Revolution was in France. The Republic had been ruthlessly suppressed by King Ferdinand.

As a result Joseph believed that the Neapolitan aristocracy preferred him to the Bourbons: 'All the property-owners have joined my side . . . there is no unpaid position, chamberlain, equerry, page, colonel, officer of the provincial guard, which is not solicited by the richest nobles, because the

Ingres, *Count de Forbin* *Count de Forbin, who became Princess Pauline's lover in 1806, had the reputation of being 'the most agreeable man in the high society of France'. After he fell from favour he went to Rome, where this drawing was made. He became Director of the Louvre under Louis XVIII.*

Bourbons annoyed them, because they governed through foreigners and the dregs of the nation.' Indeed, the 'dregs of the nation', that is to say the poor, were the most faithful supporters of the Bourbons and were hated by the Bonapartes. The Emperor, who had been an enthusiastic supporter of Robespierre during the Reign of Terror, wrote in a characteristic letter to Joseph: 'The beggars who stabbed the French officials should be shot mercilessly .... It is only through a salutary terror that you will inspire respect in the Italian mob.'[22]

Aiming to be the king of the nobles and the rich, Joseph had a large court: the Prince of Colonna Stigliano, one of whose relatives had been executed for supporting the Revolution of 1799, was Grand Chamberlain, at the head of thirty-four chamberlains, all but four of whom were princes or dukes. The Duke of San Teodoro was Grand Master of Ceremonies. The Duke of Cassano Serra was Grand Huntsman. His wife, who had been declared 'Mother of the Fatherland' by the Republic in 1799, and sent into exile by King Ferdinand, became principal lady-in-waiting of the Queen. Although King Joseph's household was basically Neapolitan, a French element remained. General Mathieu Dumas had the key position of Grand Marshal of the Palace. The equerries, the aides-de-camp and the officers of the guard — in other words the people most concerned with the King's security — were French; so was his cook, Monsieur Méot, one of the most admired of the day.

Joseph held regular court receptions after Sunday Mass. The etiquette of the Tuileries was introduced, the habit of kissing the king's hand was dropped and non-noble officials, as well as nobles, were admitted. The King was not, at first, joined by the Queen, born Julie Clary from Marseilles. Although perfectly capable of adapting to court etiquette and behaving with royal formality, Queen Julie was happier living at their beautiful château of Mortefontaine, surrounded by her relatives. Moreover, her husband was a dedicated womanizer and, like many Bonapartes, he used his court to supply himself with lovers. The daughter of the Grand Chamberlain, the Duchess of Atri, was his mistress, and bore him a son in 1807.[23]

Queen Julie finally came to Naples in April 1808, but by then the Emperor had other plans for his brother. The last remaining Bourbon monarch, Charles IV, King of Spain, had been deposed by his own son, who ascended the throne as Ferdinand VII. French troops were already in Spain: and Napoleon saw this crisis as an ideal opportunity to extend his conquests. In June the Emperor summoned King Joseph to Marrac on the Spanish border. The Bourbons had gone to meet the Emperor, whom they regarded as their ally and the greatest genius of the age, in the hope that he would resolve their family feuds. Instead they were compelled to renounce the throne. On 5 July Joseph was proclaimed King of Spain and the Indies by a Junta of Grandees, summoned by the Emperor, who were surrounded by the Imperial Guard.

In a last round of rewards, Joseph distributed titles and money to his followers in Naples. Monsieur Miot, Intendant of his Household, became Count de Mélito and the Grand Chamberlain (whom Queen Julie called the Grand Imbecile) was given 37,522 ducats. Joseph's mistress's husband received 472,000 ducats. After King Joseph left Naples, his court officials repeated, with suspicious emphasis, that he had taken only 'a very restricted choice of linen, silver and books'. 'Everything has stayed in its place and the palaces were never better arranged or in better condition', wrote Mathieu Dumas. But the Neapolitans were convinced that the King was taking everything away. When Queen Julie left in July, a month after her husband, the Neapolitans said: 'The King arrived like a sovereign, and left like a brigand. The Queen arrived in rags and left like a sovereign.'[24]

Although King Joseph-Napoleon was hypocritical and corrupt, he was also committed to certain liberal principles. While King of Naples, he had introduced those reforms which everywhere accompanied the installation of a Bonaparte monarch. They included the sale of ecclesiastical property to those rich enough to afford it (his aristocratic Neapolitan courtiers were among the principal purchasers), the restriction of the jurisdiction of ecclesiastical courts, the extension of civil rights to Protestants and Jews, and the lowering of legal barriers between nobles and non-nobles. The country was transformed and modernized.

In Spain, however, he was in an impossible situation. As he rapidly realized, most Spaniards were ferociously opposed to the French invader and *el rey intruso*, the intruder king. This was made clear by the behaviour of his court. He crossed into Spain on 9 July, accompanied by most of the courtiers of Ferdinand VII, such as the Dukes of Infantado, Frias and del Parque, who had all sworn allegiance to him. Three hundred miles away in Madrid, the Emperor's lieutenant in Spain, his brother-in-law Marshal Murat, wrote that all the court officials in the Royal Palace served him as they had served the Bourbon king: 'in general I am very satisfied with the behaviour of all the em-

Prince Clary, ***The Duke of Frias*** *The Duke of Frias was one of the few Spanish Grandees who was committed to King Joseph. Prince Clary, who drew him at the wedding of Napoleon and Marie-Louise, wrote that he was ugly, badly dressed and had skin like the hide of an elephant.*

ployees of the court.'[25]

But once Spanish outrage at the treatment of the royal family had had time to develop, resistance to King Joseph and the French grew. On 12 July, halfway between the frontier and Madrid, King Joseph wrote a letter to his terrifying brother which will always do him credit. 'No one has told Your Majesty the whole truth until now. The fact is there is not one Spaniard who has come out for me except the small number of individuals . . . who are travelling with me.' Even this number was rapidly diminishing, particularly after news of the Spanish victory at Baylen on 23 July — the French army had been so burdened with the loot of Spanish houses and churches that it could hardly move.

By 25 July the Duke of Frias was the only Grandee still with King Joseph: 'the rest are cowardly and discouraged' — or, from the Spanish point of view, brave and hopeful. Although there had been sixty carriages when Joseph crossed into Spain, only three accompanied him to Madrid. The entire Spanish royal household deserted the Royal Palace of Madrid after the news of Baylen. For a time Joseph had to rely on his French courtiers and servants.[26]

When King Joseph entered Madrid there were a few scattered cries of 'Long live the King!' in the streets, but, in the words of his brother's ambassador Count de La Forest, 'the dominating feeling was amazement'. The salons of the Royal Palace were fairly full, and King Joseph's affability made a favourable impression on the officials presented to him. But most Spaniards wanted Ferdinand. Joseph bravely wrote to the Emperor: 'You are wrong. Your glory will fail in Spain.'[27]

For the next five years a war of unprecedented barbarism devastated Spain. The Spanish insurgents were supported by a British army under Wellington. As Joseph knew, only Calabria in southern Italy, where supporters of Ferdinand IV had often defeated his own forces with British help, had witnessed something similar. Joseph was often in a desperate position. In 1810 he wrote to Berthier that in one week he would not be able to pay for his own food: his court and guard had not been paid for ten months.

Nevertheless, he maintained some sort of court life, primarily due to the strength of the Emperor's army. From late 1808 to early 1813, with only one interruption in the summer of 1812, the French maintained control of Madrid and its ring of sumptuous palaces — Aranjuez, the Escorial, La Granja and the Pardo. In addition many people who attended Joseph's court were genuinely sympathetic

J.L. Rugendas, ***The second entry of King Joseph into Madrid in 1808*** *King Joseph had been forced to flee for a few weeks after the Spanish victory of Baylen, but soon returned. He had few supporters in his capital.*

to his regime. Even in patriotic Spain, under circumstances so inauspicious that they throw lasting doubt on the Emperor's political skill, the Bonapartes appealed to certain individuals and groups, who were called the *afrancesados*.

Joseph brought with him not only French soldiers but also the prospect of a more modern and efficient administration. As a result many able and enlightened ministers, such as O'Farrill, a former minister of Charles IV, were prepared to serve King Joseph — although they were furious when he insisted that the Intendant of his Household, de Mélito, and his Private Secretary, Monsieur Ferri Pisani, Count de Saint-Anastase, joined the Council of Ministers. In December 1808, the Emperor abolished feudal rights, internal customs barriers and the Inquisition, and reduced religious communities by two-thirds. His proclamation of 7 December asserted, 'A liberal constitution gives you instead of an absolute monarchy a liberal and constitutional monarchy.' As in all the 'liberal constitutions' granted by the Bonapartes outside France, one article organized the court and the Domain of the Crown.[28]

The Archbishop of Saragossa was Grand Almoner, assisted by five chaplains. Until his death in 1811 the Mayordomo Mayor (the equivalent of Grand Marshal of the Palace) was the Duke of Frias. A liberal Spanish noble, the Marquess of Montehermoso, whose wife rapidly replaced the absent Duchess of Atri as the King's mistress, became a Grandee of the first class and Grand Chamberlain. The twenty-five chamberlains included the Duke d'Esclignac, a first cousin of Louis XVIII and Charles IV, the Duke of Berwick and Alba, one of the richest nobles in Spain, and the Count of Teba (Teba's daughter, Eugenie, married King Joseph's nephew, Napoleon III, forty years later and became Empress of the French). The Prince of Masserano was Grand Master of Ceremonies, the Duke of Campo Alange Grand Equerry and Minister of Foreign Affairs.[29] The majority of King Joseph's courtiers were liberal Spanish nobles. However, since the poor were so hostile, over half his servants were French.

King Joseph-Napoleon found time to indulge in some of the pleasures of royalty. In 1810 he was planning a museum of pictures from the royal collections at the palace of Buenavista, designed 'to assemble all schools and provide every means of instruction'. It later became the Prado. He held frequent receptions in the Royal Palace of Madrid, which could be attended by anyone 'inscribed on the registers of presentation', wearing gala costume.

The Bourbons' receptions were like a procession, the Bonapartes' like a review, according to one of the King's Spanish pages. Whereas the Bourbon kings had sat on the throne, waiting for the courtiers to kneel and kiss their hands, King Joseph-Napoleon abolished such formalities. He moved from salon to salon, speaking to as many people as possible, trying to convince them of the advantages of his rule. He presented himself as the upholder of the Spanish monarchy and his enemies as dangerous revolutionaries. At one celebration of the feast of St Napoleon, now the chief annual festivity throughout the Empire, 136 ladies paid their court to King Joseph in the Royal Palace of Madrid, including 18 wives of Grandees of Spain. Like all his family, he also held informal evening parties which could be attended by the leading courtiers and officials and their spouses.[30]

However, attendance at King Joseph's court, and the cheers which welcomed the King on some of his journeys to provinces controlled by the French army, meant little. Few Spaniards wanted to be ruled by a French king and French soldiers, however modern and efficient they promised to be. Their hostility was fuelled by the appalling behaviour of the French: according to King Joseph himself, pillage had become a way of life. He complained to the French Ambassador: 'The automatic excuse is that they have not been sent to Spain just for a change of air, and it is in fact so fashionable to try to make your fortune here that soldiers can be heard every day boasting of excesses which they have not committed, rather than pass as complete idiots.'

Despite his attempts to appear a devout Catholic, it is not surprising that King Joseph was never popular. Posters appeared in the streets of Madrid telling him to abdicate. His love affairs aroused contempt. People repeated a song that 'the lady of Montehermoso has an inkwell in which Don Jose Primero dips his pen'. King Joseph, who was an intelligent and realistic man, more realistic than the Emperor, saw things as they were. In 1810 he wrote to Queen Julie, who never came to Spain, that he wanted to go and live in Corsica — provided he was given a court there.

Anon, *General Hugo* *General Hugo was one of the seven Mayordomos of the Palace of King Joseph in Spain. One of his sons became a page; the other, Victor Hugo, was to be one of the most effective popularizers of the Napoleonic legend.*

In 1811 his brother (perhaps deliberately) put an end to any hope of Joseph inspiring Spanish loyalty by annexing the province of Catalonia, in all but name, to the French Empire. It was divided into four departments administered by French officials appointed from Paris. Thereafter there were few grand receptions at court, even on the King's feast day. The King's excuse was that they were too expensive.[31]

King Joseph now concentrated on his private interests. The Bonapartes were an ambitious family, and it would have been strange if they had not wanted to be rich as well as royal. Like most royal families, they had a passion for jewels, perhaps because they were easy to pack in a hurry as well as impressive to look at. The King of Spain had bought many French crown jewels during the Revolution, and as a result the Spanish royal collection was particularly splendid. In the chaos of May 1808 Napoleon I, Charles IV, Murat and King Joseph competed to acquire this treasure for themselves, despite protests from Spanish ministers that the crown jewels were the property of the nation and 'necessary for the splendour of the throne'. In the end King Joseph simply took the crown jewels 'according to the nature of his needs', as he later told the French Ambassador. His excuse was that his civil list was not being paid regularly. In fact 18 per cent of government expenditure and 90 per cent of the subsidy Napoleon sent from France was spent on the civil list.

Some of the finest crown jewels, including the legendary pearl La Peregrina, which can be seen in Velazquez's portraits of queens of Spain, were despatched to Queen Julie in France, who knew how to look after them. The King also transferred money from Spain to Amsterdam and London. The King lost other jewels, and two hundred pictures (including works by Titian, Rubens and Velazquez) he was removing from the royal palaces, as he retreated north in 1813: the pictures were taken by Wellington and are now in Apsley House and Stratfield Saye. Nevertheless, Joseph accumulated a fortune from his reign.[32] After the fall of the Empire, he was the richest and least generous member of the Bonaparte family. He soon sold La Peregrina which, after many adventures, has been acquired by Elizabeth Taylor. It is not as perfect as it once was, since it now bears her dog's teeth-marks.

Spain and Italy were not the only countries to be ruled by a Bonaparte. A pro-French government had ruled the 'Batavian Republic' (as the Netherlands was renamed) since the expulsion of the Princes of Orange in 1795. In June 1806 it was persuaded to ask for the Emperor's third brother Louis as King of Holland. Like the installation of Elisa in Lucca, his reign is an example of the swing to monarchy in early nineteenth-century Europe. Although there was a wealthy land-owning nobility in Holland, it was not the dominant class, and Holland had been a commercial republic for two hundred years. However, after 1806 King Louis-Napoleon established both a powerful monarchy and an aristocratic court.

At first, more than any of his brothers or sisters, King Louis-Napoleon kept a largely French household. The Grand Chamberlain was Count d'Arjuzon, the son of a pre-1789 tax official like so many Napoleonic courtiers. The Grand Marshal of the Palace was a merchant from Toulouse, Monsieur Sénégra. The Grand Equerry, General Caulaincourt, was a brother of the Emperor's Grand Equerry. The Grand Huntsman and Governor of the palace of the Hague was General Noguès, the King's favourite courtier. The only prominent Dutch court official was the Grand Master of Ceremonies, Count van Brantsen, who helped form the court with Sénégra. The Queen, Hortense de Beauharnais, also had a large household although she was rarely there; inevitably one of her ladies-in-waiting, Madame de Huyghens, became the King's mistress (Queen Hortense soon dismissed her).[33]

At first the court resided in the Hague, but its inhabitants were attached to the exiled Stadtholders, the Princes of Orange. In October 1807 the King moved to Utrecht, on the grounds that it was in the centre of his kingdom. But there was no suitable palace, and the court moved again in April 1808 to Amsterdam. This move was an outward demonstration that monarchy had come to Holland.

King Louis-Napoleon chose to inhabit the former town hall. It is a magnificent building, erected in the middle of the seventeenth century when Amsterdam was the financial centre of the world. It contained warehouses and the offices of the main bank, and Sénégra reported to the King that 'the inhabitants appear to be very attached to this building', which they considered one of the wonders of the world. Despite 'murmers', however,

Von der Kooi, ***Jonkheer Twent, Count van Rosenberg*** *Twent was a chamberlain and Minister of the Interior of King Louis-Napoleon.*

AUGERES
SALUS
PATRIÆ

the town hall became the King's palace. The citizens' hall was turned into a reception room, the magistrates' court became the throne room, a royal chapel replaced the High Court of Justice. An immense quantity of tabourets and a splendid silver-gilt table service by Biennais, modelled on the Emperor's, were ordered from Paris.[34]

Louis-Napoleon, like all his family, had a taste for splendour and held frequent receptions, balls and concerts. At the first balls, some of the ladies wore the local costume of Zeeland or north Holland, to the amusement of his smart French courtiers. One recorded that, 'The Dutch had such an awkward appearance that you could not look at them without appearing to be laughing at them.' (Even Queen Hortense, on her two brief visits from Paris, laughed at or ignored her Dutch courtiers.) A Parisian actor, Monsieur Morcuitrier, was imported to teach the Dutch what to wear and how to behave at court.[35] Such French contempt for foreign customs was characteristic of the 'family courts': the courtiers of King Joseph-Napoleon thought the ladies of Naples were ugly, badly dressed and vulgar as fishwives.

The Dutch ruling classes quickly adapted to the ways of a court. The French minister was amazed at how easily, almost without noticing, they were adopting 'monarchical manners'. In May 1807, when on a mission from King Joseph to King Louis, Stanislas de Girardin wrote from the Hague that: 'The court presents the most brilliant appearance. The costumes of the public and court officials are magnificently embroidered. The intention seems to be to compensate them for never having worn embroidery in this country.' The King took a deep personal interest in the costumes of his courtiers and the uniforms of his guard.[36]

King Louis was the only idealist in the Bonaparte family. He wanted to serve his people rather than his dynasty or his pocket. Unlike his brothers in Spain or Westphalia, he bothered to learn to speak his subjects' language. His determination to be a Dutch king alienated many of his French courtiers, who still hoped for a career in the French army or administration. Between 1807 and 1809 Louis replaced all his senior French court officials by Dutch nobles. The new Grand Chamberlain was Count

Anon, ***Entry of King Louis-Napoleon into Amsterdam, 20 April 1808*** *King Louis-Napoleon is arriving at the former town hall of Amsterdam, which has been transformed into his residence. It is still a royal palace, and full of Empire furniture.*

van Zuylen van Nyevelt, a member of one of the grandest Dutch noble families; the Grand Marshal of the Palace was a special favourite of the King, General Roest van Alkemade. With one exception all the sixteen chamberlains were now Dutch.

As a result of the King's intelligent, independent policies, and of the reforms he introduced, such as the Code Napoléon, he became extremely popular. Even the most hostile Dutch Republicans accepted him as their king. When King Louis returned to Amsterdam from a tour of his kingdom in September 1808, he was received 'with the loudest cheers from an immense crowd of people . . . people of different parties and opposite opinions hastened to go to court' — many more than had gone for the feast of St Napoleon on 15 August. In the evening 'the court ball was very well attended and very brilliant'.

The King's new Dutch courtiers knew how to address him in the adoring, submissive language he enjoyed. When Louis was on a visit to Paris, Count van Zuylen van Nyevelt wrote, in French, that his return was desired 'no less universally than ardently and sincerely', and he signed himself, 'Sire, of Your Majesty, the very humble and very obedient Servant and devoted Subject'.[37] Surrounded by his aristocratic Dutch court, King Louis became increasingly opposed to the demands of his brother's government. The Emperor's Berlin Decree of 1806, which imposed the Continental System and prohibited trade between the Continent and Britain, was particularly disastrous for a trading country like Holland; King Louis had to allow infractions. The Emperor was furious; his ambassador in Holland blamed the court. In July 1809, for example, he reported that the King was at his principal country palace of Het Loo, without his ministers and surrounded by Dutch courtiers of both sexes. The First Chamberlain Count van Pallandt, 'the proudest person at court', was particularly anti-French and influential.

A break with the Emperor was rapidly approaching. The French ambassador reported in February 1810 that 'the most absurd remarks against the family of their sovereign' started in the royal antechambers. Soon the last Frenchmen were sacked from the royal household, then the French ambassador and his servants were insulted on their way to court.[38] Faced with increasing French demands, and the invasion of his kingdom by French troops, King Louis abdicated on 1 July and fled to Austria, where he passed the time writing a bad novel. His sons were taken to Paris to live with their mother. Just as his kingdom was absorbed into the Empire, so his servants were taken into the Emperor's household, either in Paris or in its new branch in Amsterdam. When the Emperor visited Amsterdam in October 1811 he was received with enthusiasm. But the merchants of the city warned him that the economy was close to collapse.[39]

Kinson, ***King Jerome*** *The Bonapartes made a habit of being painted in front of the palaces they had acquired. Behind King Jerome is his palace of Napoleonshöhe.*

In contrast to King Louis-Napoleon, the youngest of the Bonapartes, Jerome-Napoleon, King of Westphalia, never identified himself with his subjects or learnt their language. Jerome was the most aristocratic, extravagant and sensuous of all the Bonapartes: his court carried to an extreme tendencies which were more restrained at the other family courts. After the Emperor's victory over Prussia in 1806, the Kingdom of Westphalia was formed in north-west Germany out of Hesse-Cassel, Brunswick, and parts of Prussia. Jerome, who was only twenty-three, was married to the Princess Catherine of Württemberg, large, proud and soon deeply in love with her husband. The new young King and Queen of Westphalia arrived at their capital Cassel in December 1807. They lived just outside in one of the most splendid palaces in Europe, formerly the residence of the Elector of Hesse-Cassel, called Wilhelmshöhe. Inevitably, King Jerome renamed it Napoleonshöhe.

Their court was composed of both French and Germans. The King's great favourite, Monsieur Lecamus, was one of the many French bourgeois who took to court life under the Empire with extraordinary ease. The son of a Lyons shopkeeper, he seemed to the Queen to be 'a perfect gentleman, perfectly brought up'. He became First Chamberlain and Grand Master of the Wardrobe. Another friend of the King from their days in the navy was Monsieur Meyronnet, the son of a cook, who tried to prove that he was descended from the ancient family of the Marquis de Meyronnet. He became Grand Equerry and Count of Wellingerode, but was dismissed for corruption in 1812.[40]

Even though the King was frivolous, extravagant, indeed in many ways a joke, some Germans were prepared to serve him. Like Prince Borghese, and half of Europe, they believed that the Emperor was 'the Greatest Man in the World'. Perhaps his family offered a greater chance of progress and prosperity

Anon, ***Lecamus, Count of Fürstenstein*** *Frank and loyal, Fürstenstein was described as an excellent favourite but a bad minister for his master, King Jerome. The son of a Lyons shop-keeper, he never learnt to pronounce his new title properly, but his children became Germans and served the King of Prussia.*

Anon, ***Prince Ernest of Hesse-Philippsthal*** *By serving King Jerome, Prince Ernest quarrelled with his family, but more than quadrupled his income. In 1813 he was quick to join the Russian army which invaded Westphalia and expelled King Jerome.*

than a German dynasty; perhaps the Bonapartes would be the saviours of society. Indeed, with the imposition of the egalitarian Code Napoléon in 1807 it seemed that these hopes might become reality. All legal barriers between nobles and non-nobles were removed, as well as those between Christians and Jews.

Among the most prominent Germans at court was the Grand Chamberlain, the Prince of Hesse-Philippsthal, a cousin of the last Elector. King Jerome obtained his services by paying his debts and giving him land (his income rose from 16,000 francs a year before 1807 to 84,000 francs under Jerome). He was loyal in the crisis of 1809 when much of Westphalia supported Austria's attack against Napoleon. The Queen had to withdraw to Strasbourg, and Count and Countess Waldburg-Truchsess, the first Grand Chamberlain and Grand Mistress of the Queen's Household, were dismissed because they were anti-French. Austria was defeated at Wagram, but the crisis was a revelation of the unpopularity of the regime.

Another German courtier was Prince Löwenstein, a chamberlain who was described by the French minister, Count Reinhard, as a bad prince and a bad husband. His artful and attractive wife, one of the ten ladies-in-waiting, was the King's chief mistress: the King seduced most of the other ladies-in-waiting as well. Princess Löwenstein attended the court even when eight months pregnant.[41]

Like all his family, Jerome used his courtiers in his government. Lecamus became Minister of Foreign Affairs; two Grand Equerries and a Grand Master of the Queen's Household served as Ministers of War. However, King Jerome was more interested in pleasure and display than in the business of government. As the French minister reported, Jerome had 'a passionate desire to be and to

Grandjean de Montigny, ***Throne of King Jerome in the Palace of the Estates in Cassel*** *The canopy was crimson velvet lined with gold. Grandjean de Montigny later introduced the Empire style to Brazil.*

appear King'. Like all his family he insisted on a rigorous etiquette at his court — more severe than the people of Cassel were used to — and was determined to enhance its prestige. When an official matter had to be settled between the Grand Huntsman and the Minister of War, he told his ministers that it was for the minister to consult the court official, not the other way around.

He was so intoxicated by his own status that he refused to go to a Te Deum in 1809 because there was no canopy for him to walk under. Superb court uniforms, more luxurious than Cassel had ever seen, were ordered from Maison Picot, the Paris embroidery firm which still looks back on the First Empire as its (literally) golden age. Rambuteau, who was sent to Cassel to announce the birth of the King of Rome in 1811, remembered: 'Never in my life have I seen such a galaxy of pretty women as those who clustered round the Queen and never have I witnessed greater luxury than was displayed by members of the King's household. There was more gold embroidery on their uniforms than there was silver on ours.' King Jerome was so fond of clothes he took seven different wardrobes with him on Napoleon's invasion of Russia in 1812. In addition to hundreds of lesser garments, they contained eighteen different uniforms and sixteen crates of eau-de-Cologne.[42]

At first the Germans and the French at court would not mix. French courtiers complained that living in Westphalia was like being in exile: Cassel was quite different from Paris.[43] However, with time the French became more tolerant and the Germans less alien. There were even a few marriages between them. Lecamus, Count of Fürstenstein, married a daughter of the Grand Huntsman, Count Hardenberg; a sister of the Prince of Hesse-Philippsthal married Count de La Ville-sur-Illon, Governor of the Palace.

French and Germans got to know each other at the unending round of entertainments at court and in the houses of the leading courtiers and ministers. The balls were particularly enjoyable. In the carnival season of 1810, Count Bucholtz, the Grand Master of Ceremonies, gave several masked balls. At one there was a Chinese quadrille and the King and Queen danced in a ballet. At another, the King changed costume so often that he seemed like a chameleon. The Queen did her best to keep up: she appeared as an old Jewess, a Red Indian and a peasant woman from the Black Forest in one evening. Cassel had never seen anything like it: indeed, sitting stolidly in their dominoes, the deputies to the Estates appeared to be registering all these marvels in order to describe them when they went home.

At another ball even Count Siméon, the aged minister who had been responsible for the rapid and efficient introduction of the Code Napoléon into Westphalia, wore fancy dress; and the King, dressed as Figaro, danced to the sound of castanets, throwing flowers to his guests. It is hardly surprising that the Emperor's Foreign Minister wrote primly: 'As a general rule a King ought not to dance.'[44]

King Jerome also entertained his courtiers on 'journeys' to Napoleonshöhe, lasting a week. Guests wore a special blue costume embroidered with silver. There were drives in the park, walks, concerts, plays and endless games of whist. Although the King usually ate alone, there were many opportunities for people to talk to him. There were usually eight resident guests, four men and four women. As the French minister reported, with special emphasis: '*Husbands and wives are rarely invited together.*'

To his subjects' dismay, the court of King Jerome absorbed as much as a quarter of all government expenditure. Perhaps the King was so extravagant because he did not believe in his kingdom. Like his brothers, he was more realistic than the Emperor, and may have felt that Westphalia would either be absorbed by the French Empire, or subverted from within. In 1811, when the Emperor appeared to be at the height of his power, the Continental System was ruining Germany as well as Holland. The Rhine was unnaturally quiet: the boats that used to ply up and down had no goods to carry. King Jerome wrote to warn the Emperor that discontent was at its height, that the wildest hopes were being entertained, and that the French were hated.[45]

The Emperor's brother-in-law, Marshal Murat, also received a German monarchy, although it was much smaller than the Kingdom of Westphalia. In 1806, as part of his reorganization of Germany after the battle of Austerlitz, the Emperor gave Murat the Grand Duchy of Berg between Westphalia and the Rhine. Although he formed a small household of local nobles, Murat did not spend much time in Berg. In 1808 he was promoted to King of Naples on Joseph's transfer to Spain. The

G. Forte, ***The Duke of Roccaromana*** *He always accompanied Murat in the campaigns of 1812–15; he lost three fingers through frost-bite during the retreat from Moscow.*

Dunouy and Carle Vernet, ***View of the palace of Benrath in 1807***
Benrath was Murat's principal palace in the Grand Duchy of Berg. Caroline Murat and her children are driving past. Murat took this picture with him when he lost Berg and was promoted to King of Naples. Another version still hangs in his former Paris residence, the Elysée.

elder son of King Louis of Holland, Napoleon-Louis, was subsequently made Grand Duke of Berg, but he never went there and never received a German household.[46]

As King of Naples, King Joachim-Napoleon (as Murat was called) inherited Joseph's court as well as his kingdom: the Prince of Stigliano Colonna and the Duke of San Teodoro served King Joachim-Napoleon as well as they had served King Joseph-Napoleon. The most important new acquisition was the Duke of Roccaromana, a great noble who had distinguished himself in the Revolution of 1799 and was created Grand Equerry in 1812. Lady Blessington called him 'the very personification of a *preux chevalier*, brave in arms and gentle and courteous in society'. In 1813 there were also 44 chamberlains (including 18 dukes and 16 princes), and the Queen had 28 ladies (including 11 duchesses and 12 princesses).[47]

Clearly the court of King Joachim and Queen Caroline was as aristocratic as those of the rest of her family. The *Etichetta della Real Corte delle Due Sicilie* regulated its ceremonial. Like all Napoleonic etiquette, it was based on the ceremonial of the Tuileries, with the significant difference that *all* officially recognized nobles could go to court, and enter the first antechamber of the palace. More people went to court, and etiquette was stricter, than under King Joseph.[48]

The Murats lived in considerable state. Years later Murat's daughter remembered being served at table by pages in red and gold livery. As at the Tuileries, the chamberlains had red uniforms, the equerries dark blue, and the prefects of the palace scarlet ones. On gala days the King wore a special costume of red velvet covered in silver embroidery, with a plumed hat.

Murat's favourite palace was at Portici by the sea. The Queen's apartments were covered in 'draperies of the richest silk', and contained 'endless suites of apartments, bathrooms, cabinets, bookrooms, green-houses'. The King's apartments were 'equally luxurious, splendid and commodious, the hangings all silk and satin'. For years afterwards the guide would say to admiring visitors: 'Everything made for Madama Murat! Every-

Anon, *Terrace of the Royal Palace of Naples*
Murat maintained such strict etiquette at his court that only he and his wife Caroline had the right to use the terrace.

thing made for Madama Murat!' When the Bourbons returned, they were overwhelmed by the lavish redecoration which had taken place during their absence. The King's youngest son said: 'Oh Papa! If only you had stayed away another ten years!'[49]

Despite his splendid court, Murat was a child of the Revolution. He was proud of the reforms he promoted in Naples, which included a commission dealing with feudal rights that favoured the communes rather than noble land-owners. His wife, however, had the aristocratic instincts of her family. She wrote him a letter in 1810 which reveals the degree to which the Bonapartes wanted to crush revolution and represent the interests of the nobility — if the nobles would let them: 'You ought to know, however, by the experience of the French revolution how dangerous it is to give in to the people which, after destroying the nobles, has never failed to overthrow the throne.' The nobles of Naples were so angry and impoverished, she complained, that only her own ladies-in-waiting came to her *soirées*.[50]

Murat and Caroline both enjoyed their royal status and were determined to preserve it. Murat tried to put down roots in Naples. Two of his nieces were brought from Gascony and married to Neapolitan chamberlains, the Prince of Caramanico and the Duke of Avalos. From 1810 he began to pursue a more 'national' policy, like his brothers-in-law in Holland and Spain. Many Frenchmen left his court as a result. Murat was suspicious that his wife might be pro-French, and excluded her from politics. Her passion for archaeology became her main occupation. She visited Pompeii or Herculaneum once a week, filled her apartments with finds and extended the area available for excavation.

The family courts reveal the Bonapartes' grandiose concept of their royal status. In Naples and Cassel, as well as Paris and Milan, they lived in greater state than their legitimate predecessors. In Lucca and Amsterdam they imposed monarchy and court life on Europe's only surviving Republics. It is true that the Bonapartes also introduced important and lasting reforms, more radical than those the Emperor introduced into France. But these were a means to an end rather than ends in themselves. The Bonapartes used the necessity for reforms to justify their own very traditional ambition to found dynasties, acquire palaces and surround themselves with magnificent courts.

Despite reforms apparently inspired by concern for the people, the Bonapartes were not at heart democratic. They were more ceremonious and aloof than the legitimate monarchs they replaced. Their attitude to their subjects is revealed by the Bonapartes' determination to keep the people at a distance from their palaces.

In the past, many of the palaces of the kings and emperors of Europe had been closely connected to the surrounding city, and indeed open for ordinary people to walk through, as the Hofburg in Vienna still was in the early nineteenth century. The Bonapartes, however, cut themselves off from their subjects by creating large squares in front of their palaces. Napoleon I had most of the houses in front of the Tuileries demolished in order to enlarge the Place du Carrousel. Elisa created huge piazzas in front of her palaces at Lucca and Massa, enraging the people of Massa by insisting that one of their churches be demolished in the process. A church was also demolished in Venice in order to clear the space in front of the Emperor's palace on the Piazza San Marco. King Joseph created an immense semi-circular piazza in front of the Royal Palace of Naples. An equestrian statue of the Emperor, the largest yet carved, was to be erected in the middle (but in the end its base and horse were used by Canova for the statue of the Bourbon King Charles III of Spain which is still there). King Joseph also created the enormous Plaza de Oriente in front of the Royal Palace of Madrid.

On one level, the Bonapartes' craving for large squares was a sign of their appetite for splendour. A square reveals the grandeur of a palace, and can be used for ceremonial display and parades. More significant, however, was the fact that a large square made it easier to defend a royal palace and made the Bonapartes feel more secure. It gave guards more room for manoeuvre and an attacking crowd less cover. Such protection was necessary in view of the fact that the poor of Amsterdam, Naples and Madrid were particularly loyal to the House of Orange and the Bourbons. Even King Louis, who was relatively popular with his subjects, was afraid of being 'at the mercy of the populace' when he moved to Amsterdam. One reason why he chose to live in the former town hall was that there was a square with room for four or five thousand soldiers in front of it.[51] Despite protests from the citizens, he enlarged this square still further. Wherever they were, the Bonapartes relied on force.

7

Power and Illusion

'Bonaparte claims that I am just a fool: he laughs longest who laughs last!'

Letter of Tsar Alexander I to the Grand Duchess Catherine, Erfurt, 26 September 1808.

French politics from 1804 to 1814 were primarily court politics. The Emperor was an all-powerful autocrat. Censorship of the press, the stage and books was of a severity rarely equalled even in the twentieth century: references to kings in the plays of Racine, for example, were severely controlled. The Emperor compelled his subjects to serve in his armies and even tried to regulate whom they should marry. Alternative power centres such as the Senate and the Legislative Body had been reduced to cowering phantoms. All ministers, except Talleyrand and Fouché, acted simply as executives carrying out orders.

Court politics under Napoleon I were dominated by the Emperor's endless wars. Although some wars were started by other powers (for example, those of 1806 with Prussia and of 1809 with Austria), their real cause was the Emperor's disregard of neutrality combined with his apparently limitless appetite for territorial expansion. By 1812 he and his family ruled half of Europe. It was often maintained that the Emperor's ambitions were encouraged by his courtiers — or, less directly, by his need to satisfy an army hungry for loot and promotion. In 1807 a foreign diplomat at the Emperor's headquarters in Poland claimed that 'the entourage and suite of the Emperor, composed of young, ambitious people, encouraged him ceaselessly to new adventures.'[1]

Indeed the court did encourage the Emperor to do anything he wanted. A visitor to the Tuileries, as early as 1801, was surprised that the First Consul was surrounded by so much 'flattery and cringing attention'. His courtiers saw it as their duty to please their master; they told him what he wanted to hear. In 1807, the Empress Josephine, in a letter to her son Prince Eugene, presumably sent by private courier and therefore unlikely to be read by the secret police, wrote: 'The Emperor is too grand for anybody to tell him the truth; everybody who surrounds him flatters him all day long.' His court flattered him in its actions as well as in its words. An Austrian visitor who came to the court in 1810 for the wedding of Marie-Louise could not believe the way the courtiers 'push and shove each other and tread on each other's toes to catch a word or a look, to be the first to enter'.

A letter written by Count Ferdinand de Rohan, a member of the grandest family of the aristocracy of the old regime, shows how Napoleon was treated. Thanking the Emperor for permission to transfer from Josephine's to Marie-Louise's household as First Almoner, he wrote: 'As long as I have a breath of life left in me it will be to devote it to you.' He added, sacrilegiously, that the Emperor was 'my tutelary deity'.[2]

Napoleon I was much too intelligent not to realize that he was surrounded by flatterers, and he frequently tried to find out the truth. In the early days, when he was still First Consul, an Irish visitor had been to the Tuileries and had found that he had 'the greatest fund of levee conversation that I suppose any person ever possessed'. Unlike many other monarchs, he wanted to talk to the people who came to court, and obtain information from them. At the right moment people could say anything to him, and found that he was a good listener.

Gosse, *The Congress of Erfurt, September 1808*
An Austrian general is presenting a letter from his Emperor to Napoleon. On the right of Napoleon are King Jerome and Tsar Alexander I (in profile). On the left are Talleyrand and Caulaincourt, who were already working with Alexander I against the Emperor's policies.

But this required exceptional bravery and unusual independence of character. For most of the time the splendour and formality of Napoleon's court prevented him from hearing the truth, while he himself had destroyed other possible sources of information, such as a free press or an unintimidated parliament. A Swiss deputy to the Legislative Body called Rivaz recounts the following story in his memoirs. When he was in Paris for the legislative session of 1813, he went to court every second Sunday. One day after Mass the Emperor noticed his uniform, and stopped to speak to him.

'From what department are you?'

'From the Simplon, Sire.'

'Ah! Rivaz.'

'Yes, Sire.'

'Well, what are the people of the Haut Valais saying? Are they happy? Speak to me frankly.'

'Sire, you treat them with so much kindness that they can only be satisfied.'

Rivaz justifies his answer by writing that he replied 'as courtiers have to reply'. He felt too embarrassed, and the presence of the Emperor and his court was too overwhelming, to tell the truth about the department's discontent with taxation and conscription. The nature of court life is shown by the fact that this brief, uninteresting conversation made people at court behave differently to Rivaz, as they believed that he was 'on the road to favour'.[3]

The Emperor was careful to ensure that no one could threaten his authority at court. He was particularly conscious of the dangers inherent in the only armed force at court, the Imperial Guard. As the Emperor knew, the more absolute the monarch, the more dangerous his guard could be, since there were no independent institutions to balance its influence. He felt that, under another Emperor, 'my Imperial Guard could also have become fatal'.[4] However he was careful to divide control of his guard between four different marshals, so that there was not one all-powerful commander who might acquire too much influence. The officers of the guard, like the officials of the court, were completely dependent on the Emperor. He was in control of the government and took decisions of his own free will. His wars were undertaken to satisfy his personal desire for power and glory; they did not reflect the wishes of his army. By 1809, or earlier, the army and its leaders were beginning to tire of fighting.

The Emperor's supreme control meant that although there were people at court who distrusted his policies they could not influence his decisions. Talleyrand, with his legendary reputation for sagacity and capacity for intrigue, was the most important figure in court politics. His behaviour shows that there was always a degree of illusion in the Emperor's apparently absolute power. For, unable to influence the Emperor directly, Talleyrand began to work against his policies in secret.

As early as 1805 Talleyrand had doubts about the Emperor. According to Metternich, he was at the head of 'the great mass of the nation and the most eminent persons in the state in an effort to restrain the destructive projects of Napoleon'. Like many Frenchmen since the reign of Louis XVI, he saw Austria as the most civilized and reliable of European powers. He called it 'the House of Lords of Europe', and tried to preserve its power and territory after its defeat at Austerlitz in 1805. Many other people at court, in particular his friend the Grand Equerry, Caulaincourt, shared his distrust of the Emperor's ambitions and his determination to restrain them. Neither of them believed that the Emperor's conquests beyond the Rhine, won after his defeat of Prussia at Jena in 1806, would survive him.[5] Both wanted peace.

At the Congress of Erfurt in September 1808, Talleyrand and Caulaincourt tried to act. This Congress was intended to cement the alliance the Emperor had signed with Tsar Alexander I of Russia at Tilsit in 1807, after France, Russia and Prussia had made peace. The Emperor said: 'I want to astonish Germany by my magnificence.' Soon the road from Paris to Erfurt was covered with waggons, horses and servants, bringing supplies and furnishings from the Emperor's palaces — champagne, Gobelins tapestries and Sèvres porcelain. Soldiers of the Imperial Guard and pages in full livery appeared in the streets of Erfurt, a small town in the middle of Germany which had never seen anything like it.

On 27 September the Emperor arrived, accompanied by innumerable courtiers, including Sapieha, Rémusat and Talleyrand, who has left a biting account of the festivities. German princes rushed to see 'he who dispensed everything, thrones, disasters, fear, hope'. Rémusat organized historic performances of Racine plays by the Comédie Française, in front of an audience of monarchs. The smaller German princes outdid themselves in flattery. The Emperor was offered a lunch by the Duke of Saxe-Weimar on the very battlefield of Jena where French soldiers had killed so many Germans two years before. As Talleyrand wrote, at Erfurt the Emperor was surrounded by princes whose armies he had destroyed, whose territory he had reduced and whose pride he had humiliated.[6]

Despite this appearance of supreme power, however, the Emperor was under attack from within his own court. Talleyrand was engaging in treasonable conversations in Erfurt with the Tsar, whom he saw every evening in the salon of the Princess of Thurn and Taxis (in the early nineteenth century a salon could shape events as easily as a political party in the twentieth). Caulaincourt also encouraged the Tsar to resist the Emperor's demand that Russia should be committed to join France in the case of war with Austria.

Two of the most important men at court were working against the Emperor's policies; hence, no doubt, the quiet confidence of the Tsar's remark to his sister: 'he laughs longest who laughs last'. It is interesting that in this letter the Tsar calls his host and ally not 'the Emperor' or 'Napoleon' but, rudely, 'Bonaparte'. By urging the Tsar not to commit himself to Napoleon I, Talleyrand and Caulaincourt indirectly encouraged Austria to attack the French Empire in 1809: Talleyrand, at least, wished it was Napoleon I, not Francis I of Austria, who was defeated.[7]

Soon after the Congress of Erfurt Talleyrand organized a reconciliation with the only minister who still had a mind of his own, his old enemy Fouché, Duke d'Otrante. Previously rivals for the Emperor's favour, they now turned against him. They began to meet in different salons, including that of Madame de Rémusat, one of Talleyrand's greatest admirers. Paris was electrified to learn that Fouché had attended one of Talleyrand's own receptions. 'Nobody could believe their eyes . . . especially when they linked arms and strolled from one room to another all through the evening.'

Talleyrand had long been opposed to the Beauharnais — the Empress Josephine and her children Eugene and Hortense. He helped to supply the Emperor with mistresses, such as Madame Gazzani and the beautiful Madame Walewska, whom he had presented to the Emperor in Warsaw in 1807. Fouché had also become an advocate of divorce. Their reconciliation may have been intended to arrange the succession of Murat if the Emperor was killed on campaign. Prince Eugene and Lavallette, the Director of Posts, who was married to a Beauharnais, denounced the conspiracy. The Emperor, who was in Spain trying to establish King Joseph on the throne, was so eager to get back to Paris that he covered 700 miles in six days. An explosion was inevitable.[8]

On 28 January 1809 Talleyrand's criticism of the Emperor's expansionism, and his reconciliation with Fouché, led to a famous scene in the Emperor's private apartments in the Tuileries. The Emperor made a violent attack on Talleyrand in front of Cambacérès and the Minister of the Marine — although there is no proof that he delivered the famous verdict that Talleyrand was nothing but 'a piece of shit in a silk stocking'. Talleyrand, who was sacked as Grand Chamberlain, commented: 'What a pity that such a great man should be so ill-bred' — a remark which explains the failure of the Napoleonic court as well as any.

Despite his disgrace, Talleyrand continued to go to court. Politics was the breath of life to him, and the court was the centre of politics. Moreover it was not in Napoleon I's interests to advertise his breach with Talleyrand, who was much too powerful. As the Emperor knew, Talleyrand had friendships with the leading men and women of Europe, as well as with those of the French Empire. So Talleyrand remained a senior figure in the state as Vice-Grand Elector. Within a few months the Emperor was almost polite to him at the *lever*, as he reported with satisfaction to Caulaincourt. The Emperor may have begun to consult Talleyrand again over foreign affairs. In November 1809 he recovered the *Petites Entrées* and joined the court on its autumn visit to Fontainebleau.[9]

At the same time Talleyrand remained in treasonable communication with Russia and Austria, and received large sums of money from both countries. By 1811 he was so important in the formation of Russian foreign policy that a diplomat was sent to Paris especially to maintain contact with him. In secret despatches to St Petersburg the French Empire was referred to as 'the Marble Palace'. Talleyrand was 'My Cousin Henry', the Tsar 'Louise', and the Emperor 'Sophie Smith'. The Emperor, whose police was not particularly efficient, never found out. Indeed, in March 1812 he planned to appoint Talleyrand ambassador in Warsaw, on the grounds that such an able diplomat, who had many Polish friends, might be able to galvanize the Poles to help the French invasion of Russia. One evening the Emperor kept Talleyrand late at the *coucher* to discuss his return to office.

Talleyrand's great rival during the Empire was Maret, Duke de Bassano, the Minister Secretary of State, who was Minister of Foreign Affairs as well from 1811. Bassano was devoted to the Emperor, whose ambitions he did nothing to discourage. The Bassanos entertained their guests to puppet-shows which made fun of Talleyrand's and Caulaincourt's love of peace: a limping devil (Talleyrand) taught the puppet representing Caulaincourt to repeat inanely 'Peace brings happiness to the world'. The Duchess de Bassano was convinced that Talleyrand would soon replace her husband as Minister of Foreign Affairs if he returned to office. She told the bad news to her friend, the chamberlain Rambuteau.

To please the beautiful Duchess, Rambuteau leaked this information at once, before Talleyrand's nomination to Warsaw had been officially announced. The Emperor was furious, blamed Talleyrand and cancelled the appointment. Even the most brilliant autocrat could be manipulated by his court, as the Emperor later admitted. If Talleyrand had returned to office in 1812, he might have remained loyal in 1814.[10]

Thus some of the Empire's most senior officials had doubts about its future, almost from the beginning. At the same time, outside the official world of the court and the government, there was another world, including people of every class, which was opposed to the regime and had as little contact with it as possible. At the very beginning of the Empire many Parisians, of all classes, were horrified by the execution of the young Bourbon prince the Duke d'Enghien. To the disgust of the court, Paris was never particularly enthusiastic about the Emperor and his victories.

In the élite of birth and wealth, there were always individuals whose attitude to the Empire was eloquently expressed by a former ambassador of Louis XVI: 'whoever touches it soils himself'.[11] Madame Récamier, the most famous beauty of the age and a friend of General Moreau, refused a post at court. In 1808 Madame de Chevreuse resigned as a lady-in-waiting rather than attend the captive Queen of Spain. A frank woman, she said that it was bad enough being a slave without being a gaoler as well.

Thirteen cardinals, including Cardinal Consalvi, a brilliant diplomat who had negotiated the concordat, refused to attend the Emperor's second marriage in 1810, because they did not believe the dissolution of the first was valid. When the Emperor saw their empty places in the chapel of the Louvre he was furious. According to Consalvi's memoirs he ordered three of them to be shot as he left the chapel after the ceremony. Such an order was given in a fit of rage and was probably not intended to be carried out. Nevertheless, when the disobedient cardinals came to pay their respects in the throne room of the Tuileries, he ordered them to be expelled. In their red cardinals' robes their departure from the palace must have been dramatic. They were exiled to the provinces where, since they were forbidden to wear their full ecclesiastical dress, they were known as the 'black cardinals', in contrast to the fourteen obedient 'red cardinals', who had attended the wedding.

The Pope had excommunicated the Emperor in 1809 for annexing the Papal States. Catholic opposition to Napoleon grew stronger after the exile of the cardinals (and the imprisonment of the Pope, see below). Even the Grand Almoner, Cardinal Fesch, turned against his nephew. In 1812 he was relieved of his duties at court and sent to live in his diocese of Lyons.[12]

Aristocratic opposition to the Empire also continued, even at the height of its power. Out of loyalty to the exiled Bourbons many nobles refused to go to court, or to be appointed chamberlains. The heads of the oldest and grandest families of the old *noblesse présentée,* such as the Dukes de Noailles, de Duras and d'Aumont, spent the Empire on their estates or abroad. The Emperor could only secure the services of younger sons and their wives, who had a greater incentive to take risks, such as Countess de La Rochefoucauld, principal lady-in-waiting of the Empress before 1810, or Count Juste de Noailles and his wife, who were a chamberlain and lady-in-waiting respectively. In November 1812, as Talleyrand reported to his mistress the Duchess de Courlande, the printed announcement of the marriage of Charles de Gontaut, another chamberlain, had the words *chambellan de l'Empereur* added *in pencil* on the cards sent to people connected to the regime. In other words, even on something as formal as a marriage announcement, one courtier preferred to please the royalist aristocracy, and not to print his official imperial title, rather than to print it, and demonstrate his allegiance to the Empire.

Many of the royalist aristocracy lived in a world of their own, called 'the Faubourg Saint-Germain', after the area of Paris where most of their houses were. Royalist ladies even dressed differently from the ladies of the Napoleonic court, with longer sleeves and lower waists.[13] The Faubourg Saint-Germain was important because many royalists were still among the richest landowners in France, and their wealth gave them power and influence. Moreover, they had names famous throughout Europe. They were the people whom foreign diplomats saw and listened to, and whom the Emperor wanted in his army and court.

An extraordinary scheme devised in 1810 showed the strength of what a government report called 'the spirit of opposition which animates them [the royalist nobles] against the present dynasty'. It also revealed the Emperor's desire for total control of his subjects, which was encouraged by the man who replaced Fouché as Minister of Police in 1810, Savary, Duke de Rovigo. Rovigo was a former aide-de-camp of the Emperor and one of his most unscrupulous servants. He instructed each Prefect to draw up 'a list of the richest heiresses not yet married' in his department.

There were to be separate columns for their name and age, the names, official positions and wealth of their parents, the size of their dowry, the nature of their religious principles and their 'physical attractions'. They were then to be married to men selected by the Emperor. When a rich heiress of Lyons married a man chosen by her own family, Rovigo wrote in a fury to the Prefect: 'The dynasty we serve has its creatures to form and there are no longer enough heiresses as rich as Mademoiselle Delglat in France for them not to be reserved for the servants of the Emperor.' Most Prefects replied vaguely, late, or not at all to the Minister. The Emperor's plan to conscript heiresses as well as soldiers was defeated by the force of social and moral convention.[14]

In the conquered territories, although there were some spectacular cases of nobles rallying to the Empire, there were equally striking examples of continued aristocratic opposition. In Rome, great noble families such as the Colonna, the Orsini and the Doria refused to serve the Empire. In Belgium, although the Arenberg and the Mercy-Argenteau served, the Cröy were hostile. When it was known the Emperor was coming to Laeken, some nobles fled abroad to avoid having to be presented.

There was also hostility to the Empire among the bourgeoisie, particularly in seaports such as Bordeaux and Marseilles, ruined by the Continental System. For many of the poor the Empire represented conscription, high taxation and, in 1810–12 when there was an economic crisis, hunger as well. Bread soared in price, there were frequent bankruptcies, the Paris bourse collapsed. In March 1812 bread in Caen was so expensive that there was a serious riot. The Emperor sent one of his aides-de-camp, Count Durosnel, to restore order. Within eighteen hours of his arrival, six people, including two women, had been executed: others were sent to prison, where they were visited by local royalists.[15]

The hostility of a large part of the population of the Empire had been one reason for the creation of the court. It was intended to be a symbol of the power, magnificence and stability of the regime. This hostility, and the insecurity of the regime, also explain the relentless grandeur of furniture, decoration, painting and music in the Empire style. The lavish use of gold leaf, N's, bees and eagles was a conscious political act as well as a display of vanity.

The Empire style lacked the simple elegance of contemporary art in Vienna, Potsdam or St Petersburg or of French art under the Directory. The Emperor was the first of his dynasty and he needed to impose his image on the public through his initial and dynastic emblems in order to counteract the memory of the Bourbons' L's and lilies. The innumerable popular cartoons of 1814–15, which pay more attention to the emblems of the Empire than to its policies, show the extent of his success. The Emperor's insecurity helps to explain why he had so many palaces, arranged in such an ultra-monarchical fashion, and why he was surrounded by such a large and formal court. Contemporary monarchs like Francis I of Austria and Frederick William III of Prussia did not need to have themselves depicted as Jupiter on a palace ceiling, or to wear a special monarchical costume like the *Petit Costume de l'Empereur* at court ceremonies. They were confident of their right to the throne and the love of their subjects.

The Emperor had many influential enemies outside the boundaries of the Empire, as well as within it. He could win the wars of soldiers and treaties with ease, but he found the war of tongues more difficult. In Vienna, St Petersburg and Berlin there were salons as hostile to the Emperor as those of the Faubourg Saint-Germain and Bordeaux. In these salons, far more than at the courts of Francis I, Alexander I and Frederick William III, enemies of the Emperor received a very warm welcome indeed. They included the Prussian Baron von Stein, the Corsican Pozzo di Borgo (who had a vendetta against the Bonapartes), the Swede Count Armfelt, and agents of the exiled Louis XVIII. Even when the monarchs of Europe had been forced to sign treaties with Napoleon I, there were always aristocrats outraged by his triumphs and dedicated to his fall.[16] Napoleon I could not stop them talking, planning and waiting for a break in his luck.

For a time it seemed as if his luck would last forever. The continued war with Britain and the Spanish insurgents in the peninsula was a minor irritation. The Emperor was able to annex Rome in 1809, Holland in 1810 and north-west Germany in 1811 without difficulty. Paris was now the capital of an empire which stretched from the Baltic to the Mediterranean and from the Atlantic to the Adriatic. To foreign visitors it seemed like a city of marvels, the source of all good and evil in Europe, ruled by the greatest man of the age.

Dessiné et Gravé par A. Godefroy
Joachim Napoléon,
Roi de Naples.
Frédéric Auguste,
Roi de Saxe.
Jérome Napoléon,
Roi de Westphalie.
Frédéric,
Roi de Wirtemberg.
Louis Napoléon,
Roi de Hollande.
NAPOLÉON,
Jo
Impératri
Esquisse représentant la réunion des Souverains ac
au Bal donné par la Ville de Pari
S. M. l'Empereur répondant au Discours de Mr. le Préfêt du
Déposé à la Bibliothèque Impériale.

A. Godefroy, ***Meeting of sovereigns at the Hôtel de Ville in Paris, 24 December 1809*** *The foreign monarchs wear uniform, the Emperor and his brothers their costumes as members of the imperial family. King Jerome looked so feminine in his that Parisians mistook him for the Empress. Duroc and Ségur stand behind the Emperor's chair. The Emperor did not allow other monarchs to wear hats in his presence.*

The Emperor was not content with political domination. A few months after the annexation of Rome, the Pope was taken from his palace and imprisoned in Savona, near Genoa. He was separated from his cardinals and household, spied upon, insulted and told to abdicate. In 1812, although he was in bad health, he was taken in secret to Fontainebleau. Napoleon's aim was to establish total control over the Catholic Church. He hoped the Pope would agree to live in Paris, and do what the Emperor wanted. But Pius VII, although gentle and occasionally malleable, would not give in.

By now, as Stendhal wrote, the Emperor's vanity had become a disease; as his Empire grew larger, he saw his court as an exclusive golden halo around his throne. In 1810 the ladies-in-waiting of the Empress received precedence over all the ladies of the Empire. In 1811 a ball planned at court for the bourgeois of Paris was cancelled. Masson comments: 'The court, that is what counts, the official world barely, the bourgeoisie not at all.' The same year, the *entrée* to the throne room was removed from the presidents of the Council of State (senior government officials, many of whom came from a revolutionary background) and given to dukes, who now had precedence after the Grand Officers of the Empire. The Maréchale de Mailly, widow of a pre-revolutionary Marshal of Louis XVI, now had the same rank as the Maréchales of the Empire.[17]

Another symbol of the increasingly aloof and aristocratic character of the court was the reintroduction of the elaborate silk or satin costume which men had worn at the court of Louis XVI, called the *habit habillé*. In January 1811, in order to encourage the silk industry of Lyons, the Emperor decreed that silk costumes should be worn by all men going to court entertainments (except officers on duty). The results, first seen at a ball given by Princess Pauline, could be comic: only the genius of Napoleon I could have compelled battle-scarred veterans of innumerable campaigns, such as Marshals Ney and Junot, to dress up in pink or green silk.[18]

In the years 1810–12, as the court grew larger and more aristocratic, it also grew more important to the Emperor. It was becoming the only world he knew. The Grand Master of Ceremonies wrote that 'the moment Their Majesties arrive somewhere it becomes their palace', and the etiquette of the court applied. Even a peasant's hut was referred to by courtiers as 'the palace' if the Emperor took shelter there. Marshal Lannes, the last Marshal who had spoken freely to the Emperor and called him *tu*, was killed at the battle of Essling in 1809. In 1810, when many aristocratic chamberlains were appointed before the Emperor's marriage to Marie-Louise, a police report recorded that the new men of the Empire regarded these courtiers as 'a barrier between them and the Emperor'. They called the chamberlains 'chamber-pots' in contempt. People noticed that the Emperor was more approachable to his chamberlains than to his officers and that he could no longer recognize his soldiers by name.[19]

Personal service to the Emperor was becoming all-important. His aides-de-camp now emerged as more powerful than the Minister of War, and officials recruited from his household began to obtain the best jobs in the diplomatic and prefectoral corps. The Emperor began to pursue a deliberate policy of appointing court officials to government positions. In 1811 he substituted three chamberlains for a minister's candidates to go on a mission in Illyria, one of whom was the future memorialist of Saint-Helena, the Count de Las Cases. Napoleon's reason was that 'three chamberlains are in Paris at the moment without work'.

Between 1810 and 1813 Las Cases was also sent on missions to Holland and to investigate prison conditions in the provinces, and he frequently accompanied the Emperor to the Council of State. It is not surprising that he became a fervent admirer, who baptised his daughter Ofrésie-Marie-Louise-Napoléone in 1813.[20] When Count de Narbonne, one of the Emperor's favourite aides-de-camp, was made Ambassador to Vienna, Narbonne insisted that he remained an aide-de-camp as well. Proximity to the Emperor was more important than the most influential embassy.

In late 1810 the Secretary of State of the Imperial Family wrote to the Grand Almoner that there was no longer to be a distinction between government and household officials in the etiquette of the court. 'It must therefore be stated that the Grand Dignitaries are the First Officers of the Household of the Emperor and that the Ministers and the Grand Officers of the Empire are also part of the Household of the Emperor.... This practice is consistent with the practice of the former French monarchy and the current practice of the other courts of Europe.'[21] The government was being absorbed into the court.

Despite continued opposition both outside and inside the Empire, and the signs of hostility or despair apparent in Spain, Holland and Westphalia, it is probable that Napoleon I and his cosmopolitan, autocratic court could have continued to rule the Empire for a long time. The birth of his long-awaited heir, the King of Rome, on 20 March 1811 was an occasion for real popular rejoicing. Stendhal listened to the cannon announcing the birth 'with transport', while he was in bed with his mistress Angelina. He wrote in his diary that the sound of cheering in the street below was like the applause at 'the entrance of a favourite actor'. Royalists were sunk in gloom, convinced that the birth meant the end of the Bourbons.

The baptism of the King of Rome on 9 June 1811 was the occasion for another glittering ceremony. Madame de Montesquiou drove to Notre Dame in a special carriage, escorted by guards and courtiers, with the baby on her lap. The Emperor and the Empress went in the coronation coach. The Emperor wore his *Petit Costume*, the Empress a white dress covered in diamonds. The ceremony was long and elaborate. The baby had his own cloak of cloth of silver, lined with ermine, which was borne by a former soldier of the Revolution, Marshal Kellerman, Duke de Valmy. The 7220 guests in the cathedral cheered with enthusiasm when the child was held up by the Emperor after the baptism.

The people outside, however, were more concerned about the economic situation, which had worsened since March. There were well-justified fears of a bad harvest and food shortages. Unemployment was rising. The splendour of the procession seems to have alienated many Parisians. Stanislas de Girardin wrote that the spectators had an 'air of marked indifference' as the procession went by. There were no cheers; there were even whistles of contempt. Police agents had to remove seditious posters.[22]

The Emperor's determination to crush the last truly independent great power left in Europe (except for Britain), and enforce the Continental System, made him decide to invade Russia in the summer of 1812. It was one of the greatest gambles of his life.

For once his courtiers spoke up. Berthier and Duroc, the two people to whom he was most likely to listen, as well as Caulaincourt, Lobau, Durosnel, Turenne and Narbonne, all warned him against the invasion. The Emperor refused to change his mind. He was indeed, as Byron wrote, a heartless gambler:

> Whose game was empire — whose stakes were thrones,
> Whose table earth — whose dice were human bones.

He wanted to push reality to the limit, to see how far he could go, to defy history, geography, nationality, climate and distance.

In late May 1812 he held a court of kings at Dresden. The Kings of Saxony, Prussia and Westphalia, and even the Emperor of Austria, came to pay their respects. Innumerable German princes attended his *lever*. Dinners, plays, concerts and receptions followed each other remorselessly.

The Napoleonic court outshone all others. The ladies of the Empress of Austria felt like Cinderellas compared to the glittering duchesses attending the Empress of the French. At dinner the first guests to enter were announced as 'Their Excellencies' or 'Their Highnesses'. They were followed by 'Their Majesties, the King and Queen of Saxony', 'Their Imperial and Apostolic Majesties, the Emperor and Empress of Austria, King and Queen of Hungary', and 'Her Majesty the Empress of the French, Queen of Italy'. Finally, when everyone else was waiting, the chamberlain announced simply: *'L'Empereur!'*[23] In walked the most powerful man in the world at the height of his power.

His armies crossed into Russia on 24 June. Napoleon was so confident that he had not bothered to win Polish support. He had also failed to stop Sweden (under Bernadotte) and the Ottoman Empire from making peace with Russia. As a result he faced the full force of the Russian armies. By 14 September he had reached Moscow. Just as the Emperor's Bourbon rival Louis XVIII, throughout his exile, always judged his different residences by the palaces he had known in his youth, so Napoleon I, in the heart of Russia, also thought of his favourite French palaces. In his letters to the Empress, and in conversation with his courtiers, he frequently compared the mild Russian autumn to autumn at Fontainebleau, when the court was in residence for the hunting season.

But even Napoleon I could not control the Russian climate. The autumn would not last forever and Alexander I, encouraged by Stein and Armfelt, non-Russian enemies of Napoleon who had become two of the Tsar's most influential advisers, refused to acknowledge defeat. On 19 October the retreat from Moscow began. The weather and the Russian army soon turned it into a rout. Characteristically for a Grand Equerry, Caulaincourt blamed the disintegration of the army on the fact that its horses, except those under his own authority in the Emperor's stables, were not properly shod. Without decent horseshoes they could not manage the snow and the ice.[24]

Meanwhile an unsuccessful coup in Paris had revealed that the Emperor's political system was as fragile as his reputation for invincibility. On 23 October, a Republican general called Malet, who had long been in a lunatic asylum, managed to

Goubaud, ***Baptism of the King of Rome in Notre Dame***
The Emperor holds up his son and heir to the cheering spectators. Outside Notre Dame, however, there were no cheers. Marie-Louise is seated in front of the Grand Chamberlain Montesquiou; his wife, the Governess of the King of Rome, is behind the Emperor, waiting for him to return the baby. Goubaud was the official painter of the children of France.

Duplessis-Berteaux, *Execution of General Malet and his followers*, **29 October 1812** *Malet, who had seized control of central Paris for a few hours, has already been executed. General Guidal, in front, only fell at the third volley.*

escape. He claimed that the Emperor had been killed in Russia and seized control of part of Paris for a few hours with the help of soldiers of the National Guard, led by other conspirators. The Minister of Police himself, the ferocious Duke de Rovigo, was put in prison, and the Prefect of Paris obeyed the conspirators' orders to prepare a meeting-hall for them. Although the conspiracy was easily defeated by the military commander of Paris, Count Hulin, it had alarming implications. Some of the most senior officials of the Empire had been strangely supine in this crisis, and had ignored the claims of the King of Rome.

Respect for the government began to diminish. For weeks the most popular joke in Paris was:

'Have you heard the news?'

'No.'

'Then you must be in the police.'[25]

When news of the coup reached the Emperor, he decided to leave his army and return to France as soon as possible. He rushed back across Europe through an avenue of dying men. 'Never has a field of battle presented so much horror', wrote Caulaincourt, who accompanied him inside his carriage, with Roustam and two coachmen outside. His household protected the Emperor from the worst horrors. Throughout the retreat, while his soldiers were dying of hunger, cold and despair, or were forced to eat horses which were still alive (they found the liver was best), the Emperor was served with his favourite food: meat, rice and vegetables, washed down by *Chambertin*. While his soldiers were freezing to death, he was wrapped in layers of wool and fur, and a bear-skin. Even this was not enough, and he took half Caulaincourt's bear-skin as well. Despite this cover, icicles formed on their noses, eyebrows and eyelashes. They finally drove into the courtyard of the Tuileries on 20 December 1812. Caulaincourt wrote that he was never so relieved as when he had delivered the Emperor 'safe and sound in his palace'.[26]

The retreat from Moscow was, as Talleyrand said, 'the beginning of the end'. How could an Empire founded by force, and extended by the sword, cope with defeat? Reality now began to destroy the splendid illusions of the Napoleonic court. Many monarchs had had to pay court to Napoleon I in humiliating circumstances, at Paris, Erfurt or Dresden: some were even forced to yield precedence to his extraordinary brothers. They had never forgiven the Emperor for his unending annexations. Now they could be themselves again.

Austria was Napoleon's most persistent enemy, with reserves of resilience which the French Empire never possessed. The Emperor Francis I of Austria was a simple, peaceful monarch, far less capable than Napoleon I; but he had the incomparable advantage that he loved his people, and they loved him. Unlike Napoleon I, who was always surrounded by a display of force, Francis I often went out without guards. There were more cheers for 'Kaiser Franz', when he rode through the streets of Vienna after yet another defeat, than there ever were for his triumphant son-in-law in the streets of Paris. In December 1812, as Napoleon I was dashing back to Paris, Francis I said: 'The time has come when I can show the Emperor of the French who I am', a devastating remark which, as Metternich wrote, needed no comment.[27] The Emperor's domination of Europe had been a temporary illusion killed, like so many of his soldiers, in the Russian snow.

At first the campaign of 1813 in Germany seemed evenly matched. But the Emperor's German allies soon joined the enemy, including the King of Bavaria, who had acquired so much territory through his alliance with Napoleon. The Emperor revealed his true instincts by presenting himself as the defender of the monarchical principle. He asserted that the Tsar and Stein, and the princes who joined them, were betraying themselves by deserting him and appealing to German popular nationalism.[28] It is true that Napoleon I had helped monarchs increase their authority over their subjects, and that the Kings of Bavaria, Saxony and Württemberg owed him their crowns. Most European rulers, however, felt that nationalism and liberalism were easier to cope with than Napoleon I and his hydra-headed family.

In the years 1813–15 the Emperor increasingly used his court officials as political and military agents, as if he felt they were the only people he could trust as his regime became weaker. Aides-de-camp such as Hogendorp, Lemarois and Narbonne were given the most important military commands in Germany. Lemarois reported from Düsseldorf that: 'His Majesty is feared here but everything French is utterly detested.' Michel Radziwill, a chamberlain, helped lead the defence of Danzig. By September 1813, according to the Grand Chamberlain Montesquiou, so many chamberlains had been appointed Prefects, or officers in the army and the National Guard, that not enough were available for service at court. Soon Montesquiou himself and Ségur were sent away from Paris on missions to defend the provinces.

The Emperor even began to employ his wife's ladies-in-waiting as political agents. Madame de

Brignole, a great friend of Cardinal Consalvi, was used to try to negotiate a concordat with the imprisoned Pope in November 1813. In February 1814 the Emperor told the Empress to persuade another of her ladies-in-waiting, the Duchess de Castiglione, to encourage her husband, Marshal Augereau, to fight with greater vigour against the enemy. Only in a desperate situation would the Emperor have condescended to use female influence with one of his own marshals.[29]

While the armies were fighting on the battlefields, the Emperor's courtiers were trying to persuade him to make peace. Each defeat gave them new strength to stand up to him in conversation, and he now occasionally asked their advice. Caulaincourt was acting Grand Marshal of the Palace as well as Grand Equerry for much of 1813 and was almost rude in his attempts to force the Emperor to agree to reasonable terms. The Emperor complained that he treated his sovereign like one of the postilions in the imperial stables. Caulaincourt desired a peace which would save what he and Talleyrand had called 'our dynasty' (and their own honours and power) so much that he held semi-treasonable conversations with foreign diplomats. Some diplomats, including Metternich, came to believe that Caulaincourt welcomed French defeats, in the hope that they would compel the Emperor to make peace. Caulaincourt felt that when the Emperor was victorious he ceased to be reasonable. Clearly the Emperor was losing control of his own court. In November 1813 he was forced to dismiss Bassano, whom public opinion accused of favouring the Emperor's exorbitant territorial claims, and to appoint Caulaincourt as Foreign Minister.[30] The Emperor was no longer an absolute monarch.

Even his military genius could not resist the

Faber du Faur, ***Scene near Pnewa in Russia*** *The Emperor has stopped and is warming himself by a fire. He dashed back to Paris in two weeks, sometimes travelling by carriage, sometimes by sleigh, which was quicker. His campaign household followed behind.*

overwhelming superiority of the Allied forces. On 19 October 1813 his armies were defeated at the battle of Leipzig (his old enemy, General Moreau, who had returned from exile in America to advise Alexander I, was killed by a French bullet). Meanwhile members of his family and their courts were being driven out of their foreign palaces and back to France. Pursued by Wellington, King Joseph had reached the French frontier with a reduced court and baggage-train in July. Only a few German courtiers — such as the Löwensteins — followed King Jerome and Queen Catherine back to France in October 1813. Holland rose to expel the French and restore the House of Orange in November. In order to save his throne Murat joined the Allies in January 1814, just as they were crossing the Rhine into France. His troops moved north towards Lombardy, forcing the Grand Duchess Elisa to flee from Florence on 2 February 1814. Her last words to her ladies-in-waiting were to ask them to use their influence with their husbands to maintain her reforms.

Surrounded by enemy armies and faced with a revival of royalism in France itself, the Emperor realized that the Empress was now a figure of crucial political importance. As a Habsburg, connected to the great family of European Catholic monarchs, and as the mother of the heir to the Empire, she might be a guarantee of its survival. Marie-Louise appeared gentle and artless, but she was in reality a sensible woman who knew how to get what she wanted. She was one of the few people who impressed the Emperor. When in 1811 he had wanted to make his favourite aide-de-camp, the Count de Narbonne, Grand Master of her household, she refused to accept the appointment and he gave in. A woman who could make the Emperor change his mind clearly had a strong personality. As the Allies poured their armies into France — 300,000 allied troops were fighting 50,000 French by March 1814 — she became the focus of mysterious intrigues which were rarely committed to paper.

Gérard, *Queen Hortense and her son* *Queen Hortense was the only member of the imperial family to stay in France in 1814. She accepted the title Duchess de Saint-Leu from Louis XVIII, but her salon became a meeting-place for people hoping for the return of the Emperor. (Coll. S.A.I. Prince Napoleon)*

Like the ill-defined but extremely important 'Queen's party' which emerged at the court of Louis XVI, the intrigues around Marie-Louise produced what was sometimes called the 'Regency party'. Its members believed that peace was impossible under Napoleon I, and that there should be a Regency by the Empress on behalf of her son, who would reign as Napoleon II. The Governess of the Children of France, Madame de Montesquiou, who was devoted to the Emperor and trusted in his genius, wrote with venom in 1817 that 'The Duchess [de Montebello] hated the Emperor and was an ardent member of the party of the regency, always alert, always active, whose head was M. de Talleyrand. This party revived each time the Emperor left the court and simply vegetated when he returned.' Among its members, she claimed, apart from the Duchess de Montebello, were Caulaincourt, Flahault and the First Doctor of the Emperor, Baron Corvisart.[31] The inclusion of the Duchess de Montebello and Baron Corvisart was particularly important in view of their intimacy with the Empress.

The personal antagonism between the Duchess de Montebello and Madame de Montesquiou helped to fuel the Regency party. The Duchess de Montebello was a forceful and outspoken woman, who was devoted to the Empress, but ready to point out her faults. She told Marie-Louise she ate too much and did not inspire enough respect. She also spread wicked stories about the behaviour of Madame de Montesquiou's daughters while under escort by French troops. Corvisart was a great friend of the Duchess de Montebello, and had a long-running feud with Madame de Montesquiou over who had responsibility for the health of the heir to the throne (as many royal doctors had had with royal governesses in the past). It is possible that Corvisart encouraged the Empress to believe that her health was too bad to allow her to sleep with the Emperor and risk having another child (the letters the Empress wrote to the Duchess de Montebello on this subject have disappeared). Certainly Méneval, the Empress's devoted secretary, who was said to be in love with her, wrote in 1815 that 'all means' had been used since 1812 to drive the Emperor and Empress apart.[32]

The Regency party and the court of Marie-Louise were important because Napoleon I had established an authoritarian monarchy. What happened in the antechambers of the Tuileries was more decisive, throughout this period, than what happened in the two chambers of the Senate and the Legislative Body. This was demonstrated at the

New Year reception in the Tuileries in 1814. In a rage the Emperor told the deputies of the Legislative Body, who had begged for peace a few days earlier: 'Everything resides in the throne . . . I alone represent the People . . . France needs me more than I need France.'[33] The next day the Legislative Body was dissolved.

Napoleon I believed in himself, his luck and his Empire so much that he did not yet take the threat of the Bourbons seriously. In 1814 he was most afraid of intrigues around the Empress — and any connection between them and Talleyrand, whom he described in a letter to his brother King Joseph, on 8 February, as 'certainly the greatest enemy of our family, now that fortune has abandoned it'. For Napoleon I politics was not about principles or nations, but a struggle between 'our family' and its enemies. He made King Joseph Lieutenant-General of the government in his absence, under the nominal authority of the Empress as Regent. His fear of the 'Regency party' led him to insist that the Empress, her court and the government should leave Paris if the Allied armies drew near.[34]

As the enemy forces closed in, the Empress reported to the Emperor that few people bothered to come to court. By 29 March the military situation had deteriorated so much that the Empress and the government decided to leave. The little King of Rome shouted as he was carried out of the Tuileries, 'I do not want to leave my house!' Nevertheless the Empress, the King of Rome, innumerable court and government officials and the crown jewels departed in the court carriages. Stendhal noted 'no sign of emotion' from the watching crowd:[35] they did not really care.

Talleyrand had arranged for Rémusat, who was an officer in the National Guard, to compel him to stay. The former Grand Chamberlain, who was still Vice-Grand Elector, was now the senior government official in Paris and the master of the political game. By March it had become clear that Talleyrand could not establish a regency for Napoleon II, controlled by himself, as it is likely he hoped to do. The reason was what he called 'the events of Bordeaux and the general evolution of opinion in France'. Bordeaux had risen in favour of Louis XVIII, whose restoration now seemed, to many Frenchmen, the best hope of peace and prosperity.[36]

Talleyrand himself had been thinking of the Bourbons as a possible solution since 1813 (his uncle was Grand Almoner of the exiled Louis XVIII). A Bourbon supporter, Aimée de Coigny, remembered that one of the arguments she used in their favour was 'the insipid monotony of the court of Bonaparte, enemy of subtlety and good taste'. This is not entirely absurd: good taste and good manners were almost as important as power and money to Talleyrand. In his memoirs he wrote with horror of the 'complete lack of dignity' and 'absurd . . . luxury' of the Bonaparte courts, and regretted their failure to adopt a 'noble simplicity'. He had forgotten that he himself was in part responsible for the errors he deplored.

On 31 March the allied armies entered Paris. As his patrons the Tsar and Metternich had long hoped, Talleyrand could now, working from within the Napoleonic system, depose the Emperor. He installed a provisional government favouring the return of the Bourbons over which he presided himself. By an irony of fate the Emperor was resting at an inn called *La Cour de France* when the news of the fall of Paris reached him: he was soon to find that he had no court left. He shouted: 'My carriage, Caulaincourt! To Paris!' There was no answer. Even Caulaincourt was worn out. General Belliard, assistant to the Emperor's Chief of Staff Berthier, said that there were no more troops and that 'he could not go himself'. The Emperor was compelled by his entourage to retreat to Fontainebleau. They were beginning to act for themselves, as well as to speak their minds.

While the Emperor was at Fontainebleau, the way was clear for Talleyrand in Paris to restore the Bourbons. The Emperor and his dynasty were deposed by a vote of the Senate, organized by Talleyrand, on 2 April. The Tsar and Metternich did not have to do anything. As the Tsar had prophesied at Erfurt six years earlier, they had the last laugh. The Tsar won all hearts in Paris by his affability, and the good behaviour of his troops — very different from the devastation wrought by the French in Moscow. He spent much of his time visiting the palaces and public works restored or erected by the Emperor, and admired the magnificence and perfect condition of the Tuileries. He told its architect, Fontaine, that he could find his way around thanks to the plans and drawings Fontaine had sent him in the years before the invasion of Russia.[37]

Back in Fontainebleau, his favourite palace, the Emperor now faced his moment of truth. He had made his court the most magnificent in Europe, and a centre of power and promotion in his Empire. But the genius of one man, even if he is called Napoleon I, and the allure of his court are not enough to found a regime (as the brief success of the Malet conspiracy had suggested). A constitution which works and independent institutions are more effective. It was desire for them, more than for the Bourbon dynasty, which made Talleyrand and the Senators turn to Louis XVIII.

By 1814 Napoleon had so isolated himself, and was so unpopular, that he could not even secure the loyalty of his court. On the night of 9/10 August 1792, when all Paris had seemed to be marching to dethrone Louis XVI, the palace of the Tuileries had been full of courtiers prepared to die for the King. In contrast, the palace of Fontainebleau began to empty in the second week of April 1814 as courtiers and officers of Napoleon I turned to the rising sun of the Bourbons. They did not feel the bond of loyalty and love which connected royalist courtiers to the King of France, even when fortune was against him.

The property the Emperor had distributed so generously to his courtiers made them determined to keep it, rather than be eternally grateful to their benefactor. The courtier he had rewarded most lavishly of all was Marshal Berthier, Grand Huntsman, Vice-Constable, Major-General of the Grand Army, Prince de Neufchâtel and Wagram, husband of a Bavarian princess, owner of the château of Chambord and a multi-millionaire. But Berthier had been worn out by the Emperor. Their relationship had never really recovered from the trauma of the invasion of Russia. Berthier summed up most courtiers' feelings when he wrote to Caulaincourt (in a letter signed *Alexandre*, since he was still sovereign prince of Neufchâtel) that he wanted to keep his rank and property and that he needed a rest: *'j'ai besoin de repos'*. The Emperor's most intimate personal servants, including Roustam, also deserted. Even his favourite aide-de-camp, Flahault (the previous favourite, Narbonne, had died on campaign in 1813), wrote to his mother from Fontainebleau: 'It was his desire to keep me with him, but I told him that I owed myself to you before everyone.'[38]

The court's desertion disgusted the Emperor, and has inspired the denunciation of high-minded historians. But it is doubtful if many courtiers felt remorse at the time, despite their broken oaths. Many who had devoted the best years of their lives to the Emperor, such as Caulaincourt and Berthier, were disillusioned. The Emperor's egotism and love of war had once been balanced by his genius and success. But since the invasion of Russia, which had been opposed by almost all the court, he appeared to be an autocrat out of touch with reality. Like France itself, the courtiers were worn out. They put peace and the prospect of greater freedom under a constitutional monarch before their oaths to the Emperor. Some of the Emperor's most favoured courtiers rallied to Talleyrand's government. De Pradt, the Almoner, paraded through the streets of Paris distributing Bourbon lilies. Rémusat, the First Chamberlain, helped organize the Paris National Guard. The Duke de Dalberg, husband of a lady-in-waiting, and de Jaucourt, First Chamberlain of King Joseph, served in the Provisional Government.

Back at Fontainebleau, the Emperor could not believe that he had been deposed. He complained that the allied monarchs were behaving like revolutionaries. On 5 April he planned to retreat south, but was forced to abandon the idea by the defection of Marshal Marmont, 'one of my oldest aides-de-camp', who had been encouraged in his disloyalty by General Souham, a former supporter of General Moreau.

Court etiquette and respect for the Emperor now broke down. At 2 am on the morning of 6 April Caulaincourt and Marshals Ney and Macdonald (another former officer of General Moreau) rudely woke the Emperor to urge him to abdicate. The courtiers and officers who were still at Fontainebleau were beginning to speak against him. The terrible void he had created around himself by his rudeness, selfishness and unrelenting ambition was revealed.

Under intense pressure from his entourage, the Emperor abdicated without conditions on 7 April. In return, the Treaty of Fontainebleau of 12 April, which Caulaincourt negotiated with the Tsar, gave the Emperor Elba, the Empress the Duchy of Parma in Italy, and the rest of *la famille* substantial incomes from the French government. No fallen monarch has ever (in theory) been treated so generously. Although he had worked against some of the Emperor's policies, in the crisis of 1814 Caulaincourt proved a devoted personal servant to his master — and, by persuading the Emperor to abdicate, of Tsar Alexander as well.

Meanwhile, Marie-Louise and her enormous treasure-laden court had rumbled from Paris to Blois in the valley of the Loire, and finally to Orléans nearer Paris. King Joseph and King Jerome behaved particularly badly, trying to extract as much money as possible out of the Empress for their 'expenses'. On 7 April the Empress reported to her husband: 'everyone here has lost their head'.

In Fontainebleau the Emperor was still giving orders to the Empress's secretary Méneval and to the commander of the Empress's guard, Count Caffarelli, who was strangely passive throughout this period. On 7 April Caulaincourt ordered the Duchess de Montebello to bring the Empress and her household to Fontainebleau. Napoleon I planned to travel with her and a reduced household from Fontainebleau to Italy. They would proceed slowly, so as not to tire her, using the horses of the imperial stables rather than post-horses. Meanwhile, to her disgust, many of the Empress's courtiers were drifting away: her First Equerry, Prince Aldobrandini, did not even bother to take his leave.[39] Ministers and government officials also deserted and returned to Paris.

The Count d'Artois, the younger brother of Louis XVIII, entered Paris in triumph on 12 April. The collapse of the Empire was so sudden and so dramatic that the Emperor tried to commit suicide that night. He had been appalled by the disloyalty of Marshals Ney, Marmont and Berthier, and was worried about the future of the Empress, their son, and France itself: 'Poor France!' he sighed repeatedly. He could not believe that his magnificent Empire had come to such a dismal end. He was also frightened of what the Provisional Government, and his own ex-subjects, might try to do to him on the way to Elba.

At about three o'clock on the morning of 13 April, he swallowed the capsules of poison which he had kept on his person since the retreat from Moscow. He summoned Caulaincourt for a last conversation. The Grand Equerry was dismayed when he realized what was happening. As the Emperor grew weaker, Caulaincourt tried to go for help. The Emperor clung to him with such force that his coat was almost torn in two. Caulaincourt later wrote: 'His skin was parched and chill; all of a sudden it was covered with an icy sweat; I thought he was about to expire in my arms . . . he called for death more eagerly than anyone has pleaded to live.'

Caulaincourt finally managed to escape to call for help; but what really saved the Emperor was that he threw up most of the poison. After a long wait, while they woke up and dressed themselves, Hubert the Emperor's valet, Constant the First Valet, Yvan the First Surgeon, Turenne the Master of the Wardrobe, Bertrand the Grand Marshal and Bassano arrived. Despite the Emperor's pleas and orders, Yvan refused to obey the Emperor and give him more poison. By seven in the morning the Emperor was better. On his instructions, his courtiers and servants agreed not to mention the suicide attempt. The court had emerged as the guardian of religious and social morality and of the Emperor himself, even to the extent of disobeying his orders. Many people regretted that he had survived, including his own brother Jerome. Like all the family, he blamed the Emperor for the collapse of the Empire.[40]

During this bewildering month, as courtiers and marshals rushed from the Emperor at Fontainebleau to pay their respects to the Count d'Artois in the Tuileries, Napoleon made a fatal blunder. Again allowing his ambition to outweigh his own best interests, he did not personally order the Empress to join him. As their world was collapsing around them, both the Emperor and the Empress turned to her father Francis I of Austria, now the most powerful monarch in Italy. They both felt that if she went to see him while the political situation was still fluid, she might be able to obtain Tuscany instead of Parma.

The Emperor knew that his Empress could not exist outside the only world she knew, the world of courts and palaces. Elba, which had no palaces, was unsuitable for her; even his own courtiers did not want to go there. But if the Empress had Tuscany, next to Elba, she would have splendid palaces and a fine duchy. They could easily visit each other; and the Emperor could see his son.[41] These considerations — the Empress's need for a suitably grand establishment, and the Emperor's desire for her to have Tuscany — led Marie-Louise to go to see her father at Rambouillet on 13 April. In doing so she left the control of Napoleon I and the Imperial Guard for that of Francis I and the Austrian and Russian Guards. She was also open to the influence of the members of her diminished court, who belonged to the Regency party, were hostile to the Emperor and were prepared to accept the Bourbons.

As so often, the correspondence of officials and courtiers is franker than that of the monarchs they served. While France was being inundated by foreign armies, and the Empire was collapsing, the Emperor and Empress maintained a strangely domestic correspondence, full of expressions of love, concern for each other's health and hopes for a reunion. The reality was different. Méneval wrote from Rambouillet on 13 April *in code* to the Emperor's secretary Baron Fain that the Empress was 'in the situation of a prisoner . . . without protection against force and insinuations'.

Méneval meant that the Empress was being urged not to rejoin her husband by the Duchess de Montebello and Corvisart, as well as by Francis I. Corvisart told her, incorrectly, that her health could not stand the journey to Elba. Neither he nor the Duchess liked the idea of life on the small and dreary island. In the end the Empress agreed to go to Vienna. She would only proceed to Italy, and perhaps Elba, after her future was decided in Vienna. She left France with her son on 2 May, having said goodbye to her ladies and the artists Isabey, Gérard and Fontaine at Berthier's château of Grosbois. She was accompanied by sixty-four courtiers and servants, including the Duchess de Montebello, Corvisart, Madame de Montesquiou and Madame de Brignole.[42]

So the Emperor left Fontainebleau without his Empress. The only relics of his magnificent court to accompany him were Bertrand, Generals Drouot and Cambronne of the Imperial Guard, guards, servants, books, liveries and about 3.8 million livres. They moved slowly down to the coast of Provence. When he was surrounded by the Imperial Guard he was cheered. When they left, he met with indifference or, particularly in Provence, hostility. He found it easier to be brave on the battlefield than when faced with the screaming, murderous mobs which threatened his carriage between Avignon and the coast. So he disguised himself in turn as a civilian, a courier and as an officer wearing a strange mixture of Austrian, Prussian and Russian uniforms. (At least the Bourbons, when they fled from France, did not put on foreign uniforms to do so.) One of his couriers, and a Russian officer, bravely consented to play the part of the fallen Emperor.[43] Princess Pauline, who was resting in a château in Provence, was appalled when she saw her brother. Her reproaches made him put on French uniform again.

Napoleon landed in Elba on 3 May, the same day that Louis XVIII, escorted by marshals and ministers, drove into Paris in triumph. When he entered the Tuileries, this fat, pacific monarch went straight to his study and started to issue orders as King. Since he had complete faith in his claim to the throne, he knew that he was in his rightful place. Even Talleyrand, the most disillusioned politician of the age, now Louis XVIII's Foreign Minister, was impressed. And for a time it seemed as if all of France was happy to be ruled by the Bourbons.

The Emperor lost the Kingdom of Italy at the same time as the French Empire. In 1813–14 the forces of Austria and its ally Murat were too strong for the Viceroy Prince Eugene. Moreover he was not popular. His French aides-de-camp and officials were detested; he himself was known to be making a fortune out of the Italian civil list and was believed not to like Italians. The Grand Chancellor of the Kingdom wrote to him of the 'profound and universal hatred against the French' in Italy. Like Kings Joseph-Napoleon in Spain and Jerome-Napoleon in Westphalia, Prince Eugene-Napoleon had no roots, because he had not adopted the nationality of the people he was ruling. For a few days in late April, backed by a group of army officers, he tried to become King of Italy but he had no real support. He left Mantua on 27 April and disappeared from Italian politics.[44]

Wars and taxation had made the Empire so unpopular that in May there was enthusiasm for the restoration of the old sovereigns, who returned to Turin, Florence and Rome as well as Paris. The reaction was more spontaneous and unanimous than anything the Bonapartes had evoked. Everywhere the monumental statues of Napoleon were toppled with joy. It seemed as if the old dynasties were bringing in a new era of freedom, prosperity and peace.

While the Emperor and his court were trying to adapt to life on Elba, the Empress arrived at her childhood home of Schönbrunn. She considered herself 'a prisoner' and was still corresponding with her husband. She showed her loyalty to the Empire by living and eating with her Napoleonic court rather than with her Austrian family. Her servants continued to wear Napoleonic livery, and her carriages to be decorated with Napoleonic emblems.

Vienna was crowded with delegates to the Congress of Vienna, who were creating a peace settlement more lasting than any imposed by Napoleon I. The Austrian court was entertaining troops of princes and diplomats (including Prince Eugene) on a scale which outshone even the most splendid entertainments of the Empire. But Marie-Louise stayed quietly in her apartment in Schönbrunn. Her behaviour gave the Emperor reason to hope that she would visit Elba in the summer. She certainly planned to reach Parma in September and sent de Bausset, a Prefect of the Palace who now served in her household, to prepare a palace for her arrival.

Indeed, the Empress was still so Bonapartist that in July, against the advice of the Duchess de Montebello, she went to Aix-en-Savoie in France for a cure. While there Marie-Louise still corresponded with her husband. She spent much of the time embroidering chair-covers for his study on Elba, and she received news of the Emperor from valets and officers in the Imperial Guard who had been on the island. In addition Corvisart came to see her with a plan to make Fouché, the most influential ex-revolutionary in France, the Governor of the King of Rome — further confirmation of the ambitions of the 'Regency party'.

Horace Vernet, *The Emperor's farewell to the Imperial Guard, 20 April 1814* *In the courtyard of Fontainebleau, after a moving speech, the Emperor is about to kiss General Petit as he leaves the palace for Elba after his abdication. A few loyal courtiers are present. The white-haired Duke de Bassano and Baron Fain (in glasses) watch immediately behind their master. General Drouot and Bertrand are fifth and sixth from the right. This picture, painted in 1825 for the Bonapartist Count de Chambure, is one of the most famous of all representations of a historical event.*

But the Emperor and the Empress were bound to be driven apart: the wonder is that she remained loyal as long as she did. Her desire to have her own duchy in Italy — 'Parma or nothing is my motto', she wrote to the Duchess de Montebello — inevitably put her in the power of Austria, which now controlled northern Italy. She was also bound to be influenced by the gradual re-establishment of contact with her Austrian friends and relations. Moreover her own court was hostile to the Emperor. Of the people who lived and ate meals with her after the departure of the Duchess de Montebello and Corvisart in June, both Madame de Brignole, a brilliantly manipulative friend of Talleyrand, and de Bausset, fat, sycophantic and ambitious, disliked the Emperor. In the Empress's own salon de Bausset said that the Emperor had slept with all her ladies-in-waiting in return for a cashmere shawl; the Duchess de Montebello alone had required three. Méneval and Madame de Montesquiou were the only courtiers still loyal to the Emperor.[45]

After her cure at Aix, love as well as ambition and environment turned the Empress against her husband. The Habsburgs, who were famous for using royal marriages to further their ambitions, now turned to seduction. Francis I sent a handsome, charming, one-eyed general, Count Neipperg, to escort his daughter to Aix. Neipperg's instructions included the order, in writing, to use 'every means' to stop the Empress from going to Elba. On the way back to Vienna, she was forced by a storm to take refuge in a mountain inn. That night she became Neipperg's mistress. She now had to choose between her lover, her father and her duchy on one side, and her husband (busy decorating a salon in Elba with frescoes symbolizing conjugal constancy) on the other. Clearly the choice was not difficult. She remained in correspondence with her husband until January. But by October Neipperg was officially a member of her household — and a constant visitor to her apartment in Schönbrunn.

In January another link with the past went when she changed her livery from Napoleonic green and gold to brown. She decided to organize her court at Parma according to Austrian rather than French etiquette. In this way, she told the Duchess de Montebello, she could combine the advantages of private and royal life: she would only see her court when she wanted to, and at ceremonies.[46] Even though Napoleonic etiquette had been so strict and Marie-Louise had spent most of the day secluded in her private apartments, she had seen too much of her courtiers for her own liking. As other monarchs had found out, only the most rigid etiquette gave effective protection from demanding and critical courtiers.

While Marie-Louise was settling down in Schönbrunn and the Emperor was reorganizing the island of Elba, the courtiers they had left behind in France were adapting to the new regime. The Emperor himself had told his courtiers at Fontainebleau that everything was finished and that they should serve their country — in other words the government of Louis XVIII.

Indeed, for many Napoleonic courtiers the change of government was a relief. By 1814 the Empire had become a nightmare of war and fear. The Emperor himself saw a letter which revealed many people's inner feelings about him. One recently created Napoleonic countess wrote to another in April 1814: 'God be praised, we will be real countesses, now that we are free of that man!' The court of Louis XVIII, which was partly organized according to Napoleonic etiquette, satisfied many Napoleonic aristocrats. All the marshals except Davout went there to be presented. Marshal Berthier, the Grand Huntsman, continued to run the hunt under Louis XVIII: the King liked him and made him a Captain of the King's Bodyguards as well.

The Duchess de Montebello coolly wrote to Marie-Louise about her forthcoming presentation to the King. What she dreaded was not the display of disloyalty but the terrible draughts in the Tuileries, from which, she reminded her mistress, they had both suffered so much. Even Maréchale Ney, who is often said to have returned from the Bourbons' court weeping with humiliation, in fact wrote to Louis XVIII that both she and her husband had been proud to say they were well treated by the King and his family. According to Madame de Staël, if only the King had made all the Napoleonic courtiers Gentlemen of the Chamber or ladies-in-waiting at his own court, they would have been satisfied.[47]

However, the court was one of the few institutions in France which was transformed in 1814. Many of the courtiers who had served the Bourbons before 1792 returned to the Tuileries from their *hôtels* in the Faubourg Saint-Germain or their estates in the country at the same time as the King. The Marquis de Dreux-Brézé, the Grand Master of Ceremonies who had ordered the Deputies of the Third Estate to disperse in 1789, when Louis XVI was trying to recover control of the Revolution, resumed his office in 1814, to the chagrin of Ségur. The Archbishop of Reims, Talleyrand's uncle and

Louis XVIII's Grand Almoner, moved into what had been the offices of the Council of State in the Tuileries. The entire royal family, with their households, came to live in the palace. So empty under the Emperor, the Tuileries was now packed from the attics to the basement. A different style of court had come to Paris, more domestic, more religious and older than the court of Napoleon I. For a time, as the cheers for the King on his way to Mass demonstrated, the court of Louis XVIII seemed to be more popular as well.

After the first enthusiasm for the restoration of the Bourbons and the return of peace wore off, however, some Napoleonic court officials did form a nucleus of discontented Bonapartists. To their dismay they no longer monopolized the top of the social and political ladder, but had to share it with the royalist aristocracy. The royalists were just as ambitious as the Bonapartists, and hundreds of royalists received unjustified promotions in the army in 1814. Even worse, with the collapse of the Napoleonic Empire, and the loss of all the French conquests since 1792 (including Belgium and the left bank of the Rhine), Napoleonic courtiers lost their *dotations* on the Domaine Extraordinaire, and so suffered a catastrophic fall in income.

The diary of Miss Burgoyne, one of the thousands of British visitors who flooded into Paris once the war was over, gives a vivid picture of what political change could mean in personal terms for a Napoleonic courtier. Her family wanted to rent the *hôtel* of the Duke de Rovigo, the Emperor's Minister of Police, who could no longer afford to live in it. His beautiful wife, a former lady-in-waiting of the Empress (and mistress of the Emperor), showed them around in December. The *hôtel* was luxurious, packed with pictures of the Emperor and the imperial family. The Duchess sang the praises of the fallen Emperor. Miss Burgoyne concludes: 'I rather liked her and she acquitted herself as well as possible in the novel situation of a Duchess become a lodging-letter.' One wonders if the Duchess liked *her* very much, or if there was any way that the Rovigos and other ambitious Bonapartists, such as the Bassanos or Flahault, could ever have been reconciled to the government of Louis XVIII, under which they suffered such a dramatic loss of status and income.

In the autumn of 1814 Queen Hortense, who had accepted the title of Duchess de Saint-Leu from Louis XVIII, reopened her salon. A British admirer, who later had an affair with Maréchale Ney, wrote that it was 'by far the most agreeable house I have seen in Paris'.[48] Although Hortense also received royalists, it soon became a centre for discontented Bonapartists such as her lover Flahault, and a former aide-de-camp of Prince Eugene, Count de La Bédoyère. She claimed to dislike politics, but she later admitted to the Tsar that her friends had spoken of their 'hopes' and 'interests' in her salon. They also drew caricatures of Louis XVIII, the King whose favours Hortense had accepted and whose protection she implored in her disputes with her husband. The intrigues which helped prepare the return of the Emperor from Elba still remain a mystery. But Napoleon did say later that Flahault had sent a message to him on Elba that 'La Bédoyère at Queen Hortense's had declared that he would go over to me' — as he did the following spring.[49] Like the salon of the Princess of Thurn and Taxis at Erfurt in 1808, the salon of Queen Hortense in Paris in 1814–15 played an important role in politics — more important than the Chamber of Deputies which, although unchanged since the Empire, joyfully accepted all measures proposed by Louis XVIII's ministers.

The salon of Queen Hortense was only one centre of discontent in France in the autumn of 1814. Other Bonapartists in touch with the Emperor were Marshal Davout, the Duke de Rovigo and the Duke de Bassano. The Emperor had at first appeared to be happy ruling Elba and improving his 'palaces'. But he was soon in financial difficulties. The French government never paid him the pension he had been promised. He switched from his favourite *Chambertin* to *vin du pays* to save money, and began to think of making another bid for the throne of France. Officials of the court and guard were now the Emperor's sole political agents. Bertrand, Grand Marshal of the Palace, was his chief minister. Captains Loubers and Hurault de Sorbée of the Imperial Guard and Cipriani, a *maître d'hôtel* from Corsica, were his political agents and spies on the Continent.

Napoleon's decision to try his luck again and leave for France on the night of 26 February 1815 was probably a surprise, even to Bertrand. He had a smooth crossing and landed between Cannes and Antibes on 1 March, accompanied by 900 guards and a few courtiers. Among the first people he talked to were a former ordonnance officer, the Prince of Monaco, and a former footman in the imperial stables. They told him news of his court and the people respectively. The footman assured the Emperor that France was waiting for him as eagerly as the Jews for the Messiah; the Prince of Monaco was less certain.[50]

On 4 March, La Bédoyère was, as promised, the

first commanding officer to lead his regiment over to the Emperor. In one of the most dramatic moments in French history, Napoleon swept up eastern France in triumph, seducing people by his glamour, and by his promises that the Empress would soon be joining him with the Allies' approval. They were also won over by his exploitation of a growing fear that the émigrés and the priests wanted the restoration of the old regime. It appeared that the Emperor was more liberal than in the past, even revolutionary. However, his courtiers knew better: Bertrand refused to countersign a decree confiscating the property of leading royalists. On 20 March the Emperor reached Fontainebleau. He was soon joined by Caulaincourt. That evening he returned to an extraordinary welcome in the Tuileries.

The King had fled in the night of 19/20 March, telling weeping royalists that he would soon be back. He had been in such a hurry that he left some of his personal possessions and papers behind. Some servants only found out that he had gone when they woke up the next morning. They left the Tuileries, with hastily packed parcels, as soon as they could.

All over Paris, white cockades were being replaced by tricolours, and Bourbon lilies by Napoleonic violets. Nevertheless many people remained royalists, in the belief that Louis XVIII stood for peace and constitutional government. Moreover, as Fontaine (who was a dedicated Bonapartist) recorded, the King 'by the appearance of kindness, and affable manners, had won the hearts of the greater number'.

On the morning of 20 March, although one crowd was shouting '*Vive l'Empereur!*' in the courtyard between the Tuileries and the Louvre, another was shouting '*Vive le Roi!*' on the other side of the palace.[51] France was divided, but the Emperor had clearly won the throne for the time being. Later in the day a mob attempted to sack the palace, but was defeated by the National Guard, the Paris middle classes in arms. The Emperor's ministers, headed by the faithful Bassano, then arrived and summoned the courtiers to return to the Tuileries. During the afternoon and evening, chamberlains, ladies-in-waiting, *maîtres d'hôtel*

Steuben, ***The Emperor's return from Elba*** *Outside Grenoble, the Emperor's magic works on the troops sent to oppose him. He reached Paris without a shot being fired.*

and valets drifted back to the palace. They were wearing their old imperial uniforms, which had wisely not been thrown away. Queen Julie, Queen Hortense, and the ravishing Duchesses de Bassano, de Frioul, d'Istrie and de Rovigo appeared in the state apartments in full court dress. They spent the long hours waiting for the Emperor unpicking the Bourbon lilies which had been sewn over the Bonaparte bees in the carpets. The carpets, like the palace itself, rapidly became imperial again.

As night fell, candles were lit all over the palace. Finally, at nine in the evening, to a roar of adoration from the soldiers on guard outside, the Emperor swept back like a fantastic apparition. His delirious supporters carried him up the staircase and into the state apartments. Marchand, his First Valet, wrote: 'You could not believe another sovereign had inhabited the palace; the court officials and servants were at their posts; it seemed as if His Majesty had simply returned from a voyage.' Next evening La Bédoyère, promoted aide-de-camp of the Emperor, attended a celebration dinner in the house of Queen Hortense.[52]

It seemed as if the reign of Louis XVIII had been nothing but a bad dream. There were fervent cries of '*Vive l'Empereur!*' at the daily parades in the courtyard of the Tuileries. As Napoleon later recalled on Saint-Helena, his *levers* were at first so crowded that he felt exhausted. It is not true that the Emperor had lost his support among the nobility. Although about half his court (including Berthier and Rémusat) now supported Louis XVIII, those courtiers who stayed loyal to the Emperor were as aristocratic as ever. The Emperor remembered with satisfaction that Ségur's heart had remained 'pure and shining with the most sincere attachment for the Emperor'. Ségur's daughter-in-law, Madame Octave de Ségur, more faithful to her Emperor than to her husband, broke with her lover Count Molé because he did not share the family's adoration of the Emperor. Napoleon I praised the Grand Chamberlain Montesquiou because 'his conduct had been constantly noble and that of a grateful and devoted subject'. He wrote with admiration of the 'truly French feelings' of other loyal chamberlains who served at court after his return, such as de Beauvau, de Choiseul and de Marmier. Even Count de Béarn, whose wife was a

Heim, *The Emperor's return to the Tuileries, 20 March 1815* *The court is waiting for the Emperor at the top of the staircase. But his enemies said that he returned like a thief in the night.*

Martinet, ***The 'Champ de Mai', 1 June 1815*** *The troops are swearing loyalty to the Emperor and the new Constitution. There was considerable enthusiasm at the ceremony on the Champ de Mars in Paris. But the Emperor's enemies were massing their armies on the frontiers of France.*

lady-in-waiting of the daughter of Louis XVI, the Duchess d'Angoulême, served the Emperor as a chamberlain during the period which, from its short duration, has become known as the Hundred Days.[53]

Although there was a revival of revolutionary sentiment in parts of France, and the *Marseillaise* was heard in the courtyard of the Tuileries, the Emperor was determined to remain the lofty, grandiose monarch he had been in the past. At the grand review and proclamation of the new, more liberal constitution on the parade-ground of the Champ de Mars on 1 June, and on other occasions, he insisted on wearing his extraordinary *Petit Costume* rather than the popular uniform of the Paris National Guard.

Byron's friend John Cam Hobhouse, who was an admirer of Napoleon like many English Whigs, saw the Emperor proceed to the ceremony in a 'large gilt coach, with glass panels, surmounted by an immense gilt crown, nearly covering the whole top of the body'. Pages clung to the carriage, which was 'drawn by eight milk white horses, dressed in lofty plumes of white, each led by a groom who scarcely could hold him down. Napoleon was distinctly seen through the glass panels, in his plumage-covered bonnet and imperial mantle; he bowed as he passed round the amphitheatre, to the shouts of the soldiers and the people.' He then sat on a throne on a raised platform. Around him were his brothers (including Lucien), Caulaincourt and Ségur. After Mass performed by the new First Almoner (de Pradt had been dismissed), deputations of the electors of the Empire and the Emperor himself swore fidelity to the Constitution. The Emperor made a speech in which he proclaimed: 'Emperor, Consul, Soldier, I owe everything to the people.'

But for many people his costume, and soon his acts, spoke louder than his words. To the fury of the Chamber of Representatives, he tried to communicate with them through a chamberlain. This caused 'the most violent murmurs'. 'Many members rose at once; some spoke from their places, others struggled to reach the tribune. At last a member declared a chamberlain a very unfit channel of official correspondence between the Emperor and the representatives of the people.'[54] This attempt to interpose a court official between the monarch and the legislature was a decisive step in turning the Chamber against the Emperor, as it had been when Louis XVI had behaved in a similar way at the opening of the States General in 1789.

The Emperor was not destined to remain on the throne for long. Half of France, and a far larger proportion of the élite of birth and wealth, supported Louis XVIII. Napoleon had appointed Fouché as Minister of Police instead of Rovigo, in order to win the ex-revolutionaries' support. But Fouché did not believe in the future of the regime, and was in touch with Louis XVIII and Metternich. The plebiscite over the new Constitution produced the miserable result of 1.4 million or 21 per cent in favour, less than half the figure in the plebiscites of 1802 and 1804. Moreover, all Europe was arming against Napoleon. He was an international outlaw; and the Empress refused to return to France.

She had wept for hours when she heard that the Emperor had landed. She had no desire to leave her safe and satisfying life at Schönbrunn, with the prospect of a court of her own at Parma, for the unending drama of her husband's court. The Emperor sent a chamberlain, the Baron de Stassart (who had been one of his secret agents at the Congress of Vienna), and his favourite aide-de-camp Flahault to Vienna to persuade his wife to return. But they never managed to see her.

Madame de Montesquiou, still passionately Bonapartist and still hoping the Empress and her beloved King of Rome would return to France, was dismissed by Marie-Louise, with assurances of esteem and regret, at the end of April. Méneval left in early May and was able to inform the Emperor of the transformation in his wife's heart and mind. Her servants were still enthusiastic supporters of the Emperor: indeed they had known when he would leave Elba.[55] But they had no influence over their mistress. Her love for Neipperg was heightened by fears for his safety when he joined the Austrian armies fighting Murat in May. Alarmed that he was about to be deposed in favour of Ferdinand IV, Murat had marched north from Naples in the first military attempt to create a united Italy. He was easily beaten by Austria, fled, and was executed four months later during an attempt to recover his throne. Francis I had defeated Napoleon I and his dynasty in the struggle for control of Italy and Germany, as well as of Marie-Louise and her son.

The Austrian court was such a forceful influence that it effortlessly turned 'Napoleon II' (retitled the Duke of Reichstadt) into a loyal Austrian officer, until his death in 1832. In a similar way the Emperor's most useful marshal, Berthier, was taken over by his wife's family the Wittelsbachs. In April 1815 he refused to rejoin the Emperor. He went to Bavaria, heartbroken at the prospect of another war and another invasion of France. Shortly afterwards he fell to his death from a window (some people believe that he was pushed). He is buried with the kings of Bavaria.

Austria, Russia, Prussia and Britain were massing their armies against France. Wellington had taken command in the Low Countries. Napoleon I had no alternative but war. He left for the Belgian frontier on 12 June, accompanied by Bertrand and his campaign household. Flahault and La Bédoyère were two of the aides-de-camp in waiting. It is said that Napoleon was so confident of victory that he had a proclamation ready, countersigned Bertrand, Grand Marshal of the Palace and dated 19 June, 'from our imperial palace of Laeken'. But he was soon to leave the world of palaces forever. On 18 June he was defeated at Waterloo. As he bolted back to Paris he consulted his courtiers — Bertrand, Gourgaud, Drouot and others — on what he should do. They had little faith in his cause, and advised him to abdicate. Although peasants and soldiers along the route were still crying '*Vive l'Empereur!*', and his army was far from annihilated, the opinions of the court were more important than the cries of the people.[56]

On 21 June the Emperor reached Paris: he went not to the Tuileries, embodiment of power and splendour, but to the Elysée, as if he knew he was about to leave the royal world. At the Elysée, Bassano and Caulaincourt also advised him to abdicate. When they heard of his defeat, the two Chambers turned against the Emperor. La Fayette made a famous speech, on the evening of 21 June, claiming that 3 million Frenchmen had died for the Emperor from Lisbon to Moscow (the real figure is nearer 900,000), and that France had done enough for him. One of his own aides-de-camp, Count Durosnel, who had so ruthlessly suppressed the bread riot at Caen in 1812, and had been Governor of Dresden in 1813, prepared to defend the Chamber of Representatives with the National Guard should the Emperor try to close it.[57] As in 1814, the moment Napoleon was defeated, he lost the support of the élite. On 22 June he abdicated in favour of his son. A Commission of Government was formed, headed by Fouché. A few loyal courtiers in the Chamber of Peers, Flahault, La Bedoyère and Ségur, spoke in favour of 'Napoleon II'. But 'Napoleon II' was in Vienna, and Louis XVIII was on the road to Paris again.

The Elysée was now emptying as fast as Fontainebleau had done in 1814. Napoleon's chamberlains, Montesquiou and Beauvau, threw coins to the crowds outside to encourage them to cry '*Vive l'Empereur!*'. But most other courtiers found compelling reasons for absence. Exceptions were the Bassanos, Flahault, La Bédoyère, Las Cases, the Duchess de Vicence and a few ordonnance officers. On 25 June, at the suggestion of the Commission of Government which now controlled Paris, the Emperor left the Elysée for Malmaison. Queen Hortense received him, in the house where the Empress Josephine had died a year before. The following days were passed in farewells and preparations for the next journey. The Emperor transferred six million francs from the civil list to his private account with the banker Lafitte. Bertrand asked the Emperor's Treasurer Ballouhey to send horses, footmen, porcelain, linen, furniture and a complete library to the United States, where they planned to live.[58]

Soon the delay in the Emperor's departure began to irritate the government. Everyone wanted to be rid of the man who, by his return from Elba, had brought another catastrophic invasion on France. Foreign armies were spreading across the country. Towns and departments all over France were turning to Louis XVIII as the inevitable solution. Davout, the most Bonapartist of the marshals and a Colonel-General of the Imperial Guard, threatened to arrest the Emperor with his own hands if he did not leave at once. On 29 June he left Malmaison for Rambouillet, where he spent his last night in a palace. The next day, on 30 June, he left the golden world of the palaces of the Ile-de-France for ever, and took the road to the Atlantic coast.

He was followed by his brother Joseph, the Duke de Rovigo, several courtiers and a large staff of servants from the different departments of the court (among them was a fanatical Bonapartist groom Louvel, who had been on Elba and later assassinated a nephew of Louis XVIII, the Duke de Berri). The Emperor arrived at Rochefort on the coast on 3 July. It was difficult to find a boat to take him to America because the British Government, alerted by Fouché, was tightening its naval blockade. Napoleon decided to surrender to Britain. Like Louis XVI planning his flight to Varennes, the Emperor was unwilling to make a quick escape on his own. Joseph did so, and was able to enjoy a prosperous exile in the United States. But the Emperor either felt such an exit was undignified, or was unwilling to abandon his courtiers to the government of Louis XVIII.

As well as impeding him from escaping to America, his court may have persuaded him to surrender to Britain. One of his aides-de-camp, General Lallemand, wrote that 'Several officers who accompa-

ABOVE **Marchand, *View of Longwood on Saint-Helena*** *The Emperor's court has shrunk to a house on an island in the Atlantic. The Emperor is standing at the entrance to the apartment where he was to die in 1821. On the left are Madame Bertrand and her children, on the right the two priests sent by Cardinal Fesch. Chinese labourers are digging in the garden. Marchand gave this drawing to Napoleon on New Year's Day 1820.*

RIGHT **Steuben, *The Emperor dictating his memoirs to Baron Gourgaud*** *Gourgaud left Saint-Helena in 1818, furious that the Emperor preferred Montholon. Steuben was one of the dedicated artists who continued to paint Napoleonic pictures (see also illustration on page 191) after Napoleon's fall.*

nied the Emperor and especially those who, being trusted by him, had free access to him and influence over him' persuaded the Emperor to hand himself over to Britain. Lallemand was referring to Bertrand (whose wife had British blood), the First Ordonnance Officer Gourgaud, the chamberlain Las Cases (who had spent years in London as an émigré) and Rovigo. They felt that the Emperor could trust to British laws and hospitality.[59]

The Emperor selected twenty-five courtiers and servants to accompany him in exile, of whom the most important were Bertrand, two chamberlains whom the Emperor hardly knew, Counts de Las Cases and de Montholon, and Gourgaud. Many more had come to Rochefort because, in contrast to 1814, they knew that they now had nothing to hope for from Louis XVIII's government. Then, on 15 July, the Emperor handed himself over to Captain Maitland of the *Bellerophon*. He was now a prisoner, and was told that he would be taken to Saint-Helena. The illusion of splendour and deference with which his court had surrounded him was extinguished.

On the long and depressing voyage to Saint-Helena, Napoleon was treated by his British captors as a captured general rather than as a royal personage. Despite this loss of status, which must have been shattering after eleven years as Emperor, he seemed easy and charming. 'His conduct was invariably that of a gentleman . . . . His manners were extremely pleasing and affable', wrote Captain Maitland. Clearly he was prepared to expend as much charm on his British captors as he had once shown to the crowned heads of Europe. Only a few recorded the other side of his character, his 'most overbearing' behaviour to his courtiers, and their 'servility . . . more abject than an Englishman who has not witnessed it can possibly conceive'. The ship landed at Saint-Helena on 17 October.

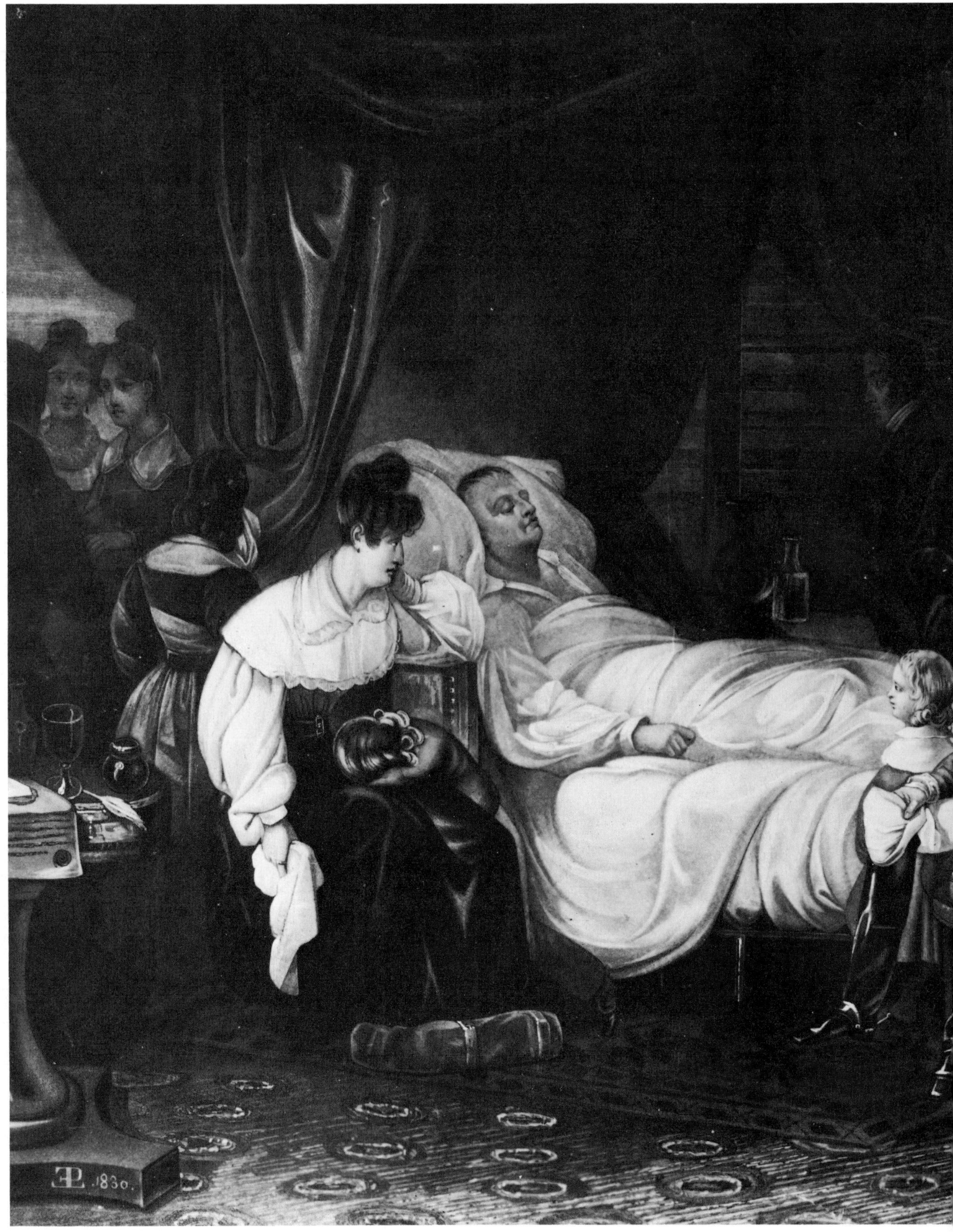
1830.

On this storm-swept rock, rising sheer out of the ocean a thousand miles from the nearest continent, the Emperor kept a minuscule but useful household. Bertrand, as Grand Marshal of the Palace, supervised the Emperor's policies — in this case his war of nerves with the British Governor, Sir Hudson Lowe. Montholon was in charge of interior domestic details, Gourgaud of the stables. They lived in an isolated house called Longwood, which was infested by rats (the Secretary of State for the Colonies, Lord Bathurst, remarked that the rats' invasion of Longwood disproved their reputation for sagacity). Lord Roseberry wrote: 'The lord of so many palaces, who had slept as a conqueror in so many palaces not his own, was now confined to two small rooms of equal size about fourteen foot by twelve, and ten or eleven high.' They were furnished with a camp bed, a table, bookshelves, and portraits of Marie-Louise and the King of Rome.[60]

However, the Emperor had kept some relics of his former grandeur. The Emperor's stable still contained *Vizir*, a horse which had been given to him by the Ottoman Sultan in 1807. His table gleamed with silver and Sèvres. When Sir George Bingham, Colonel of the 53rd foot regiment which guarded Napoleon, came to dine, he could not believe the beauty of the Sèvres coffee cups decorated with views of Egypt, or the formality of the meal. The Emperor was more attached to his possessions on Saint-Helena than he had been on the throne. He told one of his valets: 'Formerly I paid no attention to the beautiful objects I used; but now that I no longer have them I seem to miss them.'[61]

The Emperor used his courtiers on Saint-Helena as political instruments, as he had on the throne. Through them he could publicize the conditions under which he was being kept prisoner, and rewrite history. Las Cases, who became his favourite, was a skilful writer with a sense of history. He was a noble and an émigré who had followed the Emperor to Saint-Helena out of a mixture of loyalty and love of adventure. His *Mémorial de Sainte*

Steuben, ***The Emperor on his death-bed*** *The Emperor is surrounded by a small band of faithful courtiers and servants. Montholon sits, and Bertrand stands, at the foot of the bed. Madame Bertrand weeps beside the Emperor. This print was soon circulated in France.*

Hélène, published in 1823, was one of the most popular and influential books of the nineteenth century. (It sold so well that Las Cases was able to build an entire street, the Rue Las Cases in the Faubourg Saint-Germain, out of the proceeds.) It is as great a tribute to a courtier's ability to distort reality as any flattering ode.

Las Cases presents the Emperor (with the help of forged letters) as a friend of peace, a defender of the different nationalities of Europe, a representative of 'the principles of 1789' and a guardian of religion. He wrote that 'Napoleon was the type, the standard, the prince of liberal principles. If his actions occasionally seem to have been in contradiction, it is because circumstances were too powerful for him.' This fantasy Napoleon was immensely useful in creating the popular Bonapartism which was to help sweep the Emperor's nephew to power in 1848: few courtiers have done more for their master than Las Cases did for Napoleon.

Occasionally, however, even Las Cases' account cannot disguise the intoxicated autocrat. In March 1816 he records that the Emperor said: 'There was a time when one could have said that all the Courts of Europe had been brought to Paris to compose that of the Tuileries, which became the most brilliant and the most numerous which had ever been seen .... Extraordinary grandeur and magnificence were displayed there.'[62]

Stuck on a dismal island, the court inevitably became a centre of envy, hate and intrigue. Las Cases' favoured position irritated his colleagues. To their joy he left with his manuscript in 1816: it is possible that he had arranged his own expulsion. After his departure Gourgaud and Montholon were rivals for the favour of the Emperor. Gourgaud was furious that he was forced to yield precedence to Montholon, a mere chamberlain, although he was First Ordonnance Officer — a distant echo of the tensions between soldiers and civilians which had occasionally surfaced under the Empire. The Emperor preferred Montholon because he was more agreeable and intelligent than Gourgaud. He also let his wife become the Emperor's mistress. She bore a daughter, probably by the Emperor, who was christened Joséphine-Napoléone. Having unsuccessfully challenged Montholon to a duel, Gourgaud left in disgust in 1818, eager to inform the British government of the intrigues of the court of Longwood. Madame de Montholon departed in the same year.[63]

The Emperor was left with Bertrand and Montholon. Montholon was now the favourite. Like most monarchs, Napoleon I expected total devotion, and he did not like the fact that Bertrand lived in his own house with his wife and family. He only attended a few meals with the Emperor, and often made critical remarks, such as 'Your Majesty is quite wrong not to follow my advice.' As the Emperor pointed out, this would have been unthinkable at the Tuileries. Montholon ate almost every meal with the Emperor and behaved towards him like an unusually devoted son.

In reality Montholon, as well as Bertrand, was planning to leave the unbearable island. He stayed on, as the Emperor knew, partly in order to ensure that he was the main beneficiary of the Emperor's will: at Longwood, as at the Tuileries, the court was a means to wealth and power rather than an end in itself.[64] The Emperor's most devoted attendants, who did their best to look after him, were his servants Marchand, Saint-Denis and Noverraz (who had helped save him from the mob at Orgon in Provence in April 1814). But servants could not be companions for an Emperor.

In the last years the atmosphere at Longwood grew even worse. The Emperor was, literally, bored to death. The priests and doctor sent by Cardinal Fesch in his capacity as Grand Almoner were no distraction: the Cardinal, now quite mad, believed that his nephew was no longer on Saint-Helena and so had sent second-rate people. The Emperor needed distractions. He was enraged when neither Bertrand nor his doctor Antommarchi would arrange for Madame Bertrand to become his mistress.[65]

Napoleon was losing the will to live. In the past, like his courtiers, he had always worn uniform. When he had first arrived on the island, he had continued to wear the uniform of the Chasseurs of the Imperial Guard. Then he had adopted the coat of the Imperial Hunt. Now he wore a plain tailcoat like everyone else.

He did not have long to enjoy the comfortable new house supplied by the British government, which was finally ready in early 1820. He took to his bed in March 1821, ill with a stomach ulcer, but above all with the wish to die. His last dictations to his courtiers dealt with his plans for Versailles and the National Guard. He died, surrounded by courtiers and servants, on 5 May 1821 and was buried in the uniform of the Chasseurs of the Imperial Guard. As Grand Marshal of the Palace, Bertrand witnessed the Emperor's will and issued his death certificate. Montholon, Bertrand, Marchand and Las Cases were the principal beneficiaries of the will.[66] In death as in life, his court surrounded the Emperor.

8

The Return to Grandeur

'When I think of the great Emperor, in my mind's eye it is summer again, all gold and green.'

Heine

Napoleon left France weaker and smaller than he found it. In contrast, the rival monarchies of Austria, Prussia and Russia were more powerful after the Empire than before. In addition the sea of blood and tears spread through Europe by Napoleon's armies ensured that after 1815 France did not command the respect and influence it once had. Paradoxically, however, as France grew weaker, the cult of the Emperor under whom it had once been so powerful grew stronger. People who would have found him intolerable as a living monarch praised him as an immortal hero. He was more powerful dead than alive.

The return of the Emperor's remains from Saint-Helena was the culmination of this retrospective cult. On 15 December 1840 a magnificent procession escorted the hearse through the streets of Paris to the Invalides. Victor Hugo wrote that so many people were lining the route that it seemed as if the entire city had been tilted to one side. The saluting cannon, the winter sunshine, the marching troops and the sight of enemy flags won on the battlefields of Europe draping the hearse, made it the most dramatic of all the great Napoleonic ceremonies.

Napoleon was buried not as a soldier or a consul but as an Emperor. The hearse was drawn by sixteen horses (eight more than for a King) and escorted by footmen in green and gold imperial livery. It was followed by marshals and generals, by the surviving officials of the Emperor's household (including Bertrand and Gourgaud) and by soldiers of his guard in their old uniforms. This posthumous consecration as a monarch showed that one of the Emperor's most important legacies was his monarchy. The Emperor had fallen but his dynasty, courtiers and style of monarchy survived.

After the Hundred Days many of Napoleon's courtiers, such as the Montesquiou and Caulaincourt, retired to their estates to write their memoirs. They were so exhausted by the Empire that they wanted a quiet life. Others, for example the two chamberlains Rambuteau and Bondy who had had such brilliant careers under the Empire, remained hostile to the government of Louis XVIII and refused to go to the Tuileries. They lived in a world of their own, sharing the same memories and police surveillance, and going to the same parties. At a ball given in 1820 by a former aide-de-camp of the Emperor, Duke Charles de Plaisance, it was noted that: 'most of the guests came from the former court of the emperor'.[1]

Louis XVIII was succeeded on his death in 1824 by his brother Charles X. Charming, self-confident and far from stupid, Charles X was nevertheless not the material of which constitutional monarchs were made. He was a secret admirer of 'Bonaparte'. In 1830 his determination to curtail the constitution and increase his own power led to the July Revolution. He was deposed and exiled by an uprising led by the bourgeois of Paris. His clever, liberal cousin the Duke d'Orléans ascended the throne as Louis-Philippe I.

Louis-Philippe made a point of cultivating the Napoleonic aristocracy and encouraging the Napoleonic legend: it was he who had the Emperor's remains brought back in 1840. Of his fourteen aides-de-camp in 1835, six, including Gourgaud, had served at the Emperor's court. Louis-Philippe had the same Private Secretary as the Emperor, Baron Fain, and the same architect, Fontaine. Bondy, Flahault and Anatole de Montesquiou held office in the royal household. Other Napoleonic courtiers, such as Rambuteau and Stendhal, returned to government service. Even Bassano served briefly as Prime Minister (largely to get a better rating from his creditors). Thus the Bonapartes, unlike the Bourbons, did not have a group of courtiers exclusively committed to their service.

Nevertheless, those members of the family living in exile outside France did not give up hope of a return to the throne. They provided an alternative monarchy for those (in Italy as well as France) who wanted to overthrow the governments established in 1815 in the name of 'nationalism' and 'liberalism'. They believed in their own legitimacy. As the former King Joseph-Napoleon wrote to La Fayette in 1830: 'The family of Napoleon has been elected by 3,500,000 votes. Therefore it is more legitimate than the Bourbons.'[2]

This faith in their dynastic rights and future meant that some of the Bonapartes, like the Emperor on Saint-Helena, continued to surround themselves with that indispensable attribute of royalty, a court. Thanks to his Wittelsbach wife, Prince Eugene became Prince of Eichstätt in Bavaria, and First Peer of the Realm. He lived in splendour off the fortune he had acquired from the Italian civil list. He sent 800,000 francs to the Emperor's representatives, but kept the rest. His children, helped by enormous dowries, made brilliant marriages to the Crown Prince of Sweden (Bernadotte's son), the Emperor of Brazil, the Queen of Portugal and the only daughter of the Tsar of Russia.[3]

He frequently saw his sister Hortense, who settled in a palatial house in Augsburg. She was still so self-confident and so grand that she treated her sister-in-law, Princess Augusta-Amalia, as a guest in the Princess's own palace. To the amazement of Augsburg society, Queen Hortense even invited non-nobles as well as nobles to her *soirées*, which began to resemble court receptions. More than any other member of the dynasty, she lived in a Napoleonic atmosphere, surrounded by Empire portraits and furniture, dominated by faith in the future of the dynasty.[4] She also ensured that her son, the future Napoleon III, was given an extreme liberal education by his tutor.

Another Bonaparte who maintained a court in exile was the former King Jerome. His chamberlain Planat de La Faye wrote that Jerome's household was 'a miniature court .... Luxury, desire and suspicion reign there as at the court of Westphalia.' Indeed, desire was so prevalent that Jerome's wife was always changing her lady-in-waiting, as each one invariably became Jerome's mistress.[5]

But Eugene, Hortense and Jerome were exceptions. Other members of the family, either from inclination or necessity, led more private lives. When Caroline left Naples in May 1815, none of her Neapolitan courtiers followed her. She settled in Austria and was soon so poor that she had to raise money by selling the gold embroidery from Murat's uniforms and her own court dresses. Elisa was dropped by her Lucchese and Tuscan courtiers when she could no longer afford to pay them. Joseph and Louis both lived as private gentlemen.[6] Pauline, Cardinal Fesch and Madame Mère retired to Rome.

Nevertheless, with the exception of Queen Caroline, they were by no means impoverished. They had all made considerable investments, especially in jewellery, out of their incomes during the Empire, and were able to live in considerable splendour.

Princess Pauline had 'the most hospitable house in Rome'. An Irish liberal, Lady Morgan, was greatly impressed by the sight of Madame Mère's servants in green and gold imperial livery, and by the 'order, elegance and comfort' of the Bonapartes' palaces, 'not a spot uncarpeted ... anomalies in the midst of Roman dreariness and disorder'.[7] However, unlike the children of Prince Eugene, the children of Joseph, Lucien and Elisa Bonaparte lost their imperial status. They married their cousins, or other Italian nobles, and were absorbed back into the class from which they came.

A long domestic epilogue to the drama of the Napoleonic court was provided by the court of 'Her Majesty Marie-Louise, Duchess of Parma'. (Marie-Louise was as keen as Napoleon himself to maintain her imperial status after the fall of the Empire.) She finally arrived in Parma in May 1816, having just dismissed her last senior Napoleonic court official, Monsieur de Bausset. After ten years at the Napoleonic court, he said he was looking forward to being his own master again, and wanted to live peacefully in the country, surrounded by his children.

But the Empress continued to employ many junior officials and servants from her Napoleonic household, and to maintain some of its traditions and regulations. Seven of her eight maids in the 1820s were still French. Her Intendant, Monsieur Amelin, learnt Italian, and married one of her

Parma ladies-in-waiting.[8]

Marie-Louise herself missed the luxuries of Paris. She continued to order her books, silver and dresses from Paris through the Duchess de Montebello. The style and colour (*bleu Marie-Louise*) of her court dresses were the same as under the Empire, and they came from the same dressmaker. However, the size was larger. Like most people, Marie-Louise put on weight in the years of peace after 1815.

Indeed she was so busy and happy that her letters to her beloved Duchess de Montebello began to dry up in 1816. They ceased altogether after 1824, when the Duchess may have learnt of Marie-Louise's remarriage to Neipperg. Like many other stars of the Napoleonic court, the Duchess now led a retired life, devoted to her children and her books: she was dropped by almost all her former acquaintances from the court. She wrote that they now seemed as unreal as figures in a magic lantern.[9] The drama was over.

In 1848, a year after Marie-Louise's death, the drama began again. King Louis-Philippe was deposed by another French revolution, and later that year the son of King Louis and Queen Hortense, Prince Louis-Napoleon Bonaparte, helped by the glamour of his name, became the President of the Second Republic. He easily outwitted his political rivals, and after four years was able to ascend the throne as Napoleon III (the King of Rome was held to have reigned for a few days, as Napoleon II, after the Emperor's abdication on 22 June 1815).

Like his uncle, Napoleon III used splendour as a weapon, and had a large and glamorous court. The structure and etiquette were basically the same as under Napoleon I, but they were simplified and the atmosphere was more relaxed. Familiar names such as Bassano, Montebello and La Bédoyère returned to the Tuileries. The widows of Duroc and Caulaincourt were given special rank at court ceremonies. An aide-de-camp and cousin of Prince Eugene, Count Louis Tascher de La Pagerie, was Grand Master of the Household of the beautiful Spanish-born Empress, Eugenie de Montijo. Compiègne and Fontainebleau were used to entertain the court and an immense variety of guests during the autumn hunting season. Queen Victoria approved. On a visit in 1855 she wrote that 'Everything is beautifully *monté* at Court — very quiet and in excellent order.'[10]

One of Napoleon III's most important achievements also owed much to his uncle's court. From his youth Napoleon III had been determined to expel Austria from Italy. This plan was supported by the children of courtiers and followers of the Bonapartes in Italy, with names like Lecchi, Corsini and Cenami. Napoleon III's ally, who became the first King of Italy in 1861, Victor Emmanuel II of Sardinia, was the son of King Charles Albert, who had been educated in a Paris *lycée* and received the title of count and a *dotation* during the Empire. The politician who organized the alliance between Napoleon III and Victor Emmanuel II and the subsequent unification was Count Camille de Cavour. His father had been First Chamberlain of Prince Borghese in Turin and had remained a friend of the prince after the fall of the Empire. Cavour himself was a godson of Princess Pauline. She had remembered him in her will and he had inherited a fortune from one of her chamberlains.[11]

Napoleon III's foreign policy was less successful in Germany than in Italy. He was outmatched by Bismarck, and was defeated and overthrown in 1870: he died in exile in 1873. The death of his son the Prince Imperial in 1879, fighting with the British army in Zululand, extinguished the Bonapartes' hopes of a return to the throne.

Napoleon's monarchy also had a more general impact in nineteenth-century Europe. What Napoleon called the 'extraordinary grandeur and magnificence' of his court helped to inspire the return to splendour which was a characteristic of nineteenth-century monarchies. Before 1810 most monarchs had lived remarkably simply. In England there was what one Prime Minister's daughter called 'a woeful deficiency of royal splendour'. Even the simplicity of Saint James's *Palace* was too much for George III, and he moved to the Queen's *House*.

The Emperor of Austria and the King of Prussia — two of the grandest monarchs of Europe — lived very modestly in Vienna and Berlin. An English traveller wrote of Vienna: 'Admirable indeed is the simplicity which reigns at court.' In Berlin, according to another writer: 'The house in which the Royal Family lives is quite like a private gentleman's . . . the King walks about and rides without attendants.'[12]

A reaction against the 'admirable' simplicity of late eighteenth- and early nineteenth-century courts was probably inevitable: as monarchs felt less secure on their thrones, they were likely to turn to splendour and formality as weapons to counter the rising tide of democracy. But the return to grandeur was partly due to the impact of the Napoleonic courts. The rigid etiquette, dazzling costumes, hierarchical room-pattern and imperious furniture of the Napoleonic courts established a style of splendour which appealed to other monarchs.

Debret, *The Coronation of Pedro I, Emperor of Brazil, 1 December 1822* *The President of the Senate swears allegiance, watched by ministers, chamberlains and, far left, the Empress, a younger sister of Marie-Louise. The Napoleonic court was the model for the new court of Brazil.*

Gérôme, ***Reception of the Siamese ambassadors at Fontainebleau by Napoleon III and the Empress Eugenie, 27 June 1861*** *The court goes on: Napoleon III continued many of his uncle's policies, served by descendants of his uncle's courtiers. Behind the Emperor is the Grand Chamberlain, the second Duke de Bassano.*

In 1805, less than a year after the coronation of Napoleon I at Notre Dame, George III held a Garter ceremony of unprecedented magnificence at Windsor: the sequence of dates is unlikely to have been a coincidence. Thereafter the increasing splendour and formality of the English court, George IV's grandiose coronation in 1821 and his transformation of the Queen's *House* into Buckingham *Palace*, owed much to his desire to rival the Napoleonic court. Only the fact that England was at war with the French Empire prevented a more direct cultural and artistic influence.

The court of Napoleon I even appealed to his Bourbon rival Louis XVIII. Napoleon I had used courtiers and servants and adopted traditions from the court of Louis XVI. Louis XVIII did the same with the court of Napoleon I. Although the dynasty changed, there was a strong thread of continuity between the different courts. Indeed, when Louis XVIII returned to the Tuileries in 1814, he at first maintained the Napoleonic room-pattern, decoration and furniture — even (until 1822) the Emperor's throne. Only after 1815 were the eagles painted over, the N's transformed into L's and the bees on the carpets (which had simply been covered over in 1814) cut out and fleurs-de-lis segments sewn in. Louis XVIII used many of the same artists, such as Gérard and Isabey. His favourite minister, the most important man in French politics from 1818 to 1820, was also a product of the Empire. He was a bourgeois from Bordeaux called Decazes, who had been Private Secretary and confidant of King Louis-Napoleon and Madame Mère.

In 1820–1 even the inner court of Louis XVIII was remodelled on Napoleonic lines and many courtiers of the Bonapartes rallied to the Bourbons. Rapp and Princess Pauline's former lover de Forbin became Master of the Wardrobe and Gentleman of the Chamber respectively. The court services were given uniforms in the same colours as their Napoleonic equivalents — blue for the stables, violet for the ceremonies and so on. Faithful royalists were disgusted. The aged Duchess d'Escars wrote: 'Everyone who has served in the hideous court of Bonaparte wants to deprive the King of those who chose to fight and die for him.'[13] It was a process which had already begun. Talleyrand, always a law to himself, had been serving at the court of Louis XVIII in exactly the same capacity as he had served at the court of Napoleon I since 1815.

Outside France the Emperor's palaces remained as embodiments of his style after the fall of the Empire. The royal palaces of Amsterdam, Laeken, Milan and Naples were still packed with Empire furniture and tapestries and, in the words of one English tourist, 'picture after picture and bust after bust of Bonaparte'. Prince Leopold of Saxe-Coburg, who had attended the court of Napoleon I, remained an admirer of the Empire style. After he became the first King of the Belgians (with the help of other former supporters of Napoleon I like de Stassart) as Leopold I in 1830, he furnished the Royal Palace of Brussels with Empire furniture from Laeken. Like his father-in-law George IV of England, he also commissioned portraits of himself and his family standing beside particularly grandiose pieces of Empire furniture: as thrones became less secure, such glaring embodiments of splendour seemed increasingly reassuring.

The Bourbons of Naples liked the Empire style as much as their French cousins. Just as Louis XVIII said that Napoleon I had been a good concierge, so Ferdinand IV of Naples is reported to have said that Murat had been 'an excellent upholsterer and had furnished his palaces perfectly to his taste'. Ferdinand changed almost nothing on his return, except to remove, although not destroy (they can still be seen in Caserta and Capodimonte), the innumerable Bonaparte portraits he found in his palaces.[14]

Other palaces throughout western Europe still retain their Napoleonic cachet: when Napoleon III was a prisoner in Wilhelmshöhe, after his defeat in the Franco-Prussian war, he was consoled by the sight of portraits of his mother and uncle which had been there since the fall of the Kingdom of Westphalia in 1813. The Kaiser, so similar to Napoleon I in his militarism, inability to face reality and use of a grand and politically influential court, loved Wilhelmshöhe. He spent most of his summers in its Empire ambience, although it had no Hohenzollern connections at all.

A former architect of King Jerome, von Klenze, who had trained in Paris under Fontaine, remodelled Munich and the royal palaces for King Ludwig

Stieler, *Ludwig I of Bavaria* *Ludwig I's robes, crown and sceptre are almost the same as those of the Emperor on page 22, and were made by the Emperor's craftsmen in Paris. However, Ludwig I hated the Emperor's policies: he had built the temple in the background to commemorate Germany's liberation from the French.*

I after 1825. The King had hated the Emperor, but liked the Empire style. The official portraits, the crown, orb and sceptre and the royal council chamber of the Bavarian monarchy remained Napoleonic in style until its fall in 1918.

The influence of the Napoleonic court was not confined to Europe. From 1812 to 1819 King Christophe of Haiti, the 'black Napoleon', held court in his palace of Sans Souci, surrounded by an army of chamberlains and equerries, and with an elaborate etiquette based on the Napoleonic court. After 1816 the former First Architect of King Jerome, Grandjean de Montigny, redesigned Rio de Janeiro for the court of Brazil. Artists who had painted Napoleon I, such as Debret and Taunay, went to Brazil and depicted its first Emperor, Pedro I, with equal skill. Like many monarchs from legitimate dynasties, Pedro I admired Napoleon. He listened to stories of the Emperor from an exiled aide-de-camp, General van Hogendorp, and his coronation in 1822 (like that of General Iturbide as Emperor Agustín I of Mexico in the same year) was modelled on Napoleon I's in 1804.[15] Even in the twentieth century it is not hard to detect the influence of the Napoleonic court on those of two other grandiose, self-crowned Emperors, Mohammed Reza, Shah of Iran, and Emperor Bokassa of the Central African Empire.

Napoleon gave a new force, as well as a new style, to monarchy. His monarchy was a seductive combination of old and new. It was distinguished by the subordination of all independent institutions, the concentration of power in the hands of the monarch, the political importance of the court, the passion for conquests irrelevant to the national interest, the expansion of the Emperor's private funds and immense generosity to his family and followers. All these factors revealed a concept of monarchy more personal and primitive than that of his predecessors on the throne of France. Napoleon I in some ways resembles a soldier of fortune dividing booty among his followers.

The emergence of such a personal and élitist monarchy in France after 1800 suggests that the Emperor was right when he said that the Revolution had been caused by interests not ideals, ambition rather than principles. He only had to open the antechambers of the Tuileries and they were filled by some of the most ardent supporters of the Revolution, in search of titles, jobs and money. If Louis XVI had had a different style of monarchy, more military and generous to a wider circle of courtiers, perhaps he would have survived.

On the other hand Napoleon's monarchy was also a force for modernization through the spread of the Code Napoléon, the redefinition of the aristocracy to include the richest and most successful members of the bourgeoisie and the rationalization of the administration. When they recovered their lost thrones or provinces, many monarchs expressed wonder at what had been accomplished in their absence. They were happy to use Napoleonic codes, courtiers and administrators after 1815.

The modernizing personal monarchies of the Napoleonic dynasty represented a dramatic reassertion of monarchical authority in Europe. They helped to transform the robust, independent, liberal nobility of the late eighteenth century into the cautious, conservative nobility of the nineteenth. Partly as a result of the influence of the Napoleonic courts, and of their seductive combination of reforms and rewards, families like the Montesquiou, the Beauvau, the Borghese and the Caracciolo were tamer and more respectful of the monarchical principle than they had been at the end of the eighteenth century. Nobles were no longer tempted to lead revolutionary movements as they had done, after 1780, in France, Belgium and Italy. By serving the Napoleonic dynasty, they could satisfy their novel desire for reforms, at the same time as their traditional need for power and status.

The Napoleonic courts also spread an appetite for court life and monarchy among groups which had hitherto been excluded. The legal nobility, the provincial nobility, the bourgeoisie and the army were now as determined as the old *noblesse présentée* to go to court in France. A typical Napoleonic duke is described in 1814 as incapable of imagining how 'a gentleman can live far from the court'.[16] People like the Neys, the Bassanos and the Rovigos resembled this fictional duke in real life. Bourgeois such as Decazes and Stendhal, whose greatest novel *The Charterhouse of Parma* is set in a court, owed their taste for court life to their initiation at the Napoleonic court. The élites of Holland and Lucca first experienced monarchy and court life during the Empire. As the Emperor himself always maintained, his style of government strengthened monarchy in Europe, and helped it to meet the challenges of the nineteenth century.

Above all, Napoleon's style of monarchy surrounded the Emperor with an aura of splendour, and this is one reason why he has won so many passionate admirers. For many, Napoleon's appeal was magical rather than rational. The uniforms, the music, the grandiose ceremonies, the bowing princes and chamberlains, the incredible palaces, the ubiquitous N's and bees — in other words the court — contributed to the magic surrounding the Emperor. For some this outward magnificence was more spell-binding than the Emperor's victories or legal code.

As the quotation at the beginning of this chapter shows, one of the Emperor's most passionate admirers, the German poet Heine, evoked the colours of the Emperor's livery when he thought of 'the great Emperor'. The most popular French poets of the nineteenth century, Béranger and Victor Hugo, celebrated the Emperor's court of kings in verse. It has also had some surprising literary admirers. On his death-bed, in delirium, Henry James (rather like the Emperor himself on his death-bed) dictated a letter from Napoleon about the redecoration of the Louvre and the Tuileries. He praised it for achieving 'a majesty unsurpassed by any work of the kind yet undertaken in France'.[17]

But Napoleon's courtiers had to live with the monarch not the legend. They saw the ruthless egotism, the concentration of power in the hands of one man and the regimentation of every aspect of existence at first hand. Above all they endured the endless wars, including the inexcusable invasions of Spain and Russia. Their desertion in April 1814 and June 1815 showed their opinion of the Emperor and the fragility of his regime. Many courtiers would have agreed with the verdict of André Malraux. In conversation with General de Gaulle, he said that the Emperor had 'a very great mind and a rather small spirit'.

Naudin, ***Marie-Louise with her third husband, Count Charles de Bombelles*** *It is 1838 and the former Empress is walking in the park of one of her palaces outside Parma. Although she always remembered how well Napoleon had treated her, Marie-Louise was happier in Parma than in Paris.*

Sources and Bibliography

Archives

ARCHIVES NATIONALES PARIS (AN)
O^2 Papers of the Maison de l'Empereur:
1, 5, 6, 8, 28, 41, 83, 87, 108, 150, 157, 158, 159, 160, 166, 167, 217, 347, 948, 1040, 1066, 1073, 1083, 1218, 1219.
AF IV Papers of the Secrétairerie d'Etat:
332, 1221, 1231, 1311, 1726, 3177.

ARCHIVES PRIVÉES (AP):
36 AP Ségur Papers;
95 AP 11, 12, 14, 15, 22, 25, Caulaincourt Papers;
177 AP 3 letters of the Comte de Bondy, 1805–9;
181 AP papers of the Duc de Cadore;
182 AP Duroc papers;
341 AP 23 letters of Madame de Montmorency to Charles de La Grange;
349 AP 1, 2, 19, Papers of the Comte de Montesquiou;
381 AP 3, 4, 15, Papers of King Joseph;
400 AP 4 Archives Napoléon Registre de Correspondance of Duroc;
439 AP 1, 3, 4, Papers of Pierre Fontaine.

BIBLIOTHÈQUE NATIONALE, DÉPARTEMENT DES MANUSCRITS, NOUVELLES ACQUISITIONS FRANÇAISES (BN.NAF)
11399 Letters Particulières de S.E. Mgr. le Comte de Ségur
14356 Letters of the Comtesse de Montesquiou to Napoleon I

BIBLIOTHÈQUE THIERS, Place Saint Georges, Fonds Frédéric Masson (FM):
28, 32 Household of the Empress;
40, 41 Household of King Jerome;
54 Etiquette du Palais de Lucques;
100–07 Household of the Emperor;
116 Registre de Correspondance du Grand Maître des Cérémonies.

ECOLE DES BEAUX-ARTS, Pierre Fontaine, 'Notes relatives aux Fonctions que j'ai remplies depuis le 3 novembre 1799'.

HAUS- HOF- UND STAATSARCHIV VIENNA, NACHLASS MONTENUOVO (NM)
Letters of Duchess de Montebello, Comtesse de Brignole and Marquis de Bausset to Marie-Louise.

ARCHIVIO DI STATO DI PARMA
Casa e Corte di Maria Luigia 905 Matricolo della Personale.

MUSEO GLAUCO-LOMBARDI PARMA
Letters of Comtesse de Montesquiou to Marie-Louise.

Books
(Unless otherwise stated all books in French are published in Paris and all books in English in London.)

ABRANTÈS, DUCHESSE D', *Mémoires*, 4 vols., 1832.
ADDARIO, ARNALDO, 'Ascanio Mansi, la sua personalità e i suoi ideali politici 1773–1840', *Actum Luce*, April 1972, pp. 7–36.
ALMÉRAS, HENRI D', *Pauline Bonaparte*, 1906.
ANON., *Almanacco di Corte per l'Anno 1809*, Lucca, 1809.
Almanacco e Guida di Milano per l'Anno 1814.
Almanach de la Cour pour l'Année 1810, Amsterdam, 1810.
Almanach Royal de Westphalie pour l'An 1810, Cassel, 1810.
Etiquette du Palais de Leurs Altesses, Lucques, 1805.
Etichetta della Real Corte delle Due Sicilie, Naples, 1813.
APOLLO, 9, 1977, issue devoted to Palazzo Pitti.
ARIZZOLI-CLEMENTEL, PIERRE, 'Les Projects d'Aménagement Intérieur et de Décoration du Palais

Pitti pour Napoléon et Marie-Louise 1810–1814', in *Florence et la France, Rapports sous la Révolution et l'Empire*, 1979.
BACIOCCHI, ELISA-NAPOLÉON, 'Lettres Inédites . . . au Comte de Ségur', *Revue Hebdomadaire* 9, 1908, pp. 42–80.
BAILLEU, PAUL, *Preussen und Frankreich von 1795 bis 1807*, 2 vols., Leipzig, 1881–7.
BEAUFOND, EMMANUEL DE, *Elisa Bonaparte, Princesse de Lucques et de Piombino*, 1895.
BELLA BARSALI, ISA, *Il Palazzo Pubblico di Lucca*, Lucca, 1980.
BERCKHEIM, M. DE, *Lettres sur Paris*, Heidelberg, 1809.
BERGERON, LOUIS, *L'Episode Napoléonien*, 1972.
BERNARDY, FRANÇOISE DE, *Eugène de Beauharnais*, 1973;
Stéphanie de Beauharnais, 1977;
Son of Talleyrand, 1956.
BERRY, MARY, *Extracts from the Journals and Correspondence*, 3 vols., 1865.
BERTRAND, GÉNÉRAL, *Cahiers de Sainte-Hélène*, 3 vols., 1949–59.
BIGARRÉ, GÉNÉRAL, *Mémoires*, 1893.
BIVER, MARIE LOUISE, *Pierre Fontaine*, 1964.
BOULAY, DE LA MEURTHE, COMTE, *Documents sur la Négociation du Concordat*, 5 vols., 1891–7.
BOURGOING, BARON DE, *Le Coeur Secret de Marie-Louise*, 2 vols., 1938–9.
BOYER, FERDINAND, 'La Famille Bens de Cavour et le Régime Napoléonien', *Revue Historique*, CLXXXV, 1939, pp. 326–45.
CAMPAN, MADAME, *Correspondance avec la Reine Hortense*, 2 vols., 1835.
CAMPBELL, SIR NEIL, *Napoleon at Fontainebleau and Elba*, 1869.
CARAMAN, COMTE G. DE, *Notice sur La Vie Militaire et Privée du Général Marquis de Caraman*, seconde édition, 1857.
CASTELLANE, MARÉCHAL DE, *Journal*, 5 vols., 1895–7.
CASTELOT, ANDRÉ, *Napoleon's Son*, 1960.
CAULAINCOURT, COMTE DE, *Mémoires*, 3 vols., 1933.
CAUMONT–LA FORCE, MARQUIS DE, *L'Architrésorier Lebrun, Gouverneur de la Hollande 1810–1813*, 1907.
CENAMI, OLIMPIA PARENTI, *Lucca dei Mercanti Patrizi*, Florence, 1977.
CHASTENAY, MADAME DE, *Mémoires*, 2 vols., 1896–7.
CHLAPOWSKI, GÉNÉRAL DÉSIRÉ, *Mémoires*, 1908.
CHURCH, CLIVE H, *Revolution and Red Tape*, 1981.
CLARY ET ALDRINGEN, PRINCE, *Trois Mois à Paris*, 1914.
COIGNY, AIMÉE DE, *Journal*, 1981.
COLE, HUBERT, *Fouché the Unprincipled Patriot*, 1971;
The Betrayers, 1972.
COMEAU, BARON, *Souvenirs des Guerres d'Allemagne pendant la Révolution et l'Empire*, 1886.
CONSALVI, CARDINAL, *Mémoires, c.* 1890.
CONSTANT, *Mémoires*, 1967.
CORTI, EGON CESAR, CONTE, *Ludwig I of Bavaria*, 1938.
DALBIAN, DENYSE, *Dom Pedro Ier*, 1959.
DARD, EMILE, *Napoléon et Talleyrand*, 1935.
DESPRÉAUX, JEAN-ETIENNE, *Souvenirs*, Issoudon, 1894.
DU CASSE, BARON, *Les Rois Frères de Napoléon Premier*, 1883.
DUNDULIS, BRONIC, *Napoléon et la Lituanie en 1812*, 1940.
DURAND, MADAME LA GÉNÉRALE, *Napoleon and Marie-Louise*, 1886.
Empire in the Palace (catalogue of exhibition held at the Royal Palace of Amsterdam in 1983).
EUGÈNE, PRINCE, *Mémoires et Correspondance Politique et Militaire*, 10 vols., 1858.
FAIN, BARON, *Mémoires*, 1909.
FISHER, H.A.L., *Studies in Napoleonic Statesmanship, Germany*, 1903.
FLEURIOT DE LANGLE, *Elisa Soeur de Napoléon I*, 1947.
FUNCK, FERDINAND VON, *In the Wake of Napoleon*, 1935.
GABRIEL, J., *Essai Biographique sur Madame Tascher de la Pagerie*, 1856.
GACHOT, EDOUARD, *Marie-Louise Intime*, 2 vols., 1911.
GANIÈRE, PAUL, *Corvisart Médecin de Napoléon*, 1951;
Napoléon à Sainte-Hélène, 3 vols., 1957.
GARNIER, JEAN-PAUL, *Murat Roi de Naples*, 1959.
GAVOTY, ANDRÉ, *Les Drames Inconnus de la Cour de Napoléon*, 1962;
Les Drames Inconnus de la Cour de Napoléon 1805–1806, 1964;
Les Amoureux de l'Impératrice Josephine, 1961;
Amours et Aventures au Temps de Napoléon, 1969.
GIRARDIN, STANISLAS DE, *Journal et Souvenirs, Discours et Opinions*, 4 vols., 1828.
GIROD DE L'AIN, GABRIEL, *Bernadotte*, 1968;
Joseph Bonaparte, 1970.
GOURGAUD, BARON, *Journal*, 2 vols., 1896–7.
GRANDJEAN, SERGE, *Empire Furniture*, 1966.
GRANDJEAN DE MONTIGNY, *Plan . . . du Palais des Etats et Sa Nouvelle Salle à Cassel en Westphalie*, 1810.
GRAUX, LUCIEN DE, *La Comtesse de Luçay*, 2 vols., 1930.
GREATHEAD, BERTIE, *An Englishman in Paris*, 1953.
GRUNWALD, CONSTANTIN DE, 'Les Débuts de Metternich', *Revue de Paris*, 8. 1936, pp. 492–537;
'Metternich à Paris en 1808–1809', *Revue de Paris*, 10.1937, pp. 481–513.
HANOTEAU, JEAN, *Les Beauharnais et l'Empereur*, 1936;
'Journaux et Confidences de Marie-Louise', *Revue des Deux Mondes*, 15.12.1939, pp. 765–93.
HAUSSONVILLE, COMTE D', 'Souvenirs de l'Emigration et du Premier Empire', *Revue des Deux Mondes*, 1.1.1878, pp. 91–123.
HEINE, HEINRICH, *Travel Pictures*, 1887.
HÉRISSON, BARON D', *Un Secrétaire de Napoléon Premier*, 1894.
HOBHOUSE, J.C., *The Substance of some Letters . . . during the Last Reign of the Emperor Napoleon*, second edition, 1817.
HOGENDORP, DIRK VAN, *Mémoires*, La Haye, 1887.
HORTENSE, QUEEN, 'Lettres . . . au Prince Eugène', *Revue des Deux Mondes*, 15.7.1933, pp. 303–33, 1.8.1933, pp. 551–82;
Mémoires, 3 vols., 1927.

HUBERT, GÉRARD, *La Sculpture dans l'Italie Napoléonienne*, 1964.
HUGO, ABEL, 'Souvenirs sur Joseph-Napoléon', *Revue des Deux Mondes*, 1833, I, pp. 260–84, II, pp. 111–39.
JÉRÔME, KING, *Mémoires et Correspondance*, 7 vols., 1861–6.
KATHARINA, QUEEN AND JÉRÔME, KING, *Briefwechsel mit dem König Friedrich von Württemberg*, 3 vols. Stuttgart 1886–7.
KERRY, EARL OF, *The First Napoleon*, 1925.
KNAPTON, E.J., *The Empress Josephine*, 1969 ed.
KÜHN, JOACHIM, *Pauline Bonaparte*, 1937.
LABARRE DE RAILLICOURT, D., *Louis Bonaparte Roi de Hollande*, 1963.
LACHOUQUE, HENRY, *The Last Days of Napoleon's Empire*, 1966.
LA FOREST, COMTE DE, *Correspondance*, 7 vols., 1905–13.
LANZAC DE LABORIE, LOUIS DE, *Paris sous Napoléon*, 8 vols., 1905–13.
LARREY, BARON, *Madame Mère*, 2 vols., 1892.
LAS CASES, COMTE DE, *Mémorial de Sainte-Hélène*, 2 vols., 1961.
LAS CASES, COMTE EMMANUEL DE, *Las Cases Mémorialiste de Napoléon*, 1959.
LA TOUR, COMMANDANT JEAN DE, *Duroc Grand Maréchal du Palais Impérial*, 1907.
LA TOUR DU PIN, MARQUISE DE, *Journal d'une Femme de Cinquante Ans*, 2 vols., 1913.
LÉVY, ARTHUR, *Napoléon Intime*, 1893.
MADELIN, LOUIS, *La Rome de Napoléon*, 1906.
MANCINI, AGOSTINO, *Storia di Lucca*, Lucca, 1950.
MARCHAND, L.N., *Mémoires*, 2 vols., 1953–5.
MARGERAND, J., *Les Aides de Camp de Bonaparte 1793–1804*, 1931.
MARKHAM, FELIX, *Napoléon*, 3rd impression, 1966.
MARIE-LOUISE, 'Correspondance Inédite . . . et de la Reine Cathérine', *Revue des Deux Mondes*, 1.5.1928, pp. 386–425.
'Carnets de Voyage', *Revue de Paris*, 1.2, 15.2, 1.3, 1.4.1921, pp. 497–539, 701–41, 28–46, 470–506.
MARMOTTAN, PAUL, 'La Mission du Général Hédouville à Lucques en juin-juillet 1805', *Revue des Etudes Napoléoniennes*, XLVIII, 1.1922, pp. 122–36;
'Le Théâtre à la cour de Lucques sous Elisa Napoléon', *Revue des Etudes Napoléoniennes*, 2.1930, pp. 65–83;
Les Arts en Toscane sous Napoléon, 1901.
MARTINEAU, GILBERT, *Napoleon's Mother*, 1977.
MARTINET, ANDRÉ, *Jérôme-Napoléon Roi de Westphalie*, 1902.
MASSON, FRÉDÉRIC, *Napoléon chez Lui*, 1893;
Napoléon et Sa Famille, 15 vols., 1908–19;
Joséphine Impératrice et Reine, 9e ed., 1903;
Joséphine Répudiée, 3e ed., 1901;
Jadis et Aujourd'hui, 1908;
Madame Bonaparte, 1919;
L'Impératrice Marie-Louise, 2e ed., 1902;
Napoléon et Son Fils, 3e. ed., 1904;
Revue d'Ombres, 1907.
MAZE-SENCIER, A., *Les Fournisseurs de Napoléon Premier*, 1893.
MELCHIOR-BONNET, B., *Napoléon et le Pape*, 1959;
Savary Duc de Rovigo, 1962;
Jérôme Bonaparte, 1979.
MELZI D'ERIL, FRANCESCO, DUCA DI LODI, *Memorie e Documenti*, 2 vols., Milan 1865.
MÉNEVAL, BARON DE, *Mémoires pour servir a l'Histoire de Napoleon Premier*, 3 vols., 1894.
MERCY-ARGENTEAU, COMTE DE, *Memoirs*, 2 vols., New York, 1917.
MONTESQUIOU, COMTESSE DE, 'Souvenirs', *Revue de Paris*, 5, 1948, pp. 51–80.
MONTESQUIOU, ANATOLE DE, *Souvenirs*, 1961.
MORAND, PAUL, *Le Prince de Ligne. Les Plus Belles Pages*, 1964.
MORGAN, LADY, *Italy*, 2 vols., 1821.
NAPOLÉON, catalogue of an exhibition held at the Grand Palais, 1969.
NAPOLÉON I, *Correspondance Générale*, 32 vols., 1858–70.
OMAN, CAROLA, *Napoleon's Viceroy*, 1966.
PALMSTIERNA, C.F., ed., *Marie-Louise et Napoléon. Lettres Inédités*, 1955.
PERCIER, CHARLES ET FONTAINE, P.L.F., *Description des Cérémonies et Fêtes pour le Mariage de S.M. l'Empereur Napoléon*, 1810.
PICARD, ERNEST, *Bonaparte et Moreau*, 1905.
PLANAT DE LA FAYE, *Correspondance Inédite*, 1895.
PONIATOWSKI, MICHEL, *Talleyrand et le Directoire*, 1984;
Talleyrand et le Consulat, 1986.
PONS DE L'HÉRAULT, *Souvenirs et Anecdotes de l'Ile d'Elbe*, 1897;
Mémoire aux Puissance Alliées, 1899.
POTOCKA, COUNTESS, *Memoirs*, New York, 1900.
RAFFLES, THOMAS, *Letters during a Tour through Some Parts of France . . . in the Summer of 1817*, Liverpool, 1818.
RAMBAUD, JOSEPH, *Naples sous Joseph Bonaparte*, 1911.
RAMBUTEAU, COMTE DE, *Memoirs*, 1908.
RASPONI, COMTESSE LOUISE, *Souvenirs d'Enfance*, 1929.
RATH, REUBEN JOHN, *The Fall of the Napoleonic Kingdom of Italy*, New York, 1941.
RÉMUSAT, MADAME DE, *Lettres*, 2 vols., 1881;
Memoirs, 2 vols., 1880.
RIVAZ, CHARLES-EMMANUEL DE, *Mes Souvenirs de Paris*, Martigny, 1967.
RODOCONACHI, E., *Elisa-Napoléon*, 1900.
ROSEBERRY, LORD, *Napoleon the Last Phase*, 1927 ed.
ROUSTAM, *Souvenirs*, 1911.
RUTLAND, DUKE AND DUCHESS OF, *Journal of a Trip to Paris*, 1914.
SAINT-DENIS, LOUIS ETIENNE, *Souvenirs du Mamelouck Ali*, 1926.
SAINTE-AULAIRE, COMTE DE, 'Souvenirs sur Napoléon Premier', *Revue de Paris*, 6. 1925, pp. 481–97.
SANCHOLLE-HENRAUX, B., *Le Chevalier Luigi Angiolini Diplomate Toscan*, 1913.
SAVANT, JEAN, *Les Fonds Secrets de Napoléon*, 1952.

SCHAMA, SIMON, *Patriots and Liberators*, 1977.
SÉGUR, COMTE DE, *Etiquette du Palais Impérial*, An XIII, 1808.
SENFFT, COMTE DE, *Mémoires*, Leipzig, 1863.
SENKOWSKA-GLUCK, MONIKA, 'Les Donataires de Napoléon', *Revue d'Histoire Moderne et Contemporaine*, 1969, pp. 681–93.
STENDHAL, *Oeuvres Intimes*, 1966;
Napoléon, 2 vols., 1929.
STERNI, R., 'Palais Impérial du Quirinal', *Revue des Etudes Napoléoniennes*, XXVIII, 1–6. 1929, pp. 163–90, 216–44.
STEVENSON, SETH WILLIAM, *A Tour Through France, Savoy and Northern Italy in the Summer of 1825*, 2 vols., 1827;
Journal of a Tour through Part of France . . . made in the summer of 1816, Norwich, 1817.
TALLEYRAND, PRINCE DE, *Talleyrand Intime*, 1891;
'Lettres à Caulaincourt', *Revue des Deux Mondes*, 15.10.1935, pp. 782–816, 1.11.1935, pp. 142–80;
Mémoires, 5 vols., 1891–2.
THIARD DE BISSY, COMTE DE, *Souvenirs*, 1900.
THIRY, JEAN, *La Campagne de France*, 1938;
La Seconde Abdication de Napoléon I, 1945.
TULARD, JEAN, 'Les Composants d'une Fortune : le Cas de la Noblesse d'Empire', *Revue Historique*, CCLIII, 1.1975, pp. 119–38.
'La Cour de Napoléon I', in *Hof Kultur und Politik im 19. Jahrhundert*, Bonn, 1985, pp. 55–60;
Napoléon, 1977;
Napoléon et la Noblesse d'Empire, 1979;
Napoléon, Lettres d'Amour à Josephine, 1981;
Napoléon à Sainte-Hélène, 1981.
VAN YPERSELE, A. ET E., *Laeken Résidence Impériale et Royale*, Bruxelles, 1970.
VANDAL, ALBERT, *Napoléon et Alexandre Ier*, 3 vols., 1891–6.
'Le Roi et la Reine de Naples (1808–1812)', *Revue des Deux Mondes*, 1.2.1910, pp. 481–514, 15.2.1910, pp. 721–56, 1.3.1910, pp. 42–75.
VASSON, JACQUES DE, *Bertrand le Grand Maréchal de Sainte-Hélène*, Issoudun, 1935.
WARESQUIEL, EMMANUEL DE, *Général Mouton Comte de Lobau. Lettres à Cité*, Maîtrise, Paris IV, 1979.
WEIL, M.H., *Les Dessous du Congrès de Vienne*, 2 vols., 1917.
WHITCOMB, EDWARD H., *Napoleon's Diplomatic Service*, Durham North Carolina, 1979.
ZIESENISS, CHARLES OTTO, *Napoléon et la Cour Impériale*, 1980;
Le Congrès de Vienne et l'Europe des Princes, 1984.
ZIESENISS, JÉRÔME, *Berthier Frère d'Armes de Napoléon*, 1986.

Notes

I STEPS TO THE THRONE

1 Léon de Lanzac de Laborie, *Paris sous Napoléon*, 8 vols. 1905–13, I, pp. 78–80.
2 Maison Charavay, *Lettres Autographes*, Février 1983, Dubois-Crancé to Madame Dubois-Crancé, 8.3.1800; Felix Markham, *Napoléon*, 3rd impression 1966, p. 22; Jean Tulard, *Napoléon*, 1984, pp. 61–2.
3 Hubert Cole, *The Betrayers*, 1972, pp. 28–9.
4 Paul Bailleu, *Preussen und Frankreich von 1795 bis 1807*, 2 vols. Leipzig 1881–7, II, p. 17, Lucchesini to Haugwitz, 12.1.1801; Michel Poniatowski, *Talleyrand et le Consulat*, 1986, p. 55.
5 André Gavoty, *Les Drames Inconnus de la Cour de Napoléon*, 1964, p. 17; Madame Campan, *Correspondance . . . avec la Reine Hortense*, 2 vols. 1835, I, pp. 251–5, 263; Charles Otto Zieseniss, *Napoléon et la Cour Impériale*, 1980, pp. 30–1.
6 Lanzac de Laborie, pp. 111, 177.
7 Gilbert Martineau, *Madame Mère*, 1978, p. 76, Madame Mère to Napoleon, 9.5.1806.
8 Louis Bergeron, *L'Episode Napoléonien*, 1972, p. 96; Madame de Staël, *Considérations sur la Révolution Française*, 3 vols. London 1818, II, p. 258.
9 Pierre Fontaine, 'Notes relatives aux fonctions que j'ai remplíés depuis le 3 novembre 1799', Ecole des Beaux-Arts (henceforward referred to as Fontaine), 4.10.1801; Mary Berry, *Extracts from the Journals and Correspondence*, 3 vols. 1865, II, pp. 163–4, note of 30.3.1802.
10 Bailleu, II, p. 81n, Lucchesini to Haugwitz 27.9.1801; anon, *Paris as it was and is*, 2 vols. 1803, I, p. 328, article for 7.12.1801.
11 Frédéric Masson, *Napoléon et sa Famille*, 15 vols. 1908–19, II, p. 115; Zieseniss, *Napoléon*, p. 69; McClintock Papers, John Leslie Foster to Harriet Countess de Salis, 6.4.1802; Markham, pp. 82–3.
12 Comte Boulay de La Meurthe, *Documents sur la Négociation du Concordat*, 5 vols. 1891–7, V, p. 568, Count Cobenzl to Count Colloredo, 22.4.1802; *Staël*, II, p. 280; Anne Plumptre, *A Narrative of a Three Years' Residence in France*, 3 vols. 1810, I, pp. 124–5,; J.G. Lemaistre, *A Rough Sketch of Modern Paris*, sec. ed. 1803, pp. 217–19; Catherine Wilmot, *An Irish Peer on the Continent*, 1924, p. 59, letter of 25.4.1802.
13 E.J. Knapton, *The Empress Josephine*, 1969 ed. pp. 285–98; Edmond Taigny, *Jean-Baptiste Isabey*, 1859, p. 27.
14 Stanislas de Girardin, *Journal et Souvenirs, Discours et Opinions*, 4 vols. 1828, III, p. 287.
15 Bertie Greathead, *An Englishman in Paris*, 1953, p. 7, diary for 1 January 1803; Ernest Picard, *Bonaparte et Moreau*, 1905, pp. 358, 373; Stendhal, *Oeuvres Intimes*, 1966, p. 470, diary for 10.6.1804.
16 Baron Larrey, *Madame Mère*, 2 vols. 1892, I, p. 398; Baron Fain, *Souvenirs*, 1909, pp. 74–91, 119–22; Clive H. Church, *Revolution and Red Tape*, Oxford 1981, pp. 266–8.
17 Jean Tulard, *Napoléon à Sainte-Hélène*, 1981, p. 519.
18 Institut Thiers Bibliothèque Frédéric Masson, *Manuscrits* (henceforward referred to as FM), 106 'Maison de SM l'Empereur et Roi' is the basic source for the description of the household, with *Etiquette du Palais Impérial*, 1808; Maréchal de Castellane, *Journal*, 5 vols. 1895–7, I, p.95, diary for 26.5.1812; Archives Nationales (henceforward referred to as AN), 95 AP 112. *Situation comparée de l'écurie au 20 mars 1815*.
19 AN O^2 (papers of the Maison de l'Empereur) 200. Règlement of 28 Messidor An XII.
20 Baron d'Hérisson, *Un Secrétaire de Napoléon Premier*, 1894, pp. 233–43; AN O^2 167. 13, decree of 24.2.1813.
21 AN $O^2$26, Napoleon I to Duroc, 31.8.1807 (copy); AF IV (papers of the Secrétaire d'Etat) 1231, notes on

the session of 1.1.1810; Arthur Lévy, *Napoléon Intime*, 1893, p. 527.
22 A. Du Casse, *Mémoires et Correspondance Politique et Militaire du Prince Eugène*, 10 vols. 1858, II, p. 49, Eugene to Napoleon I, 16.1.1806; *Almanacco e Guida di Milano per l'Anno 1814*, passim.
23 AN 95 AP 22, 7, Duroc to Caulaincourt, 23.11.1807; FM 116, Duroc to Ségur 23, 31.3.1810.
24 Paul Ganière, *Corvisart Médecin de Napoléon*, 1951, p. 61; Zieseniss, *Napoléon*, p. 284, Napoleon to Cambacérès, 4.4.1805; FM 116, Duroc to Ségur, 20.10, 2.11.1810.
25 Church, p. 270; Fain, pp. 166–84.

2 THE EMPEROR AND HIS COURT

1 Général Bertrand, *Cahiers de Sainte-Hélène*, 3 vols. 1949–59, II, p. 215, diary for 11.4.1817; cf. Baron Comeau, *Souvenirs des Guerres d'Allemagne pendant la Révolution et l'Empire*, 1886, p. 326.
2 AN 95 AP 11, 5, Liste des personnes qui accompagnent l'Empéreur, août 1811; Méneval, II, p. 239; Fain, p. 243.
3 Roustam, *Souvenirs*, 1911, p. 209; Masson, *Napoléon chez Lui*, 1893, pp. 108–12; *Etiquette du Palais Impérial*, 1808, p. 93.
4 Cdt. Jean de La Tour, *Duroc Grand Maréchal du Palais Impérial*, 1907, passim; Napoleon I, *Correspondance Générale*, 32 vols. 1858–70, XXV, p. 368, letter to Countess de Montesquiou, 7.6.1813.
5 AN $O^2$28, Rémusat to Talleyrand, 16 Brumaire An XIII; Musée de la Chasse, Paris, Berthier to Talleyrand, 16.2.1805.
6 AN 400 AP, Archives Napoléon 4, Registre de Correspondance of the Grand Maréchal du Palais, Duroc to Talleyrand, 10.1.1808; Emile Dard, *Napoléon et Talleyrand*, 1935, p. 226, Talleyrand to Napoleon I 2.9.1809.
7 Madame de Rémusat, *Lettres*, 2 vols. 1881, I, p. 66, letter to Monsieur de Rémusat, 30.3.1805; Baron de Méneval, *Mémoires pour Servir à l'Histoire de Napoléon Premier*, 3 vols., III, p. 545.
8 Jérôme Zieseniss, *Berthier, Frère d'Armes de Napoléon*, 1986, passim.
9 FM 116, Fontanes to Ségur, 20 Vendémiaire An 13; Stendhal, *Oeuvres Intimes*, 'Souvenirs d'Egotisme', p. 1412.
10 *Etiquette du Palais Impérial*, pp. 93, 98; FM 106 Entrées Particulières, 21.11.1813; *Talleyrand Intime*, 1891, pp. 18, 31, 97, letters to Duchesse de Courlande, 6, 14.1., 16.2.1814.
11 Louis Etienne Saint-Denis, *Souvenirs du Mamelouck Ali*, 1926, pp. 24–7; *Fain*, pp. 64–73, 191–6; Comte de Bausset, *Mémoires sur l'Intérieur du Palais Impérial*, 2 vols. 1827, I, p. 205; Comte de Las Cases, *Memorial of Saint Helena*, 4 vols. 1823, III, p. 81.
12 Jean Tulard ed., *Napoléon. Lettres d'Amour à Joséphine*, 1981, p. 262, Napoleon to Josephine, 13.3.1807.
13 André Gavoty, *Les Drames Inconnus de la Cour de Napoléon*, 1964, pp. 25, 122; Queen Hortense, *Mémoires*, 3 vols. 1927, I, p. 202; Bertrand, III, p. 258, diary for 1.1819.
14 Henri d'Alméras, *Pauline Bonaparte*, 1906, pp. 159, 180.
15 Charles Percier et P.F.L. Fontaine, *Description des Cérémonies et Fêtes pour le Marriage de S.M. l'Empereur Napoléon*, 1810, passim.
16 Masson, 'Marie-Louise et ses Carnets de Voyage', *Revue de Paris*, 1.4.1921, p. 475.
17 Jean Châtelain, *Dominique-Vivant Denon et le Louvre de Napoléon*, 1973 passim; AN 400 AP 4, Duroc to Denon 11.10.1812; AN AF IV 1231, minutes for the session of 24.12.1809.
18 AN 400 AP 4, Duroc to Duc de Cadore, 3.11.1811; Sotheby's Sale 28.5.1986, Napoleon to Duroc, 27.8.1806.
19 Mademoiselle Cochelet, *Mémoires*, 1907, p. 12; Hans Naef, *Die Bildniszeichungen von J.A.D. Ingres, 5* vols. Bern 1978, II, p. 287.
20 AN 36 AP, Ségur Papers, Napoleon to Ségur, 15.1.1805; FM 116, Duroc to Ségur, 14.8.1810; *Etiquette du Palais Impérial*, p. 132.
21 Charles Otto Zieseniss, *Le Congrès de Vienne et l'Europe des Princes*, 1984, p. 154; Tulard, *Napoléon . . . à Joséphine*, pp. 235, 267, Napoleon to Josephine, 7.1.1807, 25.3.1807.
22 L.N. Marchand, *Mémoires*, 2 vols. 1953–5, II, p. 44; Baron Gourgaud, *Journal*, 2 vols. 1896–7, I, pp. 267, 427; Lord Roseberry, *Napoleon the last Phase*, 1927 ed., pp. 170–1.

3 A PASSION FOR PALACES

1 Masson, *Joséphine Impératrice et Reine*, 9e ed. 1903, pp. 387–8.
2 AN 400 AP 4, Duroc to Daru, 29.8.1806; Carola Oman, *Napoleon's Viceroy*, 1966, p. 179, Napoleon to Eugène, 1805; Prince Eugène, VI, p. 359, Eugène to Napoleon, 13.3.1810.
3 La Tour, p. 270, Duroc to Faget de Baur, 9.1808; Fain, p. 211.
4 Marie-Louise Biver, *Pierre Fontaine*, 1964, pp. 95, 108; Lanzac de Laborie, VIII, p. 318; AN 400 AP 4, Duroc to Daru, 4.4.1810.
5 Serge Grandjean, *Empire Furniture*, 1966, p. 54; Biver, pp. 47, 68; Jean Tulard, 'La Cour de Napoléon ler', in *Hof, Kultur und Politik im 19. Jahrhundert*, Bonn, 1985, pp. 57–8. On the other hand Saint-Cloud was, at first, furnished with furniture from Versailles, and Fontainebleau with furniture made for General Moreau.
6 A. and E. van Ypersele, *Laeken, Résidence Impériale et Royale*, Bruxelles, 1970, pp. 130, 200, 216; Gérard Hubert, *La Sculpture dans l'Italie Napoléonienne*, 1964, p. 276; Denise Ledoux-Lebard, *Le Grand Trianon*, 1975, p. 13; G. Lenôtre, *Le Château de Rambouillet*, 1930, pp. 133, 142.
7 AN 400 AP 4, *Règlement pour l'ameublement des Palais Impériaux*, 6 Thermidor an 13, Duroc to

Concierge, 1.1.1806; 36 AP1, Napoleon to Ségur, 22.8.1807.

8 FM 116, Duroc to Desmazis, 9.11.1809; A. Maze-Sencier, *Les Fournisseurs de Napoléon Premier*, 1893, p. 55; décision of 12.9.1811, Cadore to Desmazis, 25.11.1811; Fleuriot de Langle, *Elisa Soeur de Napoléon I*, 1947, p. 243.

9 AN 400 AP 4, Duroc to Fontaine, 18.12.1808; Instructions pour M. de Canouville Maréchal des Logis, 6.9.1808; Duroc to Fontaine, 31.12.1808.

10 Biver, p. 157; AN 400 AP 4, Duroc to Costaz, 18.1.1810.

11 La Tour, p. 285, Duroc to Daru, 7.3.1811; Lanzac de Laborie, VIII, pp. 315–19.

12 Marquis de Caumont-La Force, *L'Architrésorier Lebrun Gouverneur de la Hollande 1810–1813*, 1907, pp. 98, 101n, Napoleon to Lebrun, 17.7, 11.8.1810.

13 Pierre Arrizoli-Clementel, 'Les Projets d'Aménagement Intérieur et de Décoration du Palais Pitti pour Napoléon Premier et Marie-Louise 1810–1814', *Florence et la France, Rapports sous la Révolution et Le Premier Empire*, 1979, pp. 290–5.

14 R. Sterni, 'Palais Impérial du Quirinal', *Revue des Études Napoléonienne*, XXVIII, 1–9.1929, pp. 163, 168; Louis Madelin, *La Rome de Napoléon*, 1906, pp. 411–19; Stendhal, p. 1143, diary for 1811.

15 Fontaine diary for 28.1.1805; AN 439 AP (Fontaine Papers), Fontaine to Costaz 18.2.1810.

16 AN 95 AP 12, 83 Bertrand to Caulaincourt, 18.11.1813.

17 AN 300 AP III 16, Orléans to Madame de Saint-Laurent, 1 June 1814; Seth William Stevenson, *Journal of a Tour through part of France . . . made in the Summer of 1816*, Norwich 1817, p. 187, diary for 2 June 1816; Thomas Raffles, *Letters during a Tour through some Parts of France . . . in the summer of 1817*, Liverpool 1818, p. 92.

18 Benjamin Robert Haydon, *Autobiography and Memoirs*, 2 vols. 1926, I, p. 195; *Journal of a Trip to Paris by the Duke and Duchess of Rutland*, 1814, p. 19.

19 Pons de l'Hérault, *Souvenirs et Anecdotes de l'Ile d'Elbe*, 1897, pp. 68, 132, 139, 140, 295; id., *Mémoire aux Puissances Alliées*, 1899, p. 99n.

4 THE COURTIERS

1 Jean Tulard, *Napoléon*, 1977, p. 219.

2 *Hortense*, I, p. 335.

3 Tulard, *Napoléon à Sainte-Hélène*, p. 658; Madame de Chastenay, *Mémoires*, 2 vols. 1896–7, I, p. 160; Paul Morand, *Le Prince de Ligne. Les Plus Belles Pages*, 1964, p. 88.

4 Prince Eugène, I, p. 213, Eugene to Napoleon, 24.7.1805; Bertrand, III, p. 116, diary for 4.1818, p. 454, diary for 1820; Comte de Mercy-Argenteau, *Memoirs*, 2 vols., New York, 1917, I, pp. 126–7. Among the chamberlains seven were Belgian, seven Piedmontese, six Dutch, five Poles, three Rhinelanders, two Tuscans, one Roman, one Genevan. There were none from Liguria or north-west Germany.

5 Bronic Dundulis, *Napoléon et la Lituanie en 1812*, 1940, pp. 30, 46, 84.

6 Marquise de La Tour du Pin, *Journal d'une Femme de Cinquante Ans*, 2 vols. 1913, II, p. 294; Tulard, *Napoléon à Sainte-Hélène*, p. 458, diary of Baron Gourgaud, 16.12.1817.

7 Comte Molé, *Le Comte Molé . . . Sa Vie, Ses Mémoires*, 6 vols. 1922–30, I, pp. 131, 179; *Méneval*, III, p. 89.

8 Chastenay, II, pp. 69, 203.

9 Comte de Rambuteau, *Memoirs*, 1908, pp. 42, 49, 53, 65.

10 Stendhal, *Oeuvres Intimes*, p. 1108; id., *Napoléon*, 2 vols. 1929, I, p. 184.

11 Louis Thomas, *L'Esprit de Monsieur de Talleyrand*, 1909, p. 40 (I am grateful to Giles McDonogh for this reference); Prince Metternich, *Memoirs*, 2 vols., New York, 1880, I, pp. 295–7; Proust, *Le Côté de Guermantes*, Hachètte, 1954, I, p. 180.

12 AN 349 AP Montesquiou Papers I, *Registre des Présentations à S.M. l'Empéreur et Roi*; *Liste Générale des Invitations au Cercle de la Cour*; 349 AP 2, *Registre de la Cour*.

13 Lanzac de Laborie, III, p. 100n, police report of 4.3.1809; Masson, *Joséphine Impératrice et Reine*, p. 260.

14 *Ibid.*, p. 254; Girardin, IV, p. 339; Van Ypersele, p. 139; AN AF IV 3177, *Minutes des Actes du 21 décembre 1809*.

5 ENDS AND MEANS

1 Masson, *Joséphine Repudiée*, p. 237, Duchess de Montebello to Ségur, 9.3.1811; Jean Hanoteau, *Les Beauharnais et l'Empereur* 1936, p. 99, Josephine to Prince Eugene, 24.2.1812; Gavoty, *Les Amoureux de l'Impèratrice Joséphine*, 1961, p. 374.

2 Comte Emmanuel de Las Cases, *Las Cases Mémorialiste de Napoléon*, 1959, p. 125.

3 Prince Clary et Aldringen, *Trois Mois à Paris*, 1914, p. 307, diary for 9.6.1810.

4 Comte d'Haussonville, *Souvenirs*, 1885, pp. 63–4.

5 Lanzac de Laborie, III, p. 151.

6 Zieseniss, *Napoléon*, pp. 314–22.

7 De Berckheim, *Lettres sur Paris*, Heidelberg, 1809, pp. 96, 260–1.

8 Duchesse d'Abrantès, *Mémoires*, 4 vols. 1832, IV, pp. 169–70.

9 Masson, *Joséphine Impératrice et Reine*, p. 276.

10 Morand, p. 88; Countess Potocka, *Memoirs*, New York, 1900, p. 128; Général Comte François Dumonceau, *Mémoires*, 3 vols., Bruxelles 1958–63, II, p. 319.

11 Constantin de Grunwald, 'Les Débuts de Metternich à Paris', *Revue de Paris*, 8. 1936, p. 501.

12 Françoise de Bernardy, *Eugène de Beauharnais*, 1973, p. 148, Caroline to Hortense, 24.12.1805.

13 Pons de l'Hérault, *Souvenirs de l'ile d'Elbe*, p. 74.

14 Jean Savant, *Les Fonds Secrets de Napoléon*, 1953, pp. 53, 77, 93.

15 Masson, *Napoléon chez Lui*, p. 99; Monika Senkowska-Gluck, 'Les Donataires de Napoléon Premier', *Revue d'Histoire Moderne et Contemporaine*, 1969, p. 683.
16 Gourgaud, II, p. 201, diary for 1816.
17 Planat de La Faye, *Correspondance Inédite*, 1895, p. 67, letter of 24.6.1813; Edward A. Whitcomb, *Napoleon's Diplomatic Service*, Durham North Carolina, 1979, p. 35.
18 Françoise de Bernardy, *Son of Talleyrand*, 1956, p. 131; Dirk van Hogendorp, *Mémoires*, La Haye, 1887, p. 269.
19 Jean de Vasson, *Bertrand Le Grand Maréchal de Sainte-Hélène*, Issoudon, 1935, pp. 123–5.
20 Baron Désiré Chlapowski, *Mémoires*, 1908, p. 226; Comte G. de Caraman, *Notice sur la Vie Militaire et Privée du Général Marquis de Caraman*, seconde édition 1857, pp. 27, 29, 131, letters of 23.12, 9.5.1813.
21 *Sbornik* (Proceedings of the Imperial Russian History Society), XXI, p. 295, despatch of Baron de Tchernycheff, 31.12.1811.
22 Napoleon I, *Correspondance Générale*, XXXI, pp. 98–9.
23 Mercy-Argenteau, I, p. 56; Comte Anatole de Montesquiou, *Souvenirs*, 1961, p. 511.
24 AN 177 AP 3, Papers of the Bondy family, letters of Monsieur to Madame de Bondy, 5, 12.4, 9.5.1805, 4.10.1809.
25 Gourgaud, I, p. 306, diary for 1816; Stendhal, *Oeuvres Intimes*, p. 367; Fain, p. 188.
26 Bibliothèque Nationale, Nouvelles Acquisitions Françaises (henceforward referred to as BN.NAF) 11399, Lettres Particulières de Son Excellence Mgr. le Comte de Ségur, passim and letters of 5.11.1810, 11.2.1811, 24.8.1811.
27 Rémusat, *Lettres*, I, p. 269, letter of 26.9.1805; Egon Cesar Conte Corti, *Ludwig I of Bavaria*, 1938, p. 56; Comte de Senfft, *Mémoires*, Leipzig, 1863, p. 89.
28 Comte de Caulaincourt, *Mémoires*, 3 vols. 1933, I, p. 357, III, p. 381; Roustam, p. 211.
29 Oscar Browning, *England and Napoleon in 1803*, 1887, p. 117, despatch of 14.3.1803; Masson, *Napoléon et sa Famille*, VI, p. 37; Charles-Emmanuel de Rivaz, *Mes Souvenirs de Paris*, Martigny, 1967, p. 179; Bernardine Melchior-Bonnet, *Napoléon et le Pape*, 1959, p. 310.
30 Lt. Gen. de Suremain, *Mémoires*, 1902, p. 230; Gabriel Girod de l'Ain, *Bernadotte*, 1968, p. 347.
31 Naef, II, p. 287.
32 Roseberry, p. 64.
33 Masson, *L'Impératrice Marie-Louise*, 2e ed., 1902, p. 489.
34 Rémusat, *Lettres*, passim and I, pp. 214, 216, letters of 1.7, 14.9.1805; Jean Hanoteau, *Les Beauharnais et l'Empereur*, 1936, p. 155, Hortense to Eugene, 20.9.1805.
35 *Revue des Deux Mondes*, 11.1935, pp. 789, 792, Talleyrand to Caulaincourt, 10.12.1807, 12.1.1808.
36 Comtesse de Rémusat, *Mémoires*, 2 vols. 1880, II, p. 107; Ganière, p. 64; *La Rue de Varenne*, 1981, p. 76.
37 Morand, p. 81.
38 André Castelot, *Napoleon's Son*, 1960, p. 21.
39 Françoise de Bernardy, *Stéphanie de Beauharnais*, 1977, p. 44, letter of 26.1.1806; *Van Hogendorp*, p. 271.
40 Comte de Thiard de Bissy, *Souvenirs*, 1900, pp. 9, 21; Haussonville, p. 53; Van Ypersele, p. 136; Constant, *Mémoires*, 1967, pp. 146, 681.
41 Clary, p. 80; Hortense, II, p. 108; Chastenay, II, p. 131.
42 *Revue des Deux Mondes*, 3.1935, Talleyrand to Caulaincourt, 27.7.1812, AN 341 AP (Papers of the La Grange family) 23, Madame de Montmorency to Comte Charles de La Grange 14.3, 15.8, 23.5.1812, 7.12.1813, 28.6.1815.
43 Madame Durand, *Napoleon and Marie-Louise*, 1889, p. 221; André Gavoty, *Les Drames Inconnus de la Cour de Napoléon*, 1962, pp. 31, 47, 159–61.

6 THE FAMILY COURTS

1 Bailleu, II, p. 409, Lucchesini to Haugwitz, 23.11.1805.
2 Masson, *Napoléon et Sa Famille*, II, pp. 466–8; AN O^2 150, decrees of 1 Frimaire, 24 Ventôse, 9 Thermidor an XIII.
3 Roseberry, p. 133; Masson, *Napoléon et Sa Famille*, II, p. 455, III, pp. 346–7, Madame Mère to Napoleon, 9.5.1806.
4 Abbé Proyart, *Vie du Dauphin Père de Louis XVI*, 5e édition, Lyon, 1788, p. 169. I am grateful for this reference to P. Girault de Coursac; *Napoléon* (catalogue of exhibition at Grand Palais 1969), p. 172.
5 Oman, p. 304, letter of 22.5.1810.
6 J. Gabriel, *Essai Biographique sur Madame Tascher de La Pagerie*, 1856, p. 18.
7 Tulard, *Napoléon à Sainte-Hélène*, p. 409.
8 Emmanuel de Beaufond, *Elisa-Napoléon Princesse de Lucques et de Piombino*, 1895, pp. 3–5.
9 Paul Marmottan, 'La Mission du Général Hédouville à Lucques en Juin-Juillet 1805', *Revue des Etudes Napoléoniennes*, XVIII, 1.1922, p. 130, Hédouville to Talleyrand, 10.7.1805, Talleyrand to Hédouville, 4.7.1805; cf. Comte Murat, *Murat en Espagne*, 1897, p. 297, Murat to Napoleon, 26.4.1808, where he proposes that *l'éclat d'une cour digne de la nation espagnole* should be one of the reforms introduced by the Bonapartes.
10 Bibliothèque Marmottan, Manuscrits, Lucchesini to anon, 5.6.1809; Senfft, p. 8.
11 FM 116, Lucchesini to Ségur, 23.10.1810.
12 Paul Marmottan, 'Le Théâtre à Lucques sous Elisa', *Revue des Etudes Napoléoniennes*, 2.1930, p. 67, Elisa to Louis, 2.9.1805; Elisa-Napoléon Baciocchi, 'Lettres au Comte de Ségur', *Revue Hebdomadaire*, 9. 1908, p. 45, letter of 6.9.1805.
13 Agostino Mancini, *Storia di Lucca*, Lucca, 1950, p. 299; Beaufond, pp. 20–1, souvenirs of Baron

Eschasseriaux; *Revue Hebdomadaire*, 9.1908, p. 51, Elisa to Ségur, 26.5.1807; Pons de l'Hérault, *Souvenirs*, p. 256.

14 Hubert, pp. 342–57; G.I.C. de Courcy, *Paganini the Genoese*, 2 vols., Norman, 1957, I, pp. 86–112.

15 Fleuriot de Langle, p. 154; AN 400 AP 4, Napoleon to Elisa, 3.4.1809; FM 116, Decree of 7.6.1809.

16 Fleuriot de Langle, p. 198, Elisa to Fouché, 11.4.1809; cf. E. Rodoconachi, *Elisa-Napoléon*, 1900, p. 177.

17 Joachim Kühn, *Pauline Bonaparte*, 1937, pp. 108, 129; *d'Alméras*, p. 188, Pauline to Michelot, 21.4.1810; Un Inconnu, 'Le Piémont, l'Empire et la Cour du Prince Borghese', in *Mémoires de Constant*, 6 vols. 1830, VI, p. 247.

18 Kühn, pp. 129, 162n, 125; J. de Norvins, *Mémorial*, 3 vols. 1869–70, III, p. 113.

19 Ferdinand Boyer, 'La Famille Bens de Cavour et le Régime Napoléonien', *Revue Historique*, CLXXXV, 1939, pp. 326, 344, 345, Philippine de Cavour to Madame de Cavour, 1811.

20 B. Sancholle-Henraux, *Le Chevalier Luigi Angiolini Diplomate Toscan*, 1912, p. 237, letter of March 1812.

21 Bailleu, II, p.301, despatch from Lucchesini, 20.10.1804; Girardin, IV, p. 12.

22 King Joseph, *Mémoires et Correspondance*, 10 vols. 1854. II, pp. 235, 300, Joseph to Napoleon, 14.5. and 15.6.1806; p. 88, Napoleon to Joseph, 6.3.1806.

23 AN 381 AP Papers of King Joseph 4, 2 lists of the Royal Household; Joseph Rambaud, *Naples sous Joseph Bonaparte*, 1911, p. 516; Gabriel Girod de l'Ain, *Joseph Bonaparte*, 1970, pp. 149, 190.

24 AN 381 AP 4, Rapport au Roi, 4.7.1808; Charles Ross, *The Reluctant King*, 1976, p. 285.

25 Paul Le Brethon, *Lettres et Documents de Joachim Murat*, 8 vols. 1908–14, VI, p. 103, letter of 13.5.1808.

26 Girod de l'Ain, *Joseph Bonaparte*, p. 197; King Joseph, IV, p. 384, Joseph to Napoléon, 25.7.1808; Girardin, IV, pp. 119–20, 145.

27 Comte de La Forest, *Correspondance*, 7 vols. 1905–13, I, pp. 180–1.

28 Masson, *Napoléon et Sa Famille*, VII, p. 254; *La Forest*, II, p. 127, despatch of 15.3.1809; Gabriel Lovett, *Napoléon and the Birth of Modern Spain*, 2 vols. New York 1965, I, p. 311.

29 AN 381 AP 15, Etat Nominatif des Grands Officiers de la Couronne, Officiers Civils et des personnes qui ont traitement de cour à l'époque du 8 janvier 1813; *La Forest*, v 133, despatch of 20 March 1812. The King also had ten equerries, seven mayordomos, three huntsmen, eleven aides-de-camp, eight ordonnance officers and six adjutants of the palace.

30 AN 381 AP 15, 6, Count de Mélito to Joseph 17.8.1810; La Forest, V, p. 108, despatch of 25.6.1811, II, p. 225, despatch of 1.5.1809; Abel Hugo, 'Souvenirs sur Joseph-Napoléon', *Revue des Deux Mondes*, 1833, I, p. 274; 381 AP 15, 6, Lista General de las Senoras que fueron combinadas a palacio en la noche de 15 agosto.

31 La Forest, IV, p. 564, despatch of 30.3.1811; Gavoty, *Amours et Aventures au Temps de Napoléon*, 1969, p. 97; La Forest, VI, p. 80n.

32 *Ibid.*, V, pp. 264–6, 301, VI, p. 121, despatches of 18.6, 22.9.1811, 13.3.1812; Girod de l'Ain, *Joseph Bonaparte*, pp. 266, 272.

33 D. Labarre de Raillicourt, *Louis Bonaparte Roi de Hollande*, 1963, p. 180; anon., *Mémoires sur la Cour de Hollande*, 1820, passim and pp. 4, 10.

34 AN AF IV 1726, papers of King Louis, Sénégra to Louis 25.7.1806; Baron Ducasse, *Les Rois Frères de Napoléon Premier*, 1833, p. xv, Dupont to Cadore, 13.2.1808; *Empire in the Palace* (catalogue of exhibition held in the Royal Palace, Amsterdam 1983), pp. 9, 35.

35 *Mémoires sur la Cour de Hollande*, p. 17; Hortense, I, p. 373, II, p. 74.

36 Labarre de Raillicourt, p. 222n, despatch of 5.2.1807; Girardin, III, p. 403; AN AF IV 1726, Sénégra to Louis, 3.9.1806.

37 *Almanach de La Cour pour l'année 1810*, Amsterdam, 1810 passim; Du Casse, pp. xxxv, xliii, Prince Dolgoruky to Count Romanzov, 3.9.1808, La Rochefoucauld to Cadore, 6.3.1809; AN AF IV 1726, Van Zuylen van Nyevelt to King Louis 15.12.1809. For other examples of courtiers' flattery, see letters from Noguès and René de Villeneuve, 11.8, 30.12.1806.

38 Du Casse, pp. lii, liv, lxxxiii, lxxxvii, despatches of 29.5, 6.7.1809, 15.2, 27.4.1810 from La Rochefoucauld to Cadore.

39 La Force, pp. 104, 240, 244n.

40 Königin Katharina, *Briefwechsel mit dem König Friedrich von Württemberg*, 3 vols. Stuttgart, 1886–7, I, p. 67, letter of 22.9.1807; Masson, *Napoléon et Sa Famille*, VII, p. 107.

41 Du Casse, pp. 229, 431, 453, 475; King Jérôme, *Mémoires et Correspondance*, 7 vols., 1861–6, IV, p. 163, Journal of Catherine, 21.2.1812.

42 Du Casse, p. 242; Jérôme, IV, p. 313; Rambuteau, p. 44; FM 40.422, Garderobe du Roi, Campagne de Russie, avril 1812.

43 Jérôme, III, p. 201.

44 Du Casse, pp. 341–2, bulletin of 23.2.1810; Jérôme, V, 88, Cadore to Reinhard, 11.2.1811.

45 Du Casse, p. 452, bulletin of 14.5.1813; André Martinet, *Jérôme Napoléon Roi de Westphalie*, 1902, pp. 148–9, letter of 15.2.1811.

46 Charles Schmidt, *Le Grand Duché de Berg*, 1905, p. 80.

47 Harold Acton, *The Bourbons of Naples*, second edition, 1974, p. 698; *Almanacco Reale*, Naples, 1813, passim.

48 Rambaud, p. 518; Le Brethon, VI, p. 468n, Aubusson to Cadore, 24.12.1808.

49 Comtesse Rasponi, *Souvenirs d'Enfance*, 1929, pp. 90–92; Lady Morgan, *Italy*, 2 vols., 1821, II, pp. 340–1.

50 Albert Vandal, 'Le Roi et la Reine de Naples', *Revue des Deux Mondes*, 15.2.1910, pp. 772–4, Caroline to

Murat, 24.8.1810.
51 Du Casse, pp. lxvi, La Rochefoucauld to Cadore, 23.11.1809; AN AF IV 1726, Sénégra to Louis, 25.7.1806.

7 POWER AND ILLUSION
1 Emile Dard, *Napoléon et Talleyrand*, p. 148; cf. Ferdinand von Funck, *In the Wake of Napoleon*, 1931, p. 99.
2 J.G. Lemaistre, *A Rough Sketch of Modern Paris*, p. 162, diary for 7.3.1801; Jean Hanoteau, *Les Beauharnais et l'Empereur*, p. 48, Josephine to Eugene, 1.9.1807; Clary, p. 147, diary for 15.4.1810; Napoleon I, *Correspondance Générale*, XXI, pp. 221–2, Rohan to Napoleon, 15.2.1810.
3 McClintock Papers, John Leslie Foster to Harriet Countess de Salis, 6.4.1802; Rivaz, p. 178.
4 Comte de Las Cases, *Mémorial de Sainte-Hélène*, 2 vols., 1961, II, p. 124, diary for 10.8.1816.
5 Dard, p. 117, despatch of Metternich, 19.8.1807, p. 209; Whitcomb, p. 137; *Revue des Deux Mondes*, 15.10.1935, p. 789, Talleyrand to Caulaincourt, 10.12.1807.
6 Talleyrand, *Mémoires*, 5 vols. 1891–2, I, pp. 402, 420.
7 Grand Duke Nicholas Michailovitch, *Scenes from Russian Court Life*, 1917, p. 43, Alexander I to Grand Duchess Catherine, 26.9.1808; Dard, p. 209.
8 Hubert Cole, *Fouché the Unprincipled Patriot*, 1971, p. 182.
9 Zieseniss, *Napoléon*, p. 152; Dard, p. 245.
10 Comte de Nesselrode, *Lettres et Papiers*, 11 vols. 1904–11, III, p. 224; Caulaincourt, I, p. 322; Rambuteau, p. 66; Napoléon I, XXXI, p. 101.
11 Abbé Jacques Moulard, *Le Comte Camille de Tournon*, 3 vols., 1927–32, I, p. 46, Tournon to Madame de Tournon, 14.4, 4.7.1804; Rémusat, *Lettres*, I, pp. 21, 377, letters of 12.9.1804, 1.12.1805; Senfft, p. 101.
12 Constantin de Grunwald, 'Metternich à Paris en 1808–1809', *Revue de Paris*, 1.10.1937, p. 506, despatch of 3.6.1808; Cardinal Consalvi, *Mémoires*, n.d., pp. 236–7, 469; André Latreille, *L'Eglise Catholique et la Révolution Française*, 2 vols. 1950, II, p. 230.
13 Dard, p. 294, Talleyrand to Duchesse de Courlande, 23.11.1812; Duchesse d'Abrantès, *Memoirs*, 3 vols. 1887, III, p. 107.
14 Bernardine Melchior-Bonnet, *Savary Duc de Rovigo*, 1962, p. 145; Jean Tulard, *Napoléon et la Noblesse d'Empire*, 1979, pp. 158–9.
15 Comte de Mérode, *Souvenirs*, 2 vols. 1864, I, p. 277, cf., *La Tour du Pin*, II, p. 275; Gaston Lavalley, *Caen et ses Monuments*, Caen, 1877, pp. 21–3.
16 Comte Ouvaroff, *Esquisses Politiques et Littéraires*, 1845, p. 96.
17 AN 400 AP 4, letter of Duroc, 7.12.1810; FM 116 Duroc to Ségur, 14.8. 1810; Montesquiou to Ségur, 29.12.1810; Masson, *Napoléon et son Fils*, 3e ed. 1909, pp. 181–2.
18 Castellane, I, p. 82, diary for 1.1811.
19 AN O[2]1, Ségur to Marie-Louise, 19.5.1813; Fain, p. 238; Méneval, I, p. 336; Masson, *Napoléon chez Lui*, p. 256.
20 Emmanuel de Las Cases, pp. 137, 176, 142.
21 FM 116, Regnault de Saint Jean d'Angély to Cardinal Fesch, 4.10.1810.
22 Stendhal, *Oeuvres Intimes*, p. 1007, diary for 20.3.1811; Castelot, *Napoleon's Son*, pp. 53–5; *Sbornik*, XXI, p. 178, despatch of 5.6.1811; Albert Vandal, *Napoléon et Alexandre I*, 3 vols. 1891–6, III, p. 194; FM 266, Stanislas de Girardin, diary for 9.6.1811.
23 Caulaincourt, I, p. 385; Vandal, III, p. 415.
24 Caulaincourt, II, pp. 117, 139; Louis Madelin ed., *The Letters of Napoleon to Marie-Louise*, 1935, pp. 94, 110, 116, Napoleon to Marie-Louise, 3.9, 6.10, 19.10.1812.
25 Melchior-Bonnet, p. 211.
26 Caulaincourt, II, pp. 131, 205, 209, 353–4; Saint-Denis, pp. 51–2.
27 Dard, p. 255, Metternich to Floret, 9.12.1812.
28 Jérôme, VI, p. 279, Napoleon to Jerome, 18.1.1813. The Emperor's ambassadors had long been presenting the imperial family as the defenders of true monarchical principles against the schemers of the Cortes of Cadiz or the Faubourg Saint-Germain.
29 Commandant Gillot, *Le Général Le Marois*, 1957, p. 159, despatch of 4.2.1813 to Duc de Feltre; AN 195 AP 12, 72, Montesquiou to Caulaincourt, 26.9.1813; Méneval, III, p. 177; C.F. Palmstierna, ed., *Marie-Louise et Napoléon. Lettres Inédites*, 1955, p. 101, Napoleon to Marie-Louise, 22.2.1814.
30 Caulaincourt, III, p. 184, I, p. 112, Talleyrand to Caulaincourt, 24.8.1808; p. 138, Schouvalov to Alexander I, 19/31.5.1813, p. 155, Metternich to Francis I, 28.7.1813, p. 160.
31 *Sbornik*, XXI, p. 295, despatch of 31.12.1811; Comtesse de Montesquiou, 'Souvenirs', *Revue de Paris*, 5.1948, p. 64; cf., Anatole de Montesquiou, *Souvenirs*, 1961, p. 305.
32 Vienna Haus- Hof- und Staatsarchiv, Nachlass Montenuovo (henceforward referred to as NM), letters of the Duchess de Montebello to Marie-Louise passim, e.g. letter of 30.11.1814; Gavoty, *Amours et Aventures*, p. 113; Masson, *Napoléon et sa Famille*, XI, p. 191, Méneval to Caulaincourt, 29.4.1815.
33 Emile de Perceval, *Le Vicomte Lainé*, 2 vols. 1926, I, p. 219n; Jean Thiry, *La Campagne de France*, 1938, pp. 63–4.
34 Du Casse, p. 67, Napoleon to Joseph, 8.2.1814; Caulaincourt, III, pp. 62, 173, Méneval, III, p. 222.
35 Palmstierna, pp. 60, 132, Marie-Louise to Napoleon, 6.2, 6.3.1814; Méneval, III, p. 233; Stendhal, *Oeuvres Intimes*, p. 1409.
36 Aimée de Coigny, *Journal Intime*, 1981, p. 180; Talleyrand, II, pp. 26–7; Philip Mansel, 'How Forgotten were the Bourbons in France Between 1812 and 1814?', *European Studies Review*, XIII, 1.1983, p. 27.

37 Caulaincourt, III, pp. 57–8 ; Fontaine diary for 4.4.1814.
38 AN 95 AP 14, 64, Berthier to Caulaincourt, 9, 22.4.1814 ; Earl of Kerry, *The First Napoleon*, 1925, p. 71, Flahault to Madame de Souza, 16–19.4.1814.
39 Palmstierna, p. 198 ; Edmond Gachot, *Marie-Louise Intime*, 2 vols. 1911, II, p. 12, Caulaincourt to Madame de Montebello, 7.4.1814 ; Caulaincourt, III, p. 311.
40 Caulaincourt, III, pp. 357–67 ; Saint-Denis, pp. 55–7 ; Michel Poniatowski, *Louis-Philippe et Louis XVIII*, 1980, p. 63n, Jerome to Elisa, 9.4. 1814.
41 Palmstierna, pp. 208, Napoleon to Marie-Louise, 8.4.1819.
42 AN 95 AP 14, Méneval to Fain, 13.4.1814 ; Ganière, p. 317, note by Corvisart, 11.4.1814 ; Castelot, p. 129.
43 Caulaincourt, III, p. 402n ; Comte Schouvaloff, 'De Fontainebleau à Fréjus', *Revue de Paris*, 1.4.1897, pp. 817–8, letter to Nesselrode, 28.4.1814 ; Comte de Waldbourg-Truchsess, *Le Voyage de Napoléon de Fontainebleau à Fréjus*, 1815, pp. 20–2 ; Sir Neil Campbell, *Napoleon at Fontainebleau and Elba*, 1869, p. 191.
44 Ilario Rinieri, *Il Congresso di Vienna e il Santo Sede*, Torino, 1904, p. lxix, diary of Comte de Brignole, 20.1.1815 ; Francesco Melzi d'Eril, duca di Lodi, *Memorie e Documenti*, 2 vols. Milan 1865, II, p. 437, Melzi d'Eril to Eugene, 19, 20.4.1814 ; Reuben J. Rath, *The Fall of the Napoleonic Kingdom of Italy*, New York, 1941, p. 88.
45 Gachot, II, pp. 70, 76, 176, 137, Marie-Louise to Duchess de Montebello, 17.7, 19.7.1814, 25.2.1815, 14.11.1814.
46 Baron de Bourgoing, *Le Coeur Secret de Marie-Louise*, 2 vols. 1938–9, II, p. 95 ; Palmstierna, p. 276 ; Gachot, II, pp. 169, 137, Marie-Louise to Duchess de Montebello, 19.1.1815, 14.11.1814.
47 Tulard, *Napoléon à Sainte-Hélène*, p. 81 ; NM Duchess de Montebello to Marie-Louise, 8.1814 ; AN 300 AP II, 20 (Orléans Papers, consulted by kind permission of the Comte de Paris), Maréchale Ney to Louis XVIII, 1816 (copy) ; De Staël, III, p. 102.
48 Fontaine diary for 5.8.1814 ; Diary of Frances Burgoyne, December 1814 (consulted by kind permission of J. McCrindle Esq.) ; Ian Bruce, *Lavallette Bruce*, 1953, p. 77, letter to his father, 9.12.1814.
49 Masson, *Napoléon et sa Famille*, XII, p. 88, Hortense to Alexander I, 7.1815 ; Cochelet, p. 157 ; Gourgaud, I, p. 492.
50 John Cam Hobhouse, *The Substance of Some Letters . . . during the Last Reign of the Emperor Napoleon*, sec. ed., 2 vols. 1817, II, p. 75 ; Marchand, II, p. 76 ; Napoleon I, XXXI, p. 44.
51 Fontaine diary for 20-21.3.1815, 24.4.1815.
52 Marchand, I, p. 126 ; Hortense, II, p. 329 ; Alexandre de Laborde, *Quarante-Huit heures de Garde au Chateau des Tuileries*, 1816, pp. 19–20 ; Count Lavallette, *Memoirs*, 2 vols. 1833, II, p. 187.
53 Napoléon I, XXXI, pp. 97–8, 102 ; AN $O^2$159 trimestre d'avril, 1815.
54 Hobhouse, I, pp. 405–11, letter of 2.6.1815; I, p. 440, letter of 7.6.1815; II, p. 8, letter of 7.6.1815; *Moniteur*, 6.6.1815, p. 638.
55 Frédéric Bluche, *Le Bonapartisme*, 1980, p. 107 ; *Lanzac de Laborie*, II, p. 66 ; Museo Glauco Lombardi, Parma, Comtesse de Montesquiou to Marie-Louise, 27.4.1815 : since the Empress's letters to Madame de Montesquiou, sold at Christies in 1985, are also respectful and affectionate, their relations cannot have been as bad as is alleged ; Masson, *Napoléon et Sa Famille*, XI, p. 197 ; M-H. Weil, *Les Dessous du Congrès de Vienne*, 2 vols. 1917, II, pp. 191, 303, 333, police reports of 13.2, 9.3, 15.3.1815.
56 AN 95 AP 11, 28, Ordre de Marche, 10.6.1815 ; Gourgaud, II, p. 553, diary for 20.6.1815.
57 Baron Jean Thiry, *La Seconde Abdication*, 1945, pp. 35–6.
58 Molé, I, p. 234 ; Planat de La Faye, p. 214, letter of 26.6.1815 ; Thiry, *Seconde Abdication*, pp. 210, 246, Bertrand to Ballouhey, 29.6.1815.
59 Kerry, p. 133 ; Henry Lachouque, *The Last Days of Napoleon's Empire*, 1966, pp. 182, 229.
60 Captain F.L. Maitland, *Narrative of the Surrender of Bonaparte*, sec. ed. 1826, pp. 63, 210 ; Sir George Cockburn, *Bonaparte's Voyage to Saint Helena*, Boston, 1833, p. 23 ; J.H. Rose, *Napoleon's Last Voyages*, 1906, p. 228; Roseberry, p. 168.
61 Mansel Papers, Diary of Sir George Bingham 8.1.1816 ; Gourgaud, I, p. 375 ; Saint-Denis, p. 237.
62 Emmanuel de Las Cases, pp. 195, 367 ; *Mémorial de Sainte-Hélène*, 2 vols. 1961, I, p. 419, diary for 3.1816.
63 Paul Ganière, *Napoléon à Sainte-Hélène*, 3 vols. 1957, II, pp. 284, 295, 299.
64 *Ibid.*, I, pp. 228, 67, III, pp. 221, 243.
65 Saint-Denis, p. 59 ; Ganière, III, pp. 94, 134.
66 Saint-Denis, p. 159 ; Ganière, III, pp. 216, 234, 253.

8 THE RETURN TO GRANDEUR

1 Victor Hugo, *Choses Vues*, Gallimard, 1972, pp. 184–9, diary for 15.12.1840 ; Castellane, I, p. 387, diary for 15.1.1820.
2 Girod de l'Ain, *Joseph Bonaparte*, p. 395.
3 Oman, p. 458 ; Gourgaud, II, p. 92.
4 Masson, *Napoléon et Sa Famille*, XII, pp. 442, 451 ; Comtesse de Kielmansegge, *Mémoires sur Napoléon*, 2 vols. 1928, II, p. 165, diary for 22.1.1822.
5 Masson, *Napoléon et Sa Famille*, X, p. 52, XII, p. 392.
6 Cole, *The Betrayers*, p. 319 ; Weil, II, p. 717, Lucchesini to Marchese di Lucchesini, 16.10.1815.
7 Morgan, II, p. 266n.
8 FM 28.104, Bausset to Ballouhey, 27.2.1816 ; 107.415, Copie d'après un règlement de la Maison de l'Empereur pour ma gouverne dans l'organisation de la Maison de S.M. l'Impératrice Marie-Louise ; Archivio di Stato Parma, Casa e Corte di Maria Luigia, 905 Matricolo della Personale.
9 FM 28 149, Neipperg to Duchess de Montebello,

16.1.1816; NM Duchess de Montebello to Marie-Louise, 8. 1816.
10 Queen Victoria, *Letters*, 3 vols. 1907–08, III, p. 136 to Leopold I, 23.8.1855.
11 Masson, *Napoléon et Sa Famille*, VII, p. 364.
12 Lady Louisa Stuart, *Selections*, 1899, p. 122; Lemaistre II, p. 343; Wilmot, p. 216, diary for 22.8.1803.
13 Linda Colley, 'The Apotheosis of George III', *Past and Present*, CII, 2.1984, p. 111; Philip Mansel, The Court of France (unpublished Ph.D., London, 1978), passim; Archives X Duchesse d'Escars to Marquise de Podenas, 21.4.1821.
14 Seth William Stevenson, *A Tour in France, Savoy, Northern Italy in the Summer of 1825*, 2 vols. 1827, I, p. 108; Edith Clay, *Lady Blessington at Naples*, 1979, p. 42, diary for 31.7.1823; c.f. Paul Marmottan, *Les Arts en Toscane*, 1908, p. 223.
15 Don Lucas Alaman, *Historia de Mejico*, 5 vols., Mejico 1852, V, p. 624; Denyse Dalbian, *Dom Pedro Ier*, 1959, pp. 37, 67.
16 M.N. Balisson de Rougemont, *Le Rodeur Français ou les Moeurs du Jour*, 6 vols., 1816–21, I, p. 20, article for 20.8.1814.
17 Heinrich Heine, *Travel Pictures*, 1887, p. 146; Leon Edel, *Henry James the Master*, vol. 5, 1972, pp. 555–6.

Index

Within entries the initial N is used for Napoleon. References to illustrations are in italic.

The Imperial Family

(Only members of the family mentioned in the text are included.)

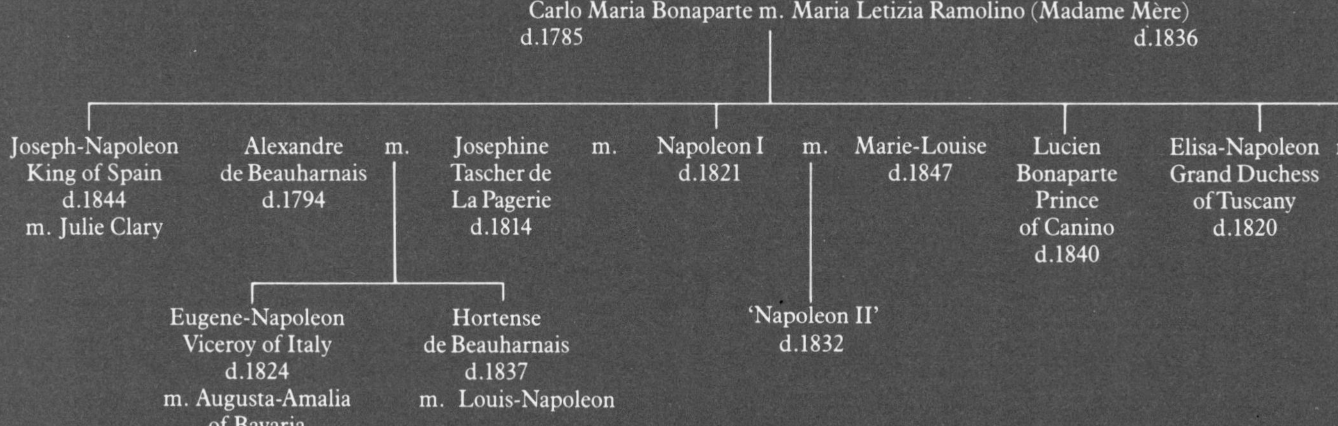